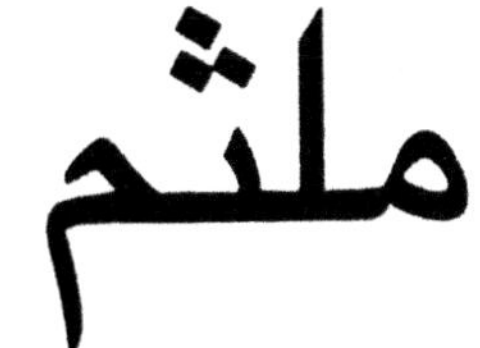

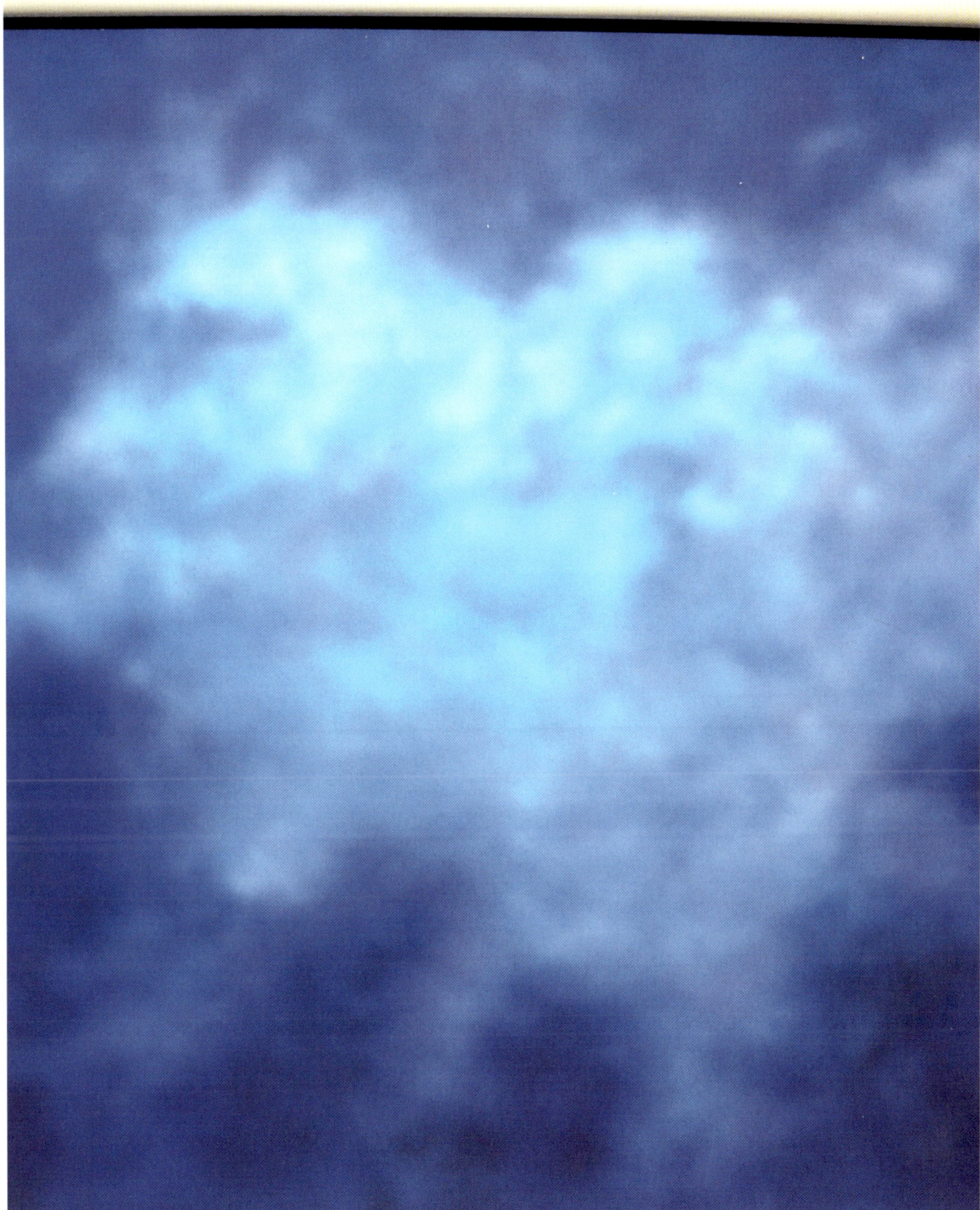

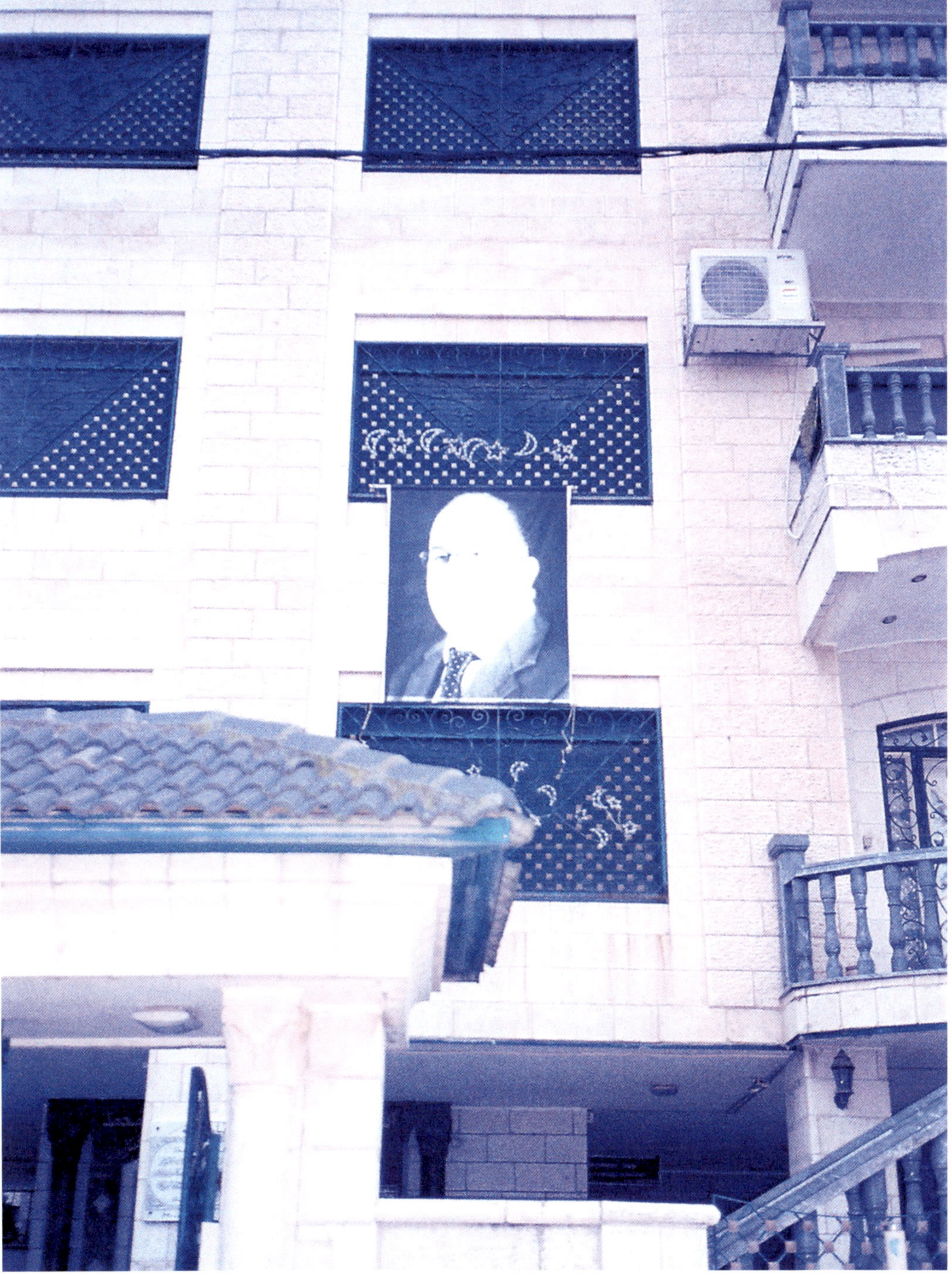

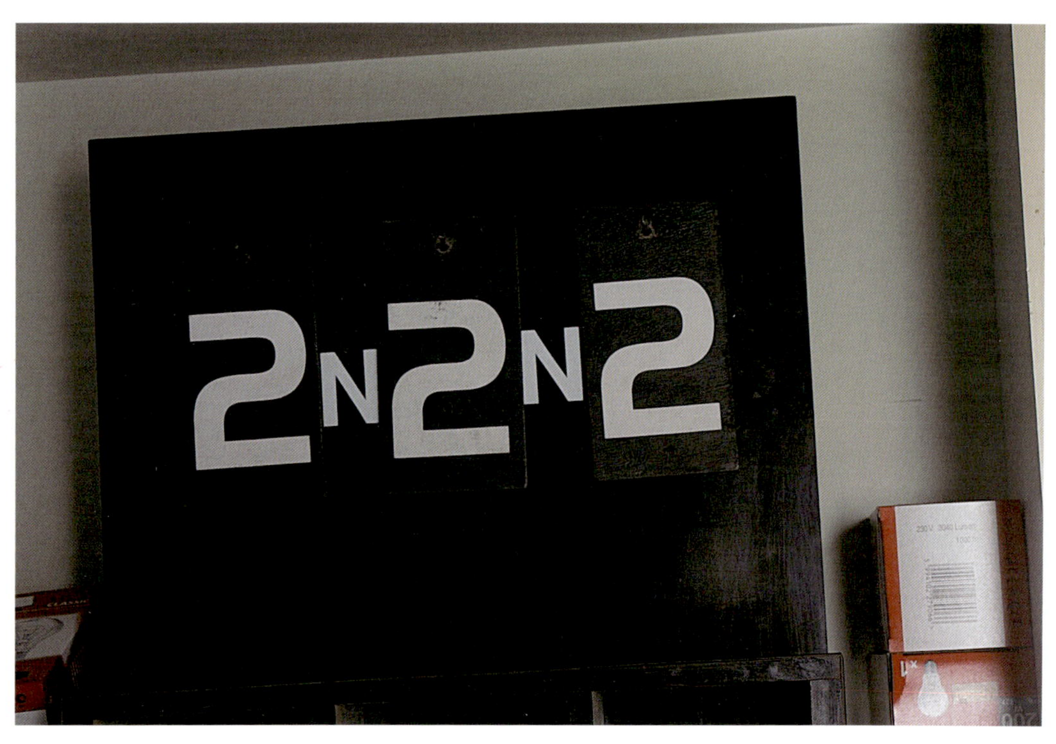2ₙ2ₙ2

MOLATHAM   SCOTT CARUTH

احنا الجيش
دير بالك رايحين نمسكك ادا منشوفك او
رايحين نئاتي على البيت

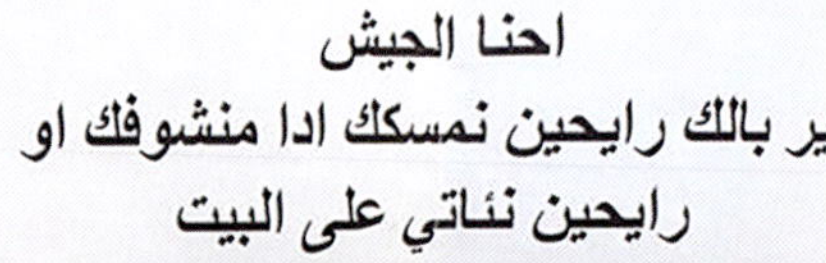
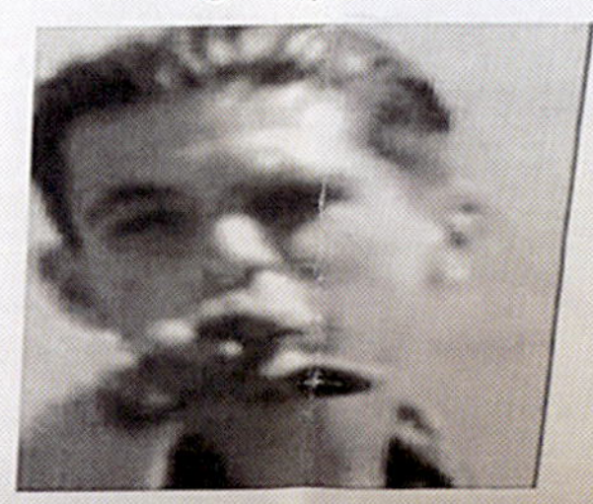

احنا الجيش
دير بالك رايحين نمسكك ادا منشوفك او
رايحين نئاتي على البيت

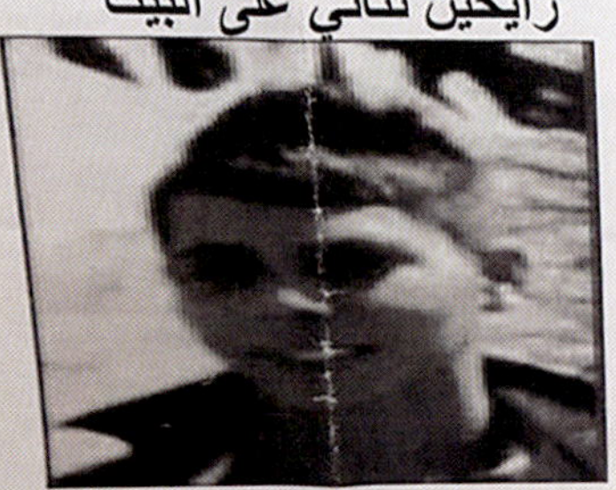

احنا الجيش
دير بالك رايحين نمسكك ادا منشوفك او
رايحين نئاتي على البيت

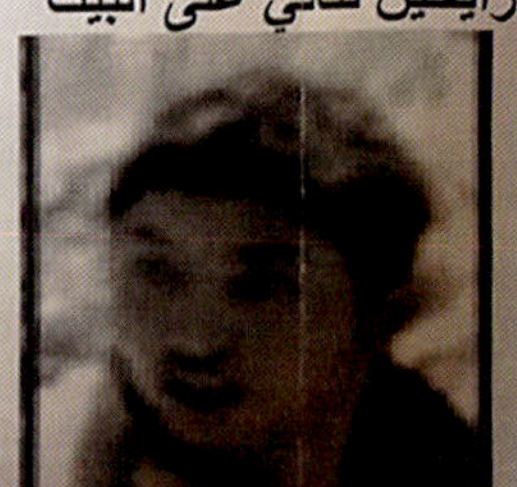

احنا الجيش
دير بالك رايحين نمسكك ادا منشوفك او
رايحين نئاتي على البيت

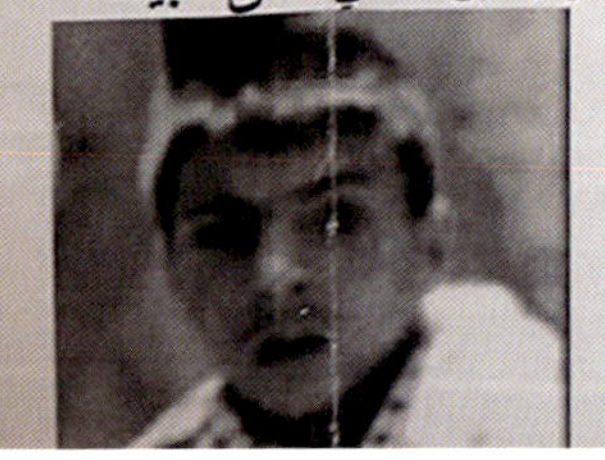

'WE ARE THE ARMY. WATCH OUT,
WE WILL CATCH YOU IF WE SEE YOU,
OR WE WILL COME TO YOUR HOUSE'

INTRODUCTION

In the summer of 2013 the residents of Kafr Qaddum, a small village near Nablus in the West Bank, woke up to find a series of photocopied flyers pasted over the village walls. They contained out of focus, grainy images of the faces of several of the village's young teenagers. The images had been taken by the Israeli Defense Forces using a telescopic lens at one of the village's weekly demonstrations against an illegal Israeli settlement nearby. The construction of this settlement had quadrupled the amount of time it took to get from the village to the nearby city of Nablus as well as cutting off many farmers from their land. The villagers had held a weekly demonstration against this every Friday since 2011. Hundreds of unarmed men, women and children (including a three year old girl) have been shot with live ammunition and many have been killed as a result.

The four grainy images on the flyer were taken during one such demonstration by the Israeli Defense Forces (IDF). The Arabic text on the side of the photograph reads 'We are the army. Watch out, We will catch you if we see you, or We will come to your house'. The four young men in the photographs were not, in any way, more wanted by the IDF than any of the other protestors present that day, they had simply left their faces uncovered.

ملثم ('Molatham'), from which this project takes its title, is an Arabic verb that translates literally as 'to cover up ones face', but is used vernacularly, in Palestine, to describe anybody resisting the Israeli occupation. The verb's application, in this context, locates the pivotal role played by the medium of photography within the Israeli occupation of the West Bank, whereby in order to resist it, Palestiians must remain anonymous whilst doing so.

"Since they were first conquered, and increasingly over the past two decades, the occupied territories have become an extended borderless photography studio whose reach may be extended at any given moment to more and more areas, including private homes"[1] Palestinian life is always under observation; from aerial reconnaissance to watch towers, from CCTV cameras to one-way mirrors at checkpoints. Whereas the Palestinian struggle has fundamentally rallied around attempts to be visible, amidst Zionist claims that 'pronounced the emptiness of the land and the non-existence of (the Palestinian) people"[2] it has also had to devise strategies to 'escape the dominating gaze of surveillance that renders them visible at all times, by finding ways to temporarily disappear or to become invisible altogether'.[3] The adoption of masks or 'Molatham' is one such strategy, resulting in images of struggle characterised by faceless entities. Synonymous with criminality, balaclava clad Palestinian subjects dominate the photographic narrative of the occupation, both locally and internationally.

Since 2012, I have spent several extended periods of time in the West Bank working as an activist with the International Solidarity Movement (ISM). ISM works with direct, non-violent and physical intervention wherever possible. For me this

*1 ARIELLA AZOULLAY , CIVIL IMAGINATION: A POLITICAL ONTOLOGY OF PHOTOGRAPHY, 2015, P.243 / *2 EDWARD SAID, PREFACE, DREAMS OF A NATION: ON PALESTINIAN CINEMA BY HAMID DABASHI, 2006, P.2/ *3 GIL Z HOCHBERG, 'VISUAL OCCUPATIONS - VIOLENCE AND VISIBILITY IN A CONFLICT ZONE', 2015, P.24

included participating in weekly demonstrations, non-violently disrupting the activities of the IDF, accompanying farmers to their fields or children to school and residing with or near families whose homes are threatened with eviction, demolition or harassment by settlers and/or soldiers.

Under an apartheid regime, the behaviour of Palestinians, Israelis and Internationals carry different consequences. Where a Palestinian can be detained indefinitely without charge, from the age of twelve, under the system of administrative detention, an international activist participating in the same activity can only be detained for a short period of time before, at the very worst, being deported. In light of this, we would directly intervene in the arrests of Palestinians in order to get ourselves arrested instead. Similarly, many Palestinians are actively targeted for recording or documenting their experience in ways that our status as Internationals could guarantee certain levels of implicit protection from.

The prioritisation of 'solidarity' forces anybody participating in such work to confront the role of photography and the camera itself within this context. The conditions of 'solidarity' mean 'Palestinian led'; whereby we would not engage in activities unless explicitly invited to do so by Palestinians. Similarly, our use of photography had to consider if it complied with such terms. Failure to do so always resulted in a reinforcement of the Palestinians' compromised position within the unequal distribution of visibility designated by the occupation. It became crucial to discern between moments where the use of a camera may act as an extension of our solidarity work and those where it would compromise it entirely.

The camera therefore, as an object, had an immediate and physical relationship with this activism. The presence of a camera on our persons made our intent to document the army explicit. An automatic response to being targeted by them would often be to hold the camera up higher, more visibly. The act of pointing cameras at the occupation's infrastructure and the vernacularly banal violence of its personnel stemmed from assumptions that it carried the capacity to rupture its normalisation. Nonetheless, our cameras were inferior before the abundance of the Israeli state's. If the use of our cameras were supposed to expose or render visible the brutality of the daily experience of occupation then it failed completely. The technological promises of justice via the camera's capacity to expose were not delivered.

The camera's perceived value as an object of self-protection, and / or bearing witness, has coincided with the increasing technological capacity for images to be published immediately and without censorship. Where as previously, the IDF would limit the gaze of press photographers through the declaration of 'Closed Military Zones', they now face the more substantial threat of everybody being equipped with cameras on their mobile phone.

It seems natural to conclude that this would make exposure of the IDF's brutality on the ground more likely and therefore carry a higher risk of evidence being produced against them in the context of international criminal justice proce-dures[4]. However such expectations have been met proportionality with an increas-ing suspicion of both the image and the human rights discourse within Israeli society, whereby 'suspicious Israeli public networks took aim at the footage itself, arguing that it had been doctored for political effect' and thereby 'labour-ing to exonerate the state through close reading of the images'[5]

Once, when maintaining a presence at a school route in Hebron where only weeks before 27 school children under the age of 15 had been beaten, blindfolded and arrested by Israeli soldiers on their way to school, a soldier looked at my camera and remarked that I "only wanted to take pictures at a specific angle to make the military look bad". He went on to suggest that I could simply set a photograph up at a specific angle creating the illusion that the rifle resting on his hip was in fact being held at the head of a small child. It struck me that the situation had been so normalized, to the soldier, that he thought I would have to manipulate the scene with my lens to make an occupy-ing army's presence at a children's school appear negative.

My sense of photographic failure within these activist experiences is not designed to be cynical nor declare resignation. The assumption that my camera alone could make any serious intervention would be as misguided as the assumption that my own personal and physical presence amidst the occupation could itself make any differ-ence. Out of many extended periods of activism, spread across 5 years with ISM, I can only guarantee that once was my attempt to intervene successful. During a particularly intense raid of a school district by the IDF in Hebron, children were running around in blind panic as the soldiers ran around arbitrarily throw-ing stun grenades and launching tear gas canisters at them. Amidst the panic I noticed one young boy with large head-phones on who was staring at the ground as he walked along, apparently oblivi-ous to the chaos around him. A group of around 15 soldiers ran towards him and only when he was encircled on all sides did the boy look up to realise that he was trapped. The ca5ptain of the platoon started to arrest him just as I squeezed myself into the circle, put my hands on the boys shoulder and calmly said 'No'. The commander looked at me, spoke Hebrew into his walkie-talkie and then clicked his fingers. At this point the entire circle of soldiers pulled out and moved away, leaving me and the boy on the spot to look at each other in bewilderment. Aside from this incident, no such literal measures of successful intervention were available. To genuinely gauge if our presence at any given incident had any modifying effect on the proportions of violence within it, we would have had to not have been there in the first place. Being able to phys-ically meet requests from Palestinians for shared presence at all was measured as successful in itself. Everything from

•4 HARRIET AGERHOLM , "ISRAEL CONSIDERING LAW TO BAN PHOTOGRAPHING OR FILMING OF IDF SOLDIERS", THE INDEPENDENT, 27 MAY 2018 -
•5 REBECCA L. STEIN , 'GOPRO OCCUPATION : NETWORKED CAMERAS, ISRAELI MILITARY RULE, AND THE DIGITAL PROMISE', 2017,P.7

that point onwards would simply be gauged through levels of ineffectiveness.

It was through these experiences, that I began to pursue evidence of photographic practices in the occupied territories that bypass the conditions of the occupier's gaze, Studio Portraiture Photography. In studios throughout the West Bank, Palestinians have, since the invention of the medium itself, utilised photography to represent themselves under conditions of their own choosing and in direct collaboration with another Palestinian photographer. This book is the culmination of a six year endeavour to document that practice. On the 25th June 2018, a new public memorial was unveiled in the Palestinian city of Ramallah. The 'Martyrs Mosaic' depicts sixteen figures including a young boy on horseback carrying a Palestinian flag, a rifle carrying resistance fighter whose face has been concealed with a Keffiyeh scarf and a woman in traditional Palestinian clothing carrying a child. Two of the sixteen figures carry framed studio portrait photographs.

Upon unveiling the memorial the mayor of Ramallah, Musa Hadid, dedicated the memorial "in the presence of the dignitaries who are absent-present".[6] Honouring a community that is made up of the living as much as it is of the dead, his dedication of the Palestinian memorial considered those who were physically absent but present in spirit, a link which can physically manifest through the object of a studio portrait photograph.

The production of a studio portrait is inherently a future oriented photographic gesture. It is designed to be revisited. As a souvenir of the self, it can stand in for those who are absent. It can represent the dead, the lost or distant. In the context of ongoing of dispossession and ethnic cleansing, the practice of studio photography in Palestine can be read as counter claim against facelessness and non- existence. It is no accident that the two figures holding studio portraits within the mosaic appear to be children, carrying forth representations of those who are no longer present but who form part of a 'collective consciousness and identification that is based on the absence of a state'.[7]

The collaborative exchange between photographer and sitter within a studio, from which such images are produced, reinstate that political agency which is denied through the occupiers use of photographic practices of surveillance or the photojournalists 'fetishised visual frame of destruction, violence or loss'[8]

Palestine was amongst the first geographies to be documented using the new technology of daguerreotype merely weeks after its invention in the nineteenth century. Photography studios established throughout Jerusalem at this time were central to the development of the medium itself. This book looks at the role played by studio portraiture from 1948 onwards, after the 'Nakbah' or forced expulsion of one million Palestinians from their homes by the advancing Israeli Army, to the occupation of the West Bank in 1967, to the first and second Intifada's (uprisings) in the 90's and 2000's, until the

*6 PA DAILY, AL-HAYAT AL-JADIDA, 'RAMALLAH MUNICIPALITY INAUGURATES MONUMENT TO "RAMALLAH MARTYRS' , 26 JUNE 2018 / *7 T J DEMOS, 'MIGRANT IMAGE: THE ART AND POLITICS OF DOCUMENTARY DURING GLOBAL CRISIS -THE RIGHT TO OPACITY: ON THE OTOLITH GROUP'S NERVUS RERUM' , 2013 , P151 / *8 GIL Z HOCHBERG, 'VISUAL OCCUPATIONS - VIOLENCE AND VISIBILITY IN A CONFLICT ZONE', 2015, P.6

present day. It looks at the status of the physical structures of the studios themselves which have often themselves been relocated, subject to restricted access or completely destroyed.

The working practices and lives of several studio photographers are detailed through transcribed interviews and selections from their archives. Developments within the photographic medium itself, from black and white hand-tinted photographs to those utilising Photoshop in the present day can be traced chronologically.

The book then moves on to explore the ways in which these personal, relatively private photographic objects go on to become the centre pieces of public gaze, widely disseminated images that form a central nexus of Palestinian resistance; within political iconography and propaganda. Finally, the book traces the medium of studio portraiture throughout the urban landscape of the West Bank.

The conditions between the use of photography within an activist context and of photography studios are different, yet find interwoven concerns stemming from their shared context of military occupation. Ariella Azoullay has argued that in 'any photographic 'event', the participation of three main parties can be identified, the photographed, the photographer and the spectator'.[9]

As seen in the flyers dropped around Kafr Kaddum by the IDF, the photographed Palestinian has conditions of total surveillance thrust upon them. The photographed

Palestinian is buffeted by external lenses that either wish to prove their criminality or expose their suffering. An activist working with the principles of solidarity must, at all times, be mindful of the ways in which their own cameras may reinforce this.

In the conditions of studio portraiture photography, the photographed Palestinian marks his or her consent within the photographic event by turning up to the studio, speaking to the photographer and commissioning their own portrait. They work with the photographer (another Palestinian) to decide upon the tone and perspective of their portrait until they are satisfied that they have been represented according to their own wishes.

The studio photographer works through their knowledge of the photographic process; exposure length, film type, lighting, filters and backdrops are all deployed with each individual subject in mind. The commissioning aspect of the exchange incurs a responsibility on each part to produce an image that both parties will be satisfied with. In other words, the photographer must ultimately answer to the photographed person in a way that honours both their own practice and working relationship. The press photographer, on the other hand, shares no such responsibility towards those that they photograph and the subjects of their photographs are often represented insofar as they conform to the roles they are expected to play within a broader terrorist / victim polarity.

9 ARIELLA AZOULAY, , 'CIVIL IMAGINATION - WHAT IS PHOTOGRAPHY?', 2015, P.17

The position of the spectator, those looking at the photographs, is slightly more complicated to deal with. It could be useful to consider a scenario I often used when I was the training co-ordinator for four months in 2016. During this time, it was my responsibility to train new arrivals to the West Bank on how to be activists with ISM. In a section called 'Violence / Non-Violence', the trainees would be presented with a series of scenarios before being asked whether what was being described was a) Violent or non - Violent and b) effective or ineffective in the context of solidarity activism. In one scenario, activists have been invited by a Palestinian council to assist in dismantling part of the Israeli separation barrier that runs through their village. A particularly violent scene is described, in which the activists assist Palestinians in using wire cutters, sledgehammers and crow bars to tear down a large section of the fence which is then trampled on by a furious crowd. Most activists assumed that this action was violent and therefore ineffective. The language used to describe the scenario is designed to sway people towards this assumption on a gut level. At this stage, I would reveal that because the Israeli barrier is illegal under international law, the activists and villagers described in the scenario are actually upholding the law. It is the fence itself that is violent. The destruction of state infrastructure coupled with the explicit invitation to do so, on behalf of a Palestinian popular committee, is regarded as being both non-violent and effective in the context of solidarity activism.

This scenario has stuck with me because it challenges many assumptions about the presence of violence throughout many of the images contained in this project. While a privately-owned studio photograph usually has a limited audience in a family home or wallet, the death or imprisonment of that same subject will see that very same photograph copied, multiplied and disseminated throughout the public domain in the form of political iconography. At this stage the spectatorship of that same studio portrait grows exponentially, but this time framed around notions of resistance and conflict. Displayed throughout the urban landscape of the West Bank, these images resonate on a local experience of injustice and collective resistance. Taken out of context however, those very same images may be held up as evidence of terrorist glorification or read as incitement for seemingly random violence. A range of assumptions may be made about the nature of this resistance, as well as moral judgements about the individual characters depicted. I would encourage readers to consider their own position within the scenario above as they navigate this book.

Scott Caruth, August 2019

INTERVIEW WITH GARO NALBANDIAN OF STUDIO GARO, EAST JERUSALEM

SCOTT   So that was the '67 war, but I'm wondering about, because of all the differ-
          ent studios I went to. Like in Jenin, Hebron or Ramallah they're all differ-
          ent, just different areas, but what I'm interested in is they all seem to
          affected by the occupation in all these different ways.

GARO   The occupation they tried to steal cameras.
          Camera's raw films, new films, things like that.
          They get to this stuff Yeah.

    S   Did anything else happen in terms of like your travel?

    G   We were not allowed to carry cameras.

    S   To the West Bank?

    G   West Bank or in Jerusalem. In Jerusalem I saw a lot of dead people and
          this and that.

    S   On the street?

    G   If you carry camera they take you, you probably be in a jail too.

    S   So you didn't carry cameras around?

    G   No! I will tell you something, would you like something to drink something?
          Sprite or something.

    S   Sprite would be great, you're not fasting though?

    G   I'm a Christian.

    S   Oh right. that would be great thanks.

          Did you get involved in the intifada?

    G   Lots of places.

    S   What do you mean?

G   What kind of involved?

S   Did you document it? Or were you participating, or what happened?

G   No, just filming, documentary and news. They ask 5 or 6 camera men, one to film each other. Before in Hebron, some cameramen had been beaten or they had their material taken. We went to film them, how the army treat them.

        I'm filming, they are filming, I am filming, another camera filming them, you know, watching each other. Every time my son says, there is journalist, there is bad luck. First in Hebrew where were filming it was very good footage and suddenly hand grenade. It didn't go off but still it is a tension. The grenade on the floor and everyone is down on the floor.

        It happened a few shots. One shot, in Ramallah, it was a sign, metal sign, I was behind it and the Palestinians were throwing stones. The army shoot at it like that; I'm in the middle-but safe side when I was filming and another guy filming me. I've been shot in Ramallah, about eight bullets.

S   By the Israelis?

G   I don't know. I was driving the car, suddenly, tat-tat-tat, all my windows went white. Many bullets.

S   You were driving by yourself?

G   With one Italian.

S   In Ramallah?

G   Yeah in Ramallah. I looked at the Italian and I say "You're alive, I'm alive." All the bullets! All the glass!

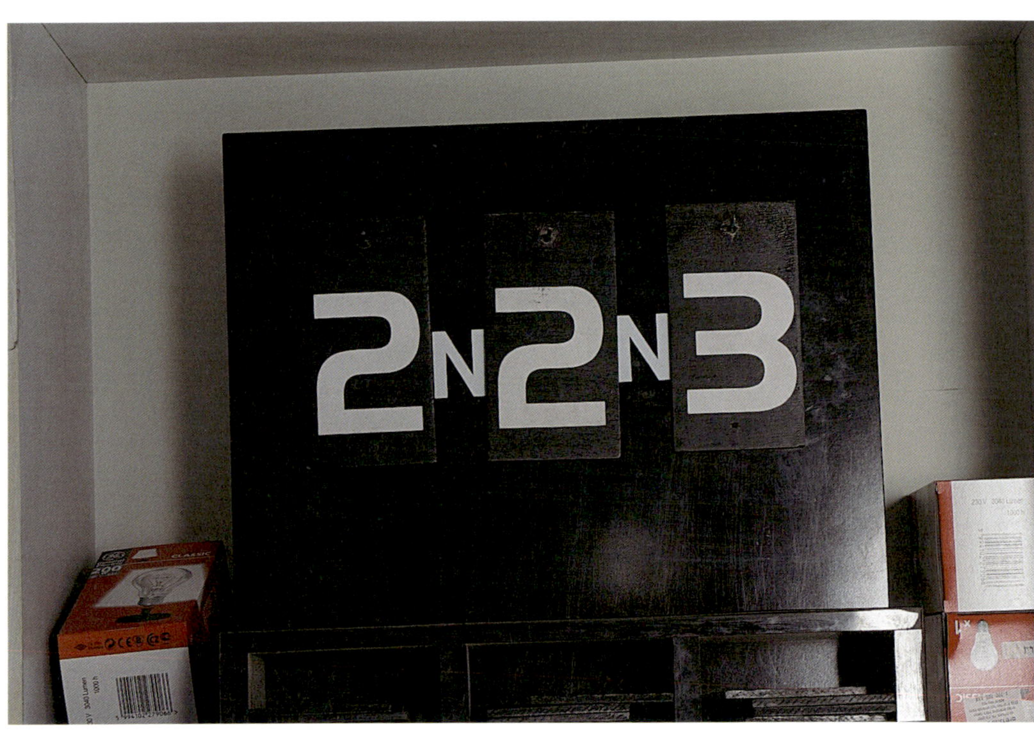
2N2N3

STUDIO HAVANA, RAMALLAH

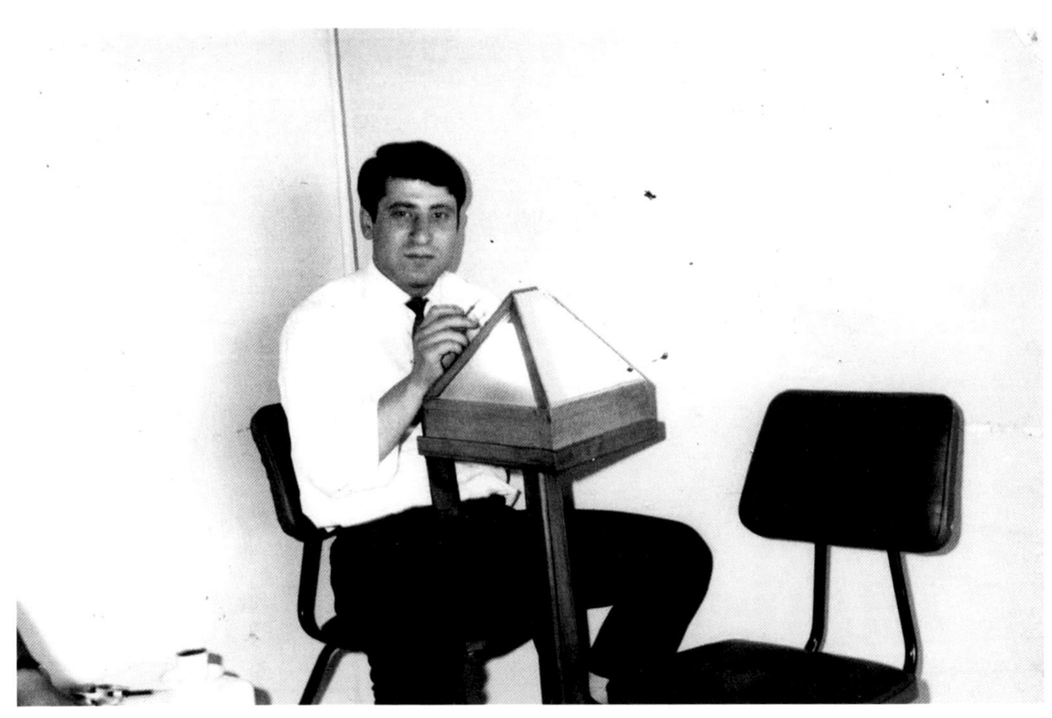

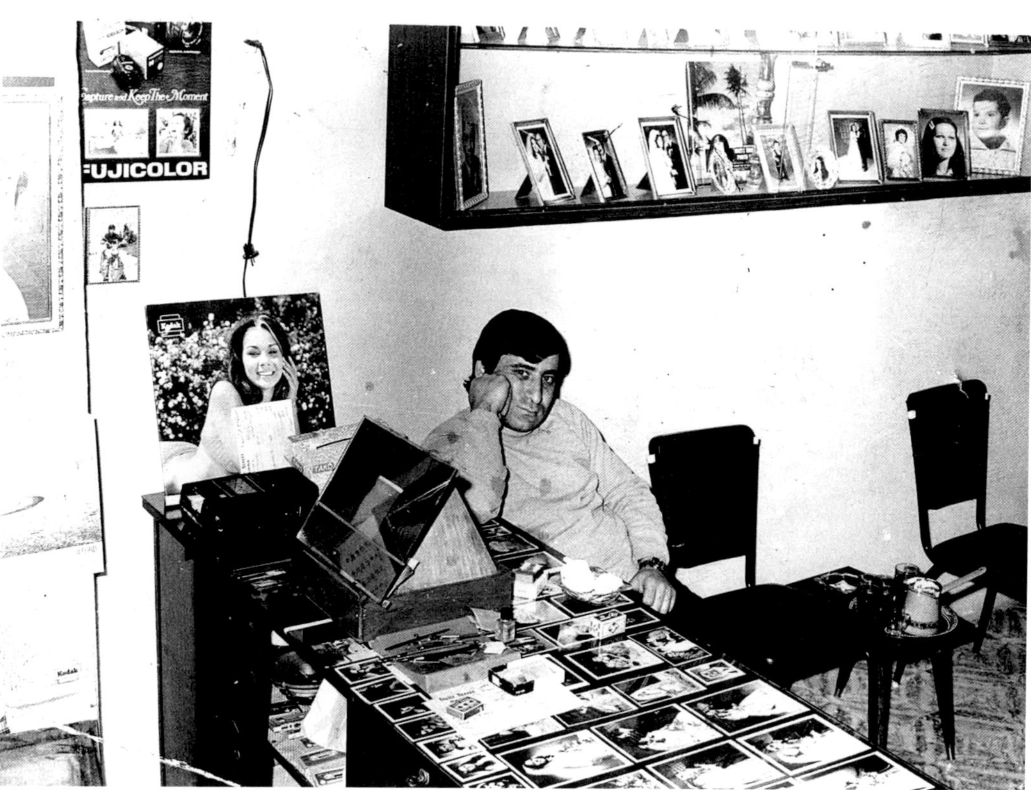

Capture and Keep The Moment
FUJICOLOR
Kodak

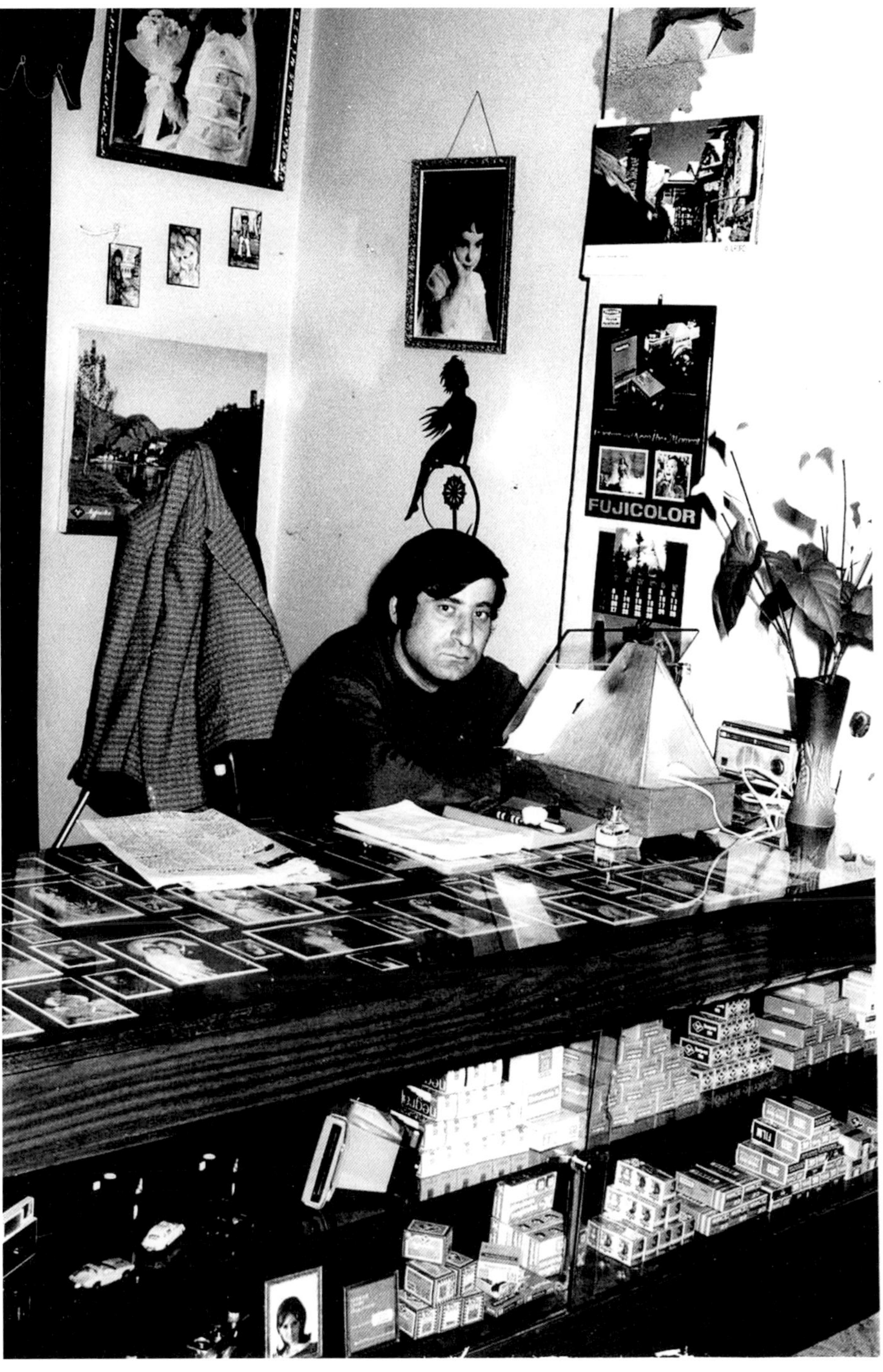
FUJICOLOR

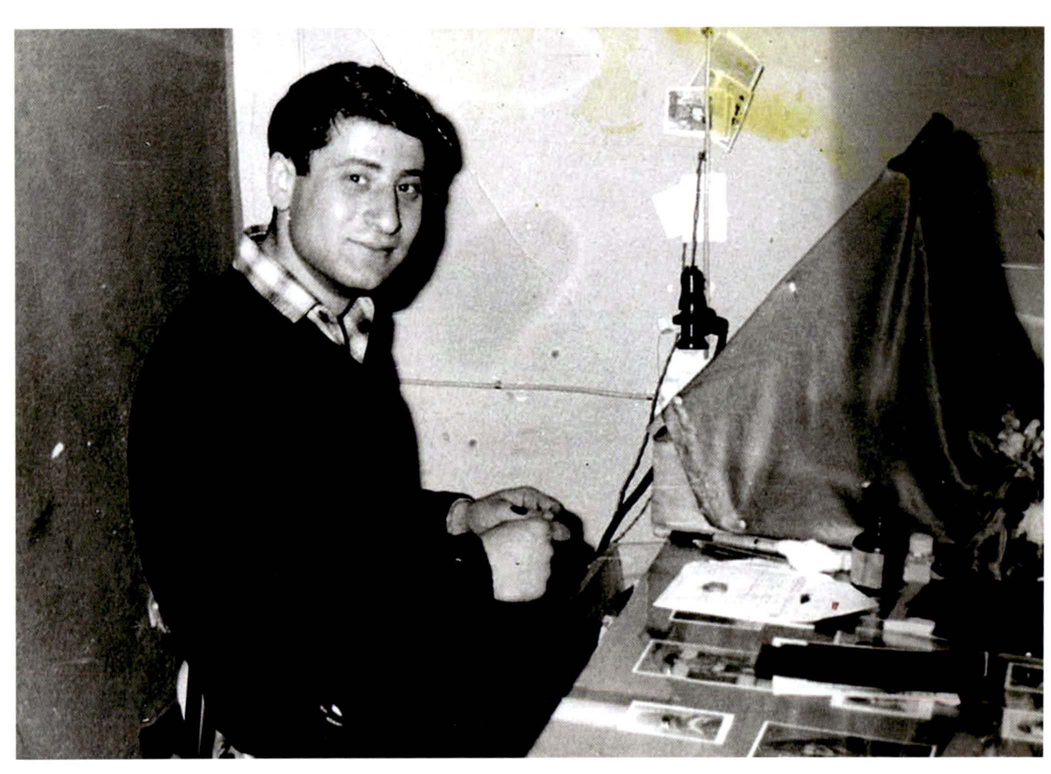

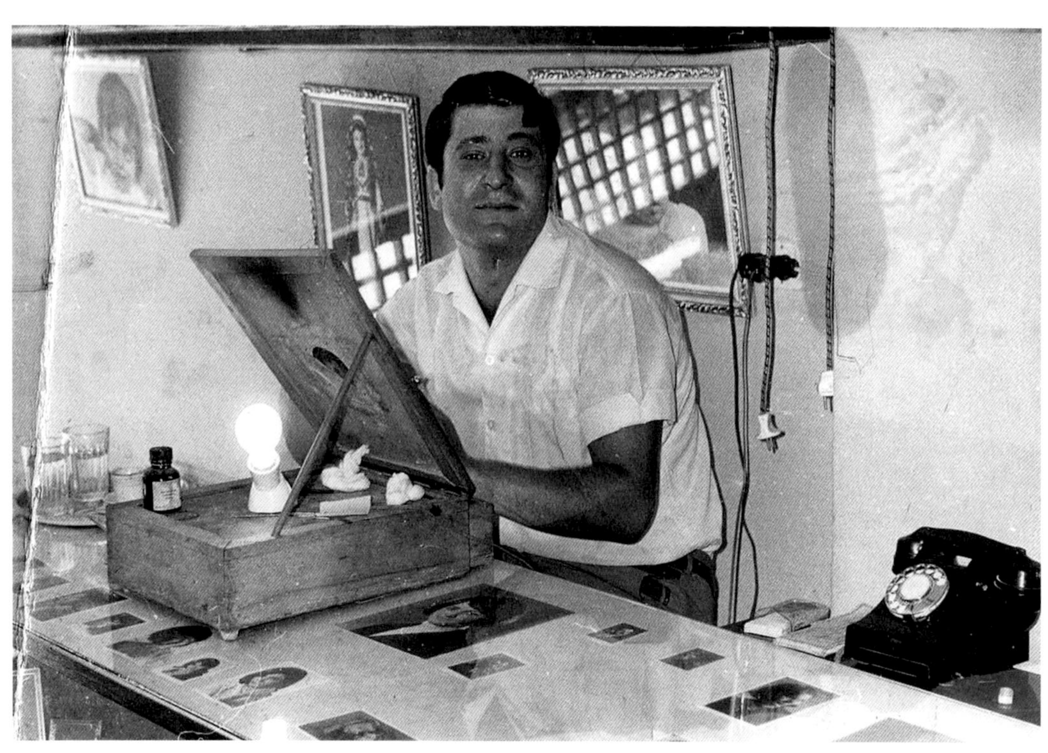

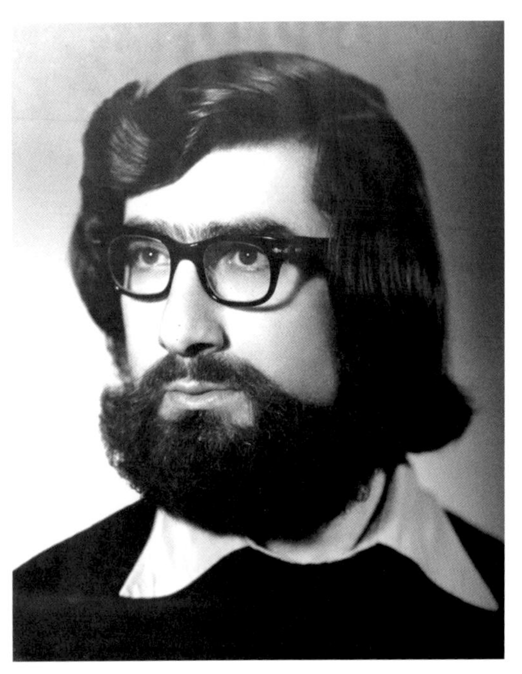 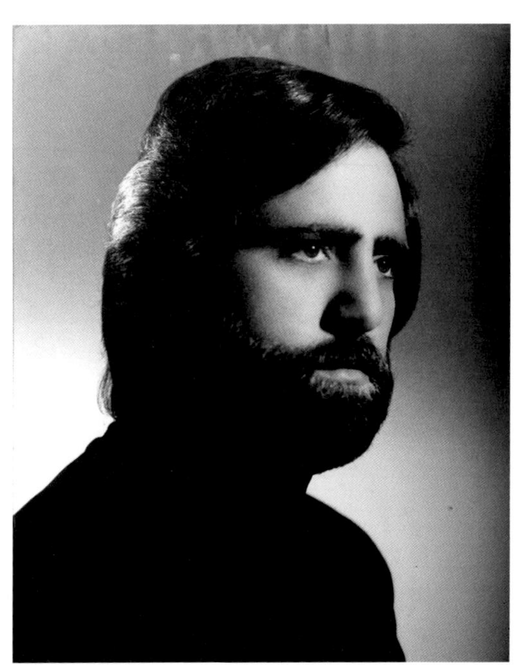

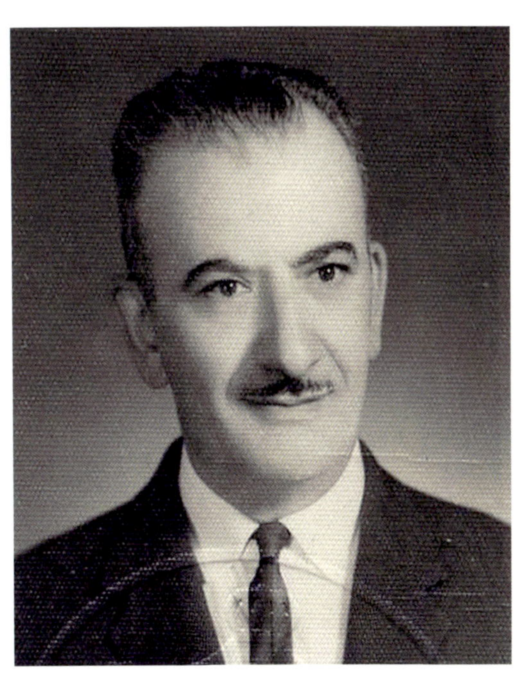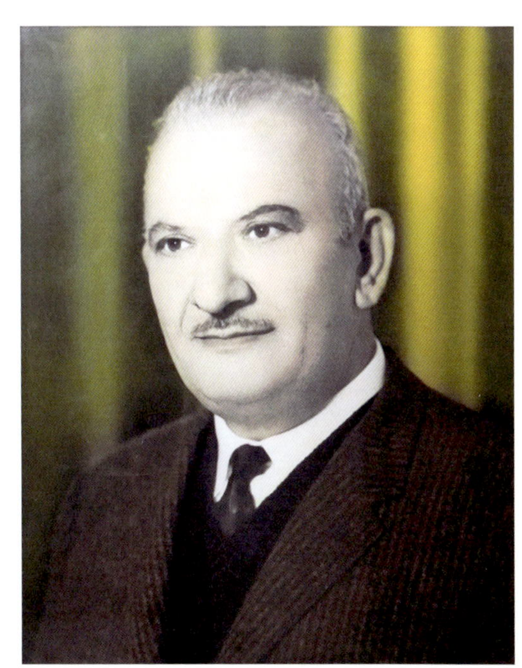

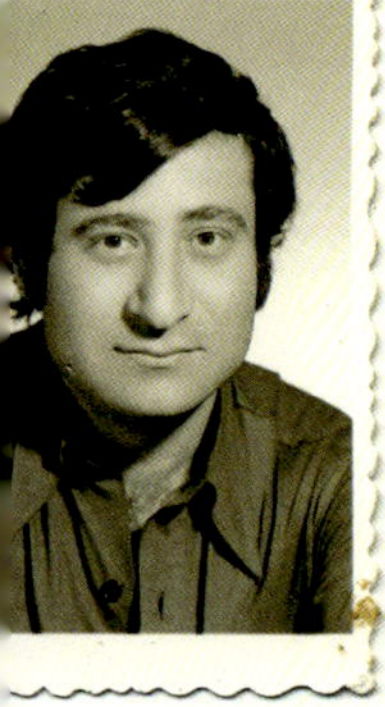

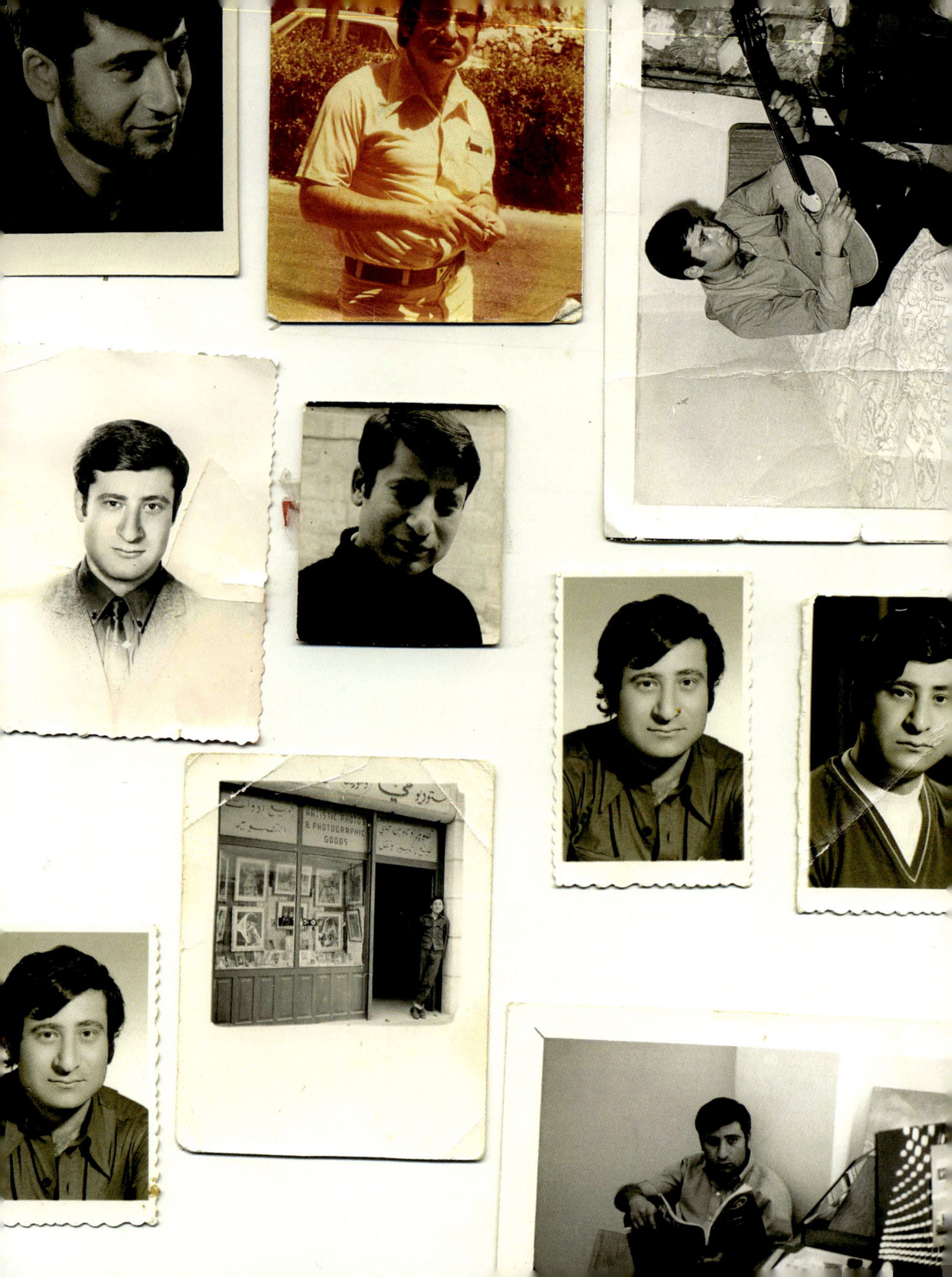

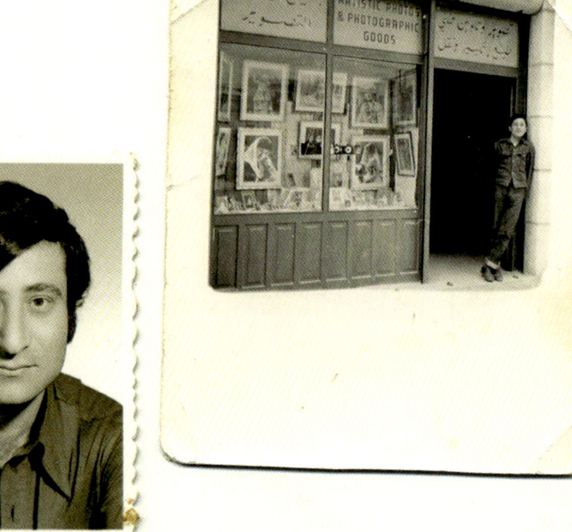

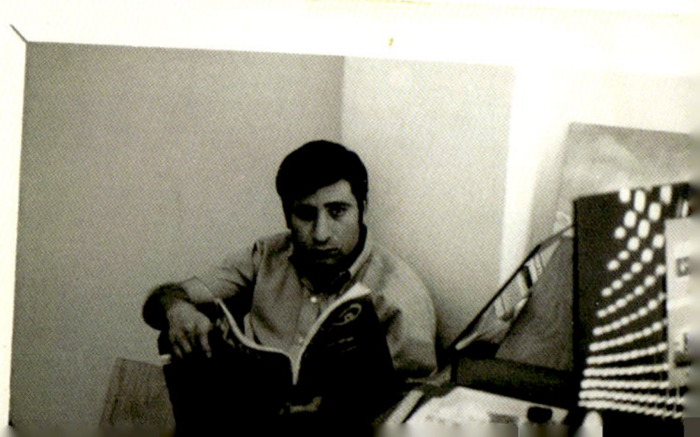

ARTISTIC PHOTOS
& PHOTOGRAPHIC
GOODS

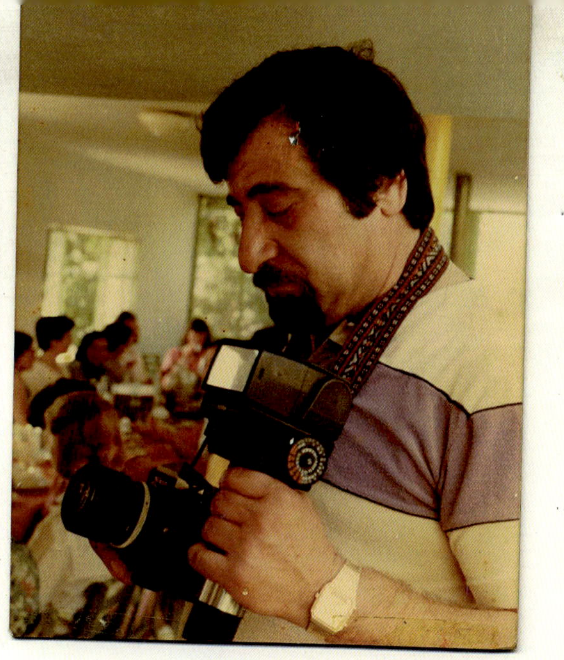

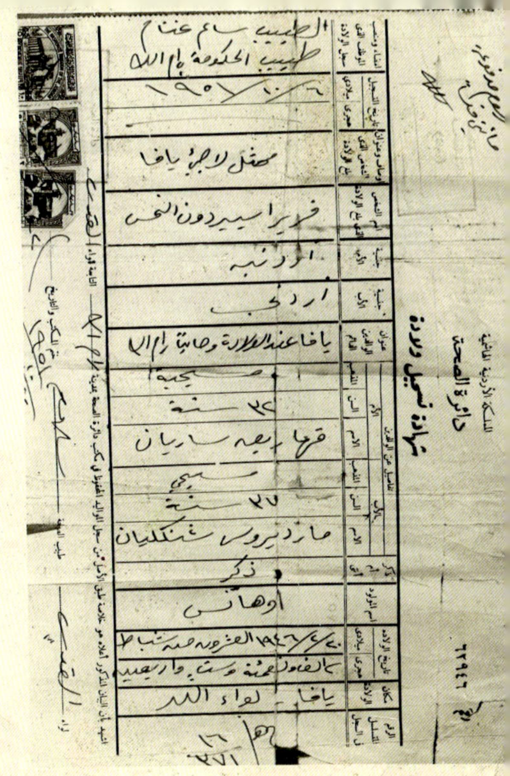

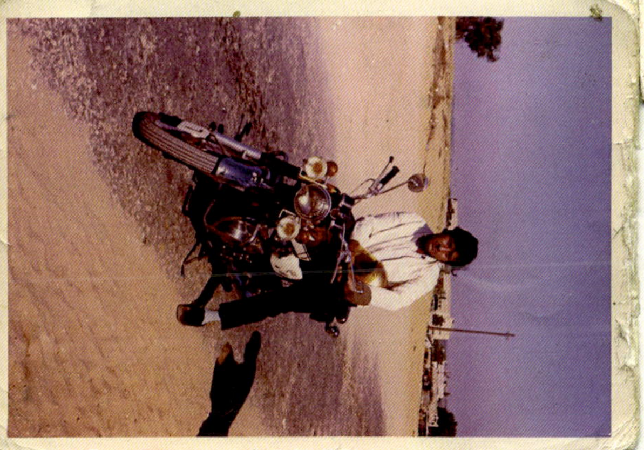

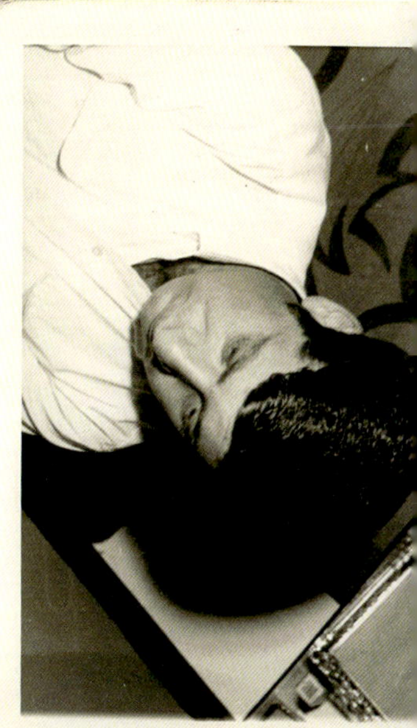

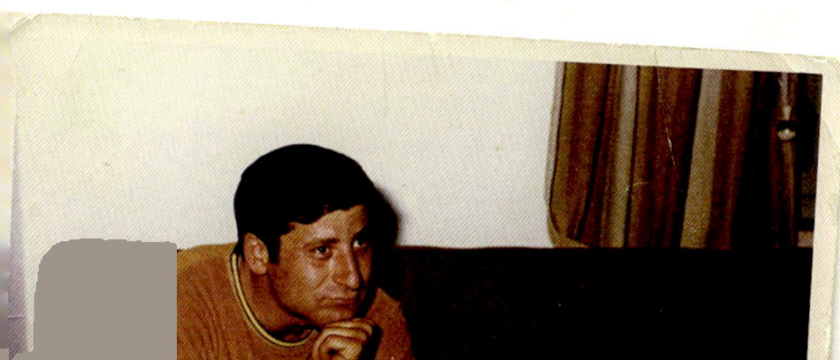

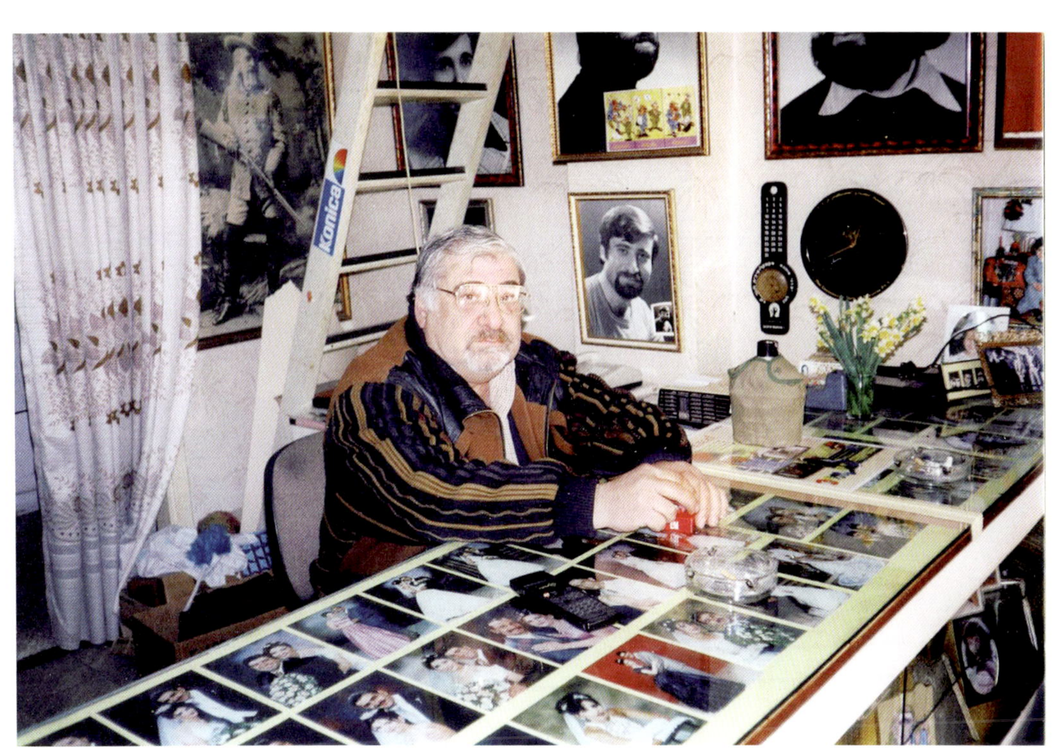

SCOTT   Why did you decide to come back here ?
         You were born in Ramallah? or somewhere else ...

CHAPL.   I born in Jerusalem, before I'm in Hebron

S   What age were you when you were born, I mean what year were you born sorry?

C   *laughter* in Jerusalem

S   Sorry, what erm..

C   What time?

S   What year...yeah

C   Erm ..1962

S   1962

C   And, I like my country, I was dreaming of how to come back here

S   Did you leave because of the war?

C   No, my father was working there 1960, before war, 65/67 was when there was
         war on and we were there in 1964

S   Okay before

C   Yes before, and when the war happened. We tried to make visa or something
         to come back and we got it in 1972

S   So six years later?

C   Yeah

S   It took a long time to get the visa was that 93 ?

C   94'. And my studio was famous before the Intifada, before the 2000 there
        was good business

S   What happened in the Intifada then ?

C   Our road there, they close it

S   For how long ?

C   For two, three years

S   Three years ?!

C   Yes *speaks in Arabic* the people was not passing from there

S   So nobody walked past ?

C   They just use *indecipherable* and also there is no good parking there and
        the business got run down

S   So on the road, did they have a checkpoint

C   Yes they close it, the end of our road there, they close it and they change
        the way and for many reason, before the people, I know them well, our
        neighbours our friends they was coming and take photo's for me and in that
        Intifada, they come with covering and with guns and they told me "make our
        photo's'. I used make lots of photo's of people and I was giving them the
        negative

S   So you didn't want to keep the negative ?

C   No because in this case it's dangerous

S   Yes

C   If the army is coming and see this negative I will be in trouble

S   So then you, yeah

C   *Arabic* And there was lots of people which they die, killed and
        I have photos of them and some children also. They come to Ramallah
        in 2002, they killed a lot of people, some of them were my customers

INTERVIEW BETWEEN SCOTT CARUTH AND STUDIO CHAPLIN, RAMALLAH

S   Can you remember, you remember them all ?

C   No I remember some of them, they come and they put their photos in the newspaper and I say "oh he's my customer"

S   Right, right, so you would begin to recognise people from that. So after the first Intifada, they opened the street again so things were good ?

      Speaks arabic They open it after maybe, ten years

S   It was closed for ten years ?

C   Yeah and after that it open for one year or something and after this only they close it again

      And now it's digital it's different from before, people was taking photos and open the computer

S   Yeah, what year did you get a digital camera?

C   2005 I think or 6, something like that

S   Did you like it?

C   All the people they was asking, "show me the photo' straight away, I was not liking. The people, the customer when I take photo they say 'show me instant now, is it nice enough". I said this is negative they told me 'oh the other studio they have', and so it was very difficult and was expensive before: I got one camera, it's normal EOS 10 D. it was around 9,000 Shekels... sometimes I spend one film, 36 shots for one customer and I was making a contact sheet and I was showing to them which one do you like, which one, this one ?" and he choose some of them....but you know, I was also looking to photo good face, nice face which I like it, I spend more, I told them it's not problem for money and if I like the photos I ask them to put it in my studio, make it framed something like this. Some people they were accept, some people no, especially girls, but for men and children, then I was choosing. You know maybe in the year, I choose one or two or three photos which I made, which I like it much. You could see in my studio....

S   I remember yeah

C   So all the government people they come in. Some of them I don't like them
         they ask which is best photographer and people say 'Chaplin', they coming.
         which they, some of them I don't like them, but I said okay

S   Why would the girls feel more self-conscious about having their photograph
         taken?

C   ...Because it's kind of community and religious stuff

S   Ah I kind of thought that

C   There was one girl, she was maybe 7/8 years and we make photo for her and
         she was nice and with wide blue eyes and something like this, I asked her
         father, I want to put photo in my shop. He says "okay", so I put the photo.
         The photo is still there after 10 years, when she was 18 years old. After
         10 years she get engagement and she come to me. I don't remember her and
         she told me "you remember me?" and she told me "I am this, this photo". I
         said "oh wow really? you look different!". She told me to put the new small
         photo's near the big photo, it was 8x10 or something like that. So I put
         the small photo there ... after maybe 6 months, one man came and he look at
         both of these photo's and he says "this is my wife, engagement" and he say,
         he don't want to have this photo here

S   Really?! that's a shame

C   I told him okay, I remove the glass, I took the small photo and I give to
         him. After maybe one year. she was pregnant and get baby and she come and
         she told me "why is my photo gone?", I said "your husband came... and she
         said' "let him! go away! put it again!"...so I put it again there. I had a
         chair with colours and hearts for nice photos for children, she bring her
         baby and she wants to put him in the chair to make photos.... I asked her
         "why?" she said because I stay in this chair when I was child I want my son
         to be in the same chair as my photo. I stayed around there for 20 years and
         the children was 5/6....

S   And they come back later on?

C   Yes, it's nice story. Now what do you want, you want to go to my house and
         see negative or something? or you want to comeback after few days, what
         do you want?

S   If you have time now that would be good

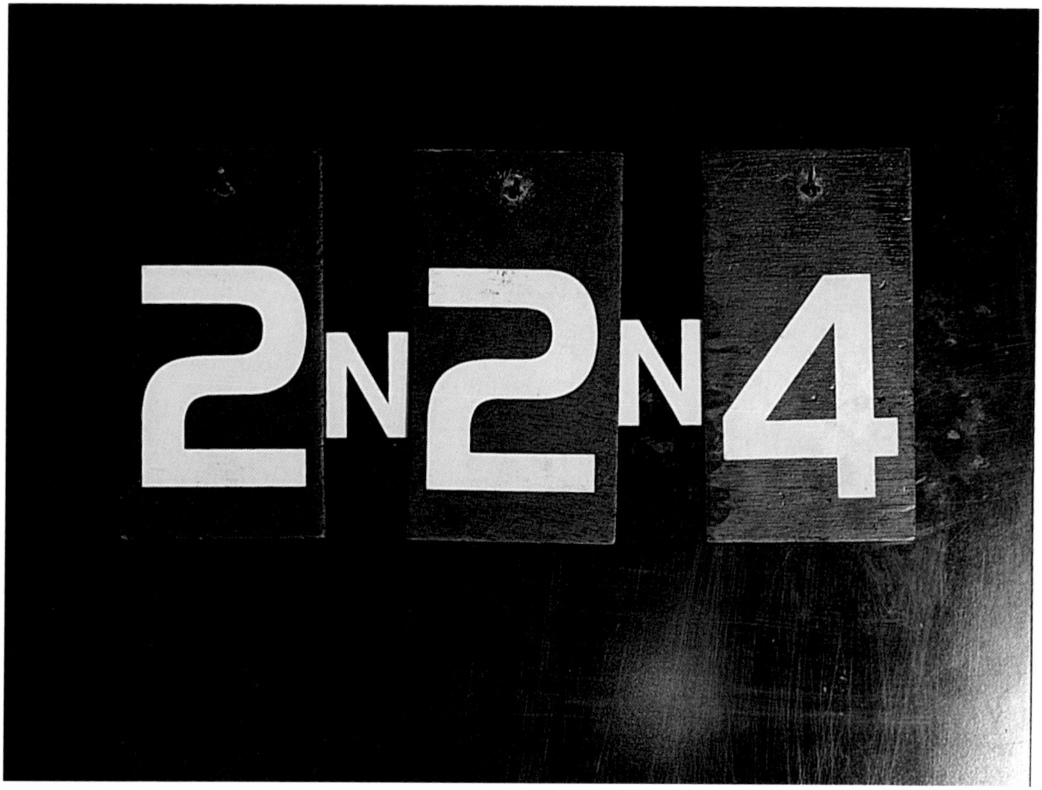

2N2N4

STUDIO CHAPLIN, RAMALLAH

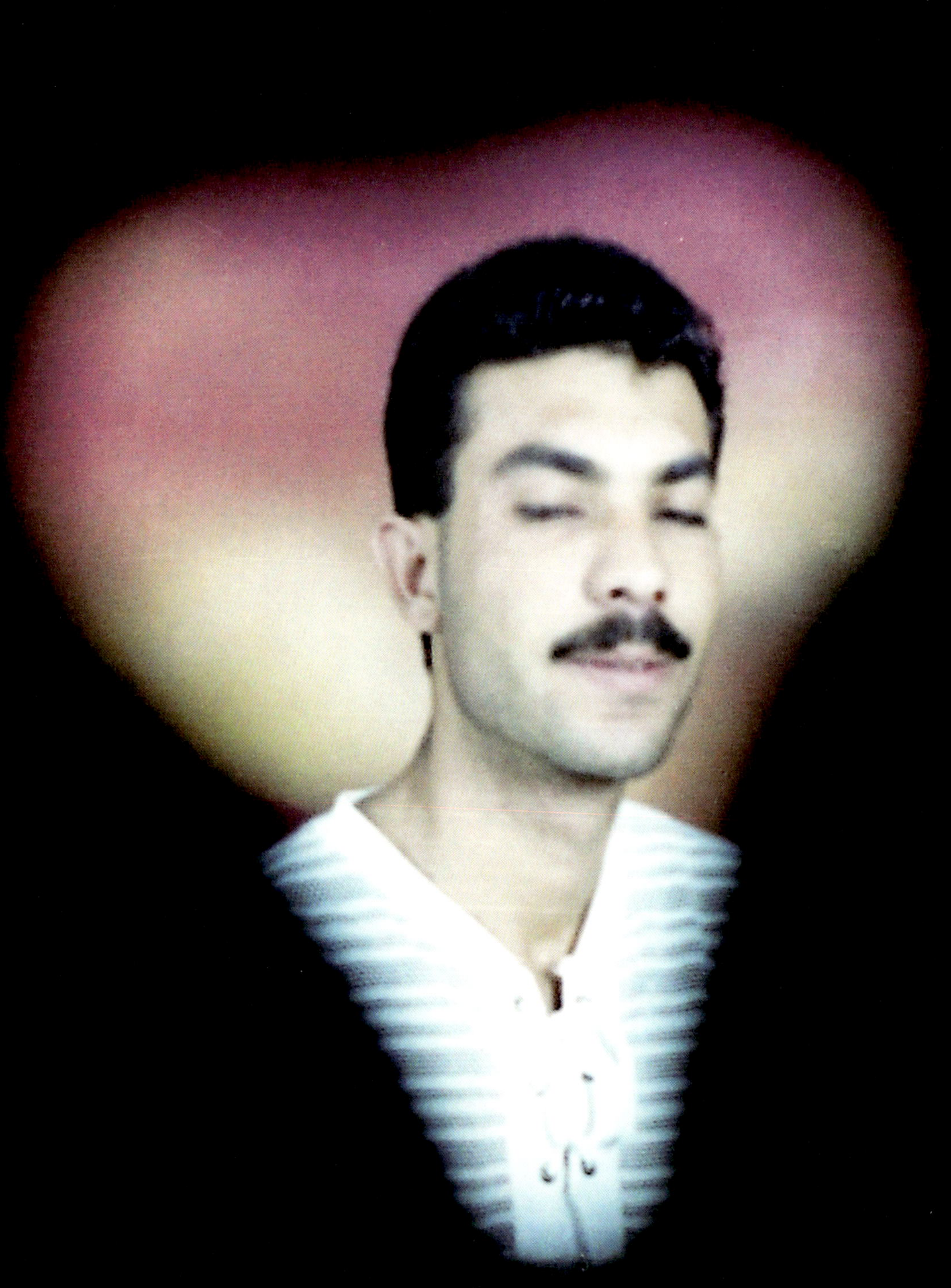

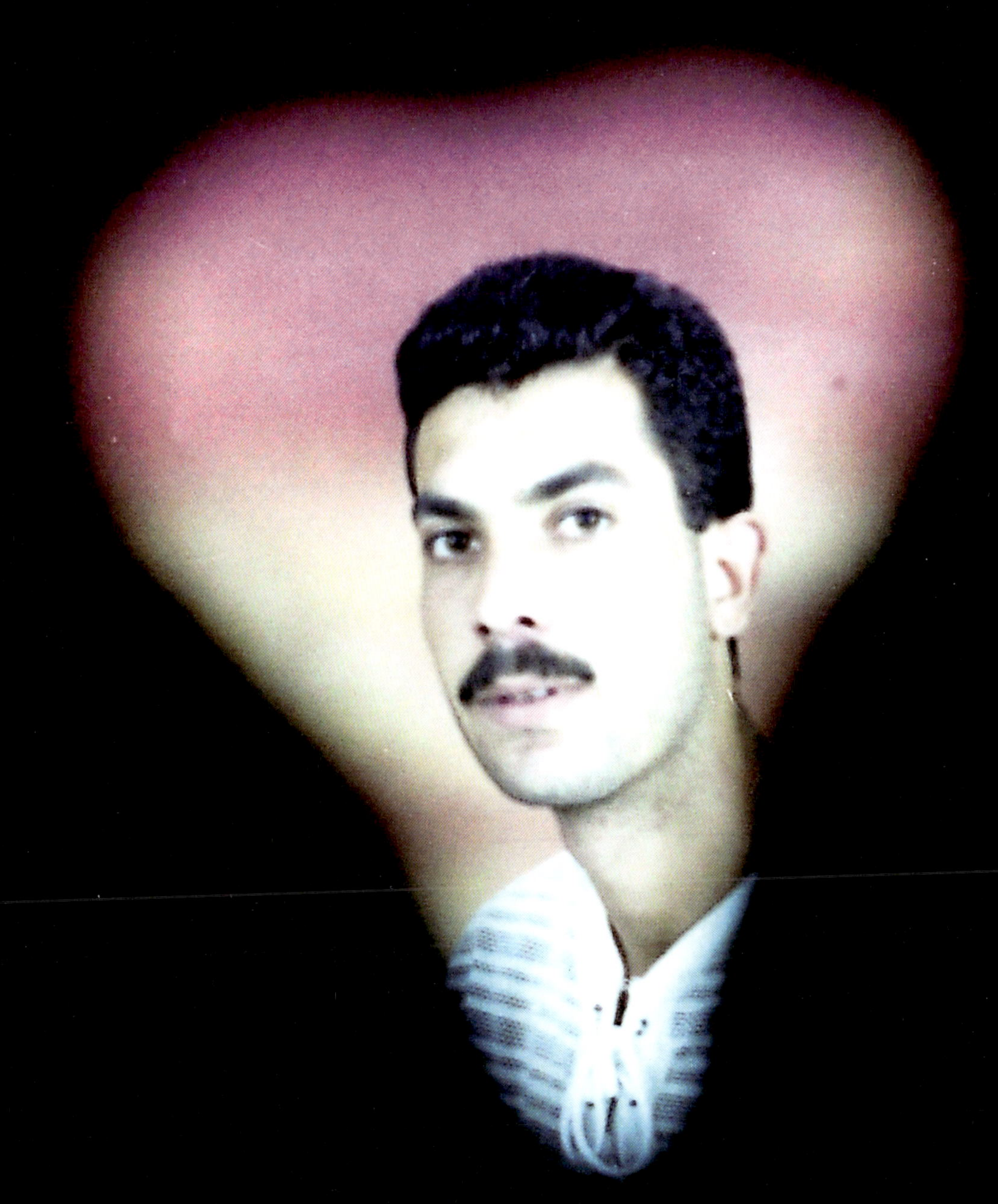

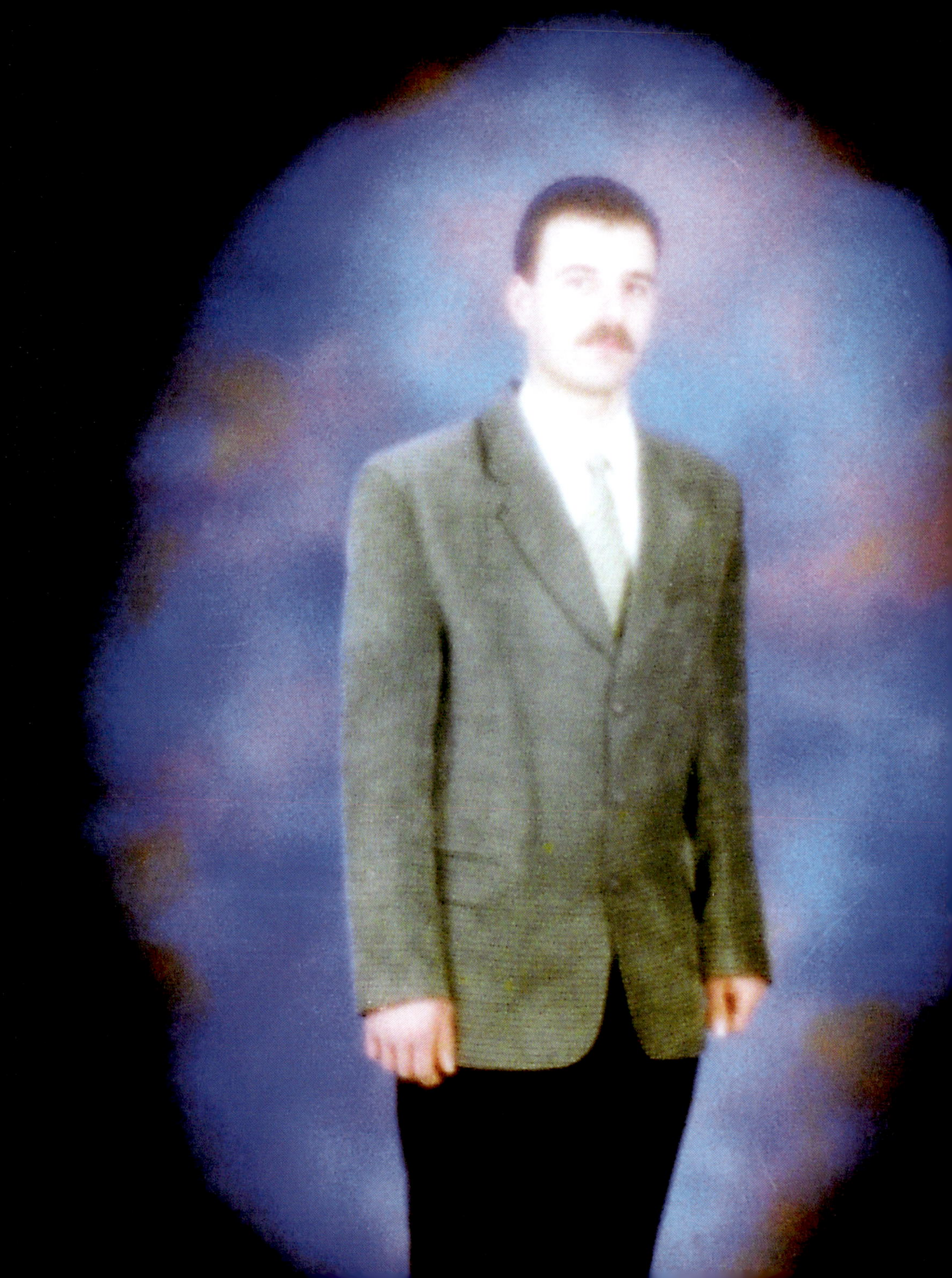

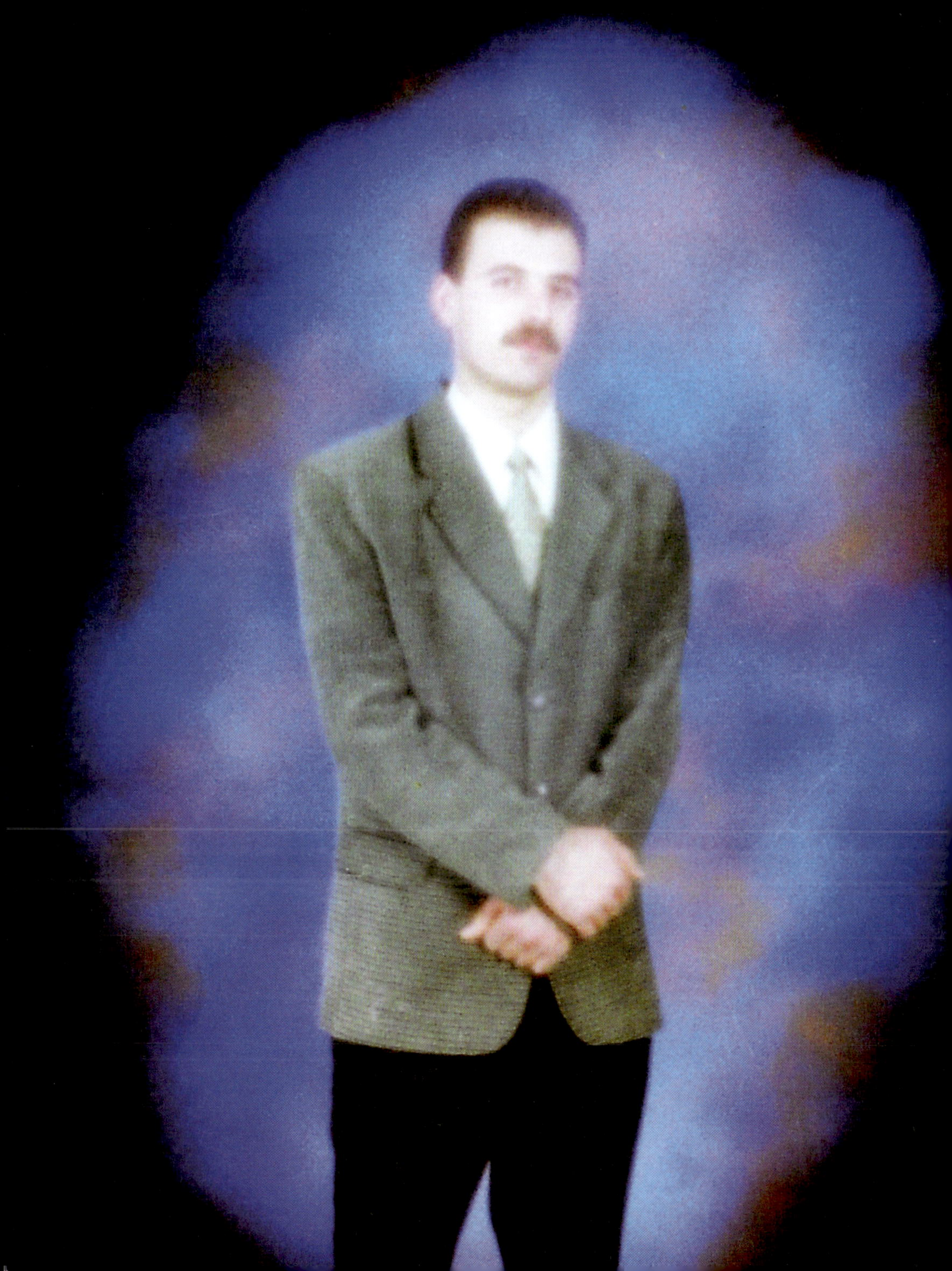

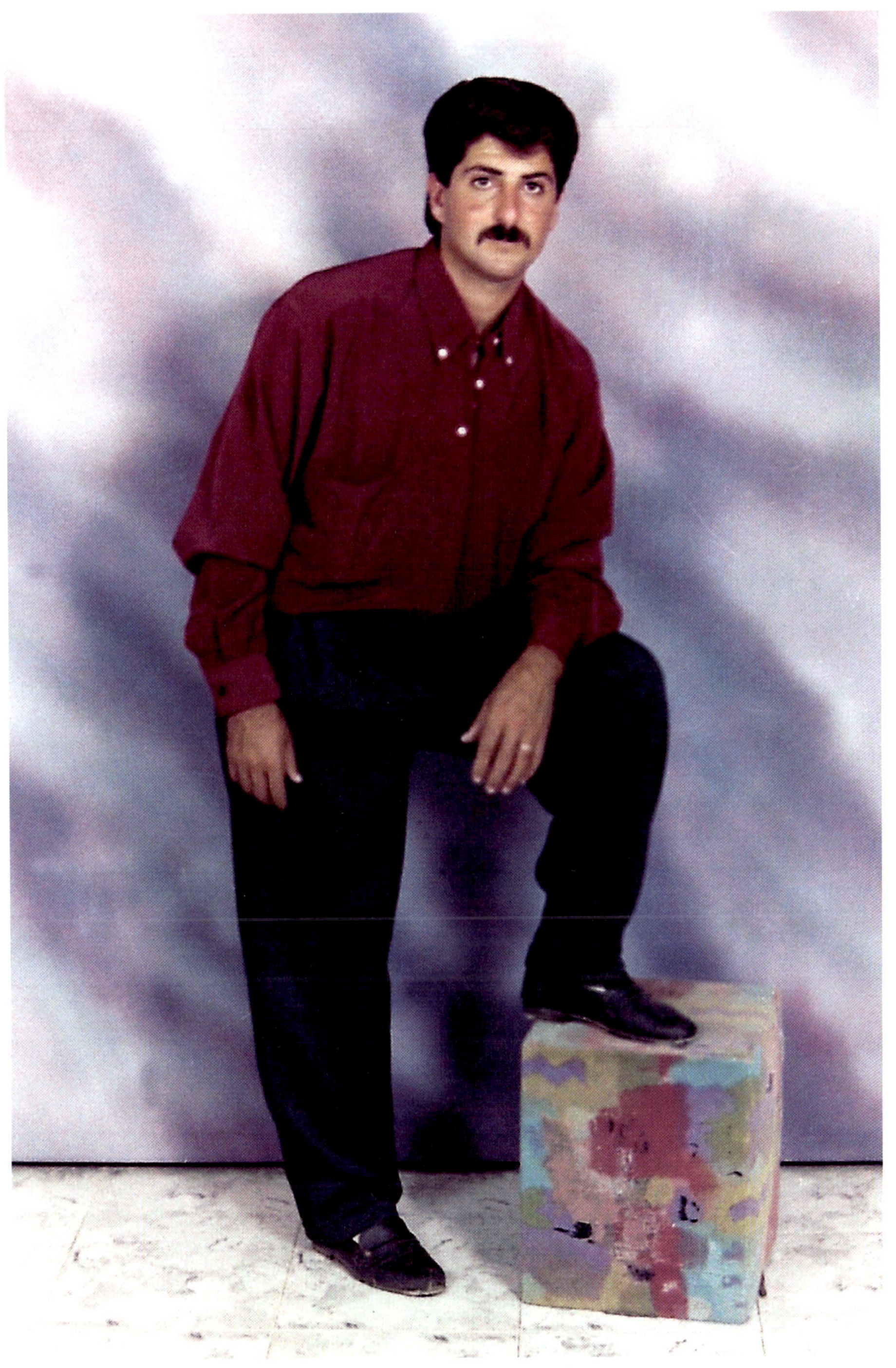

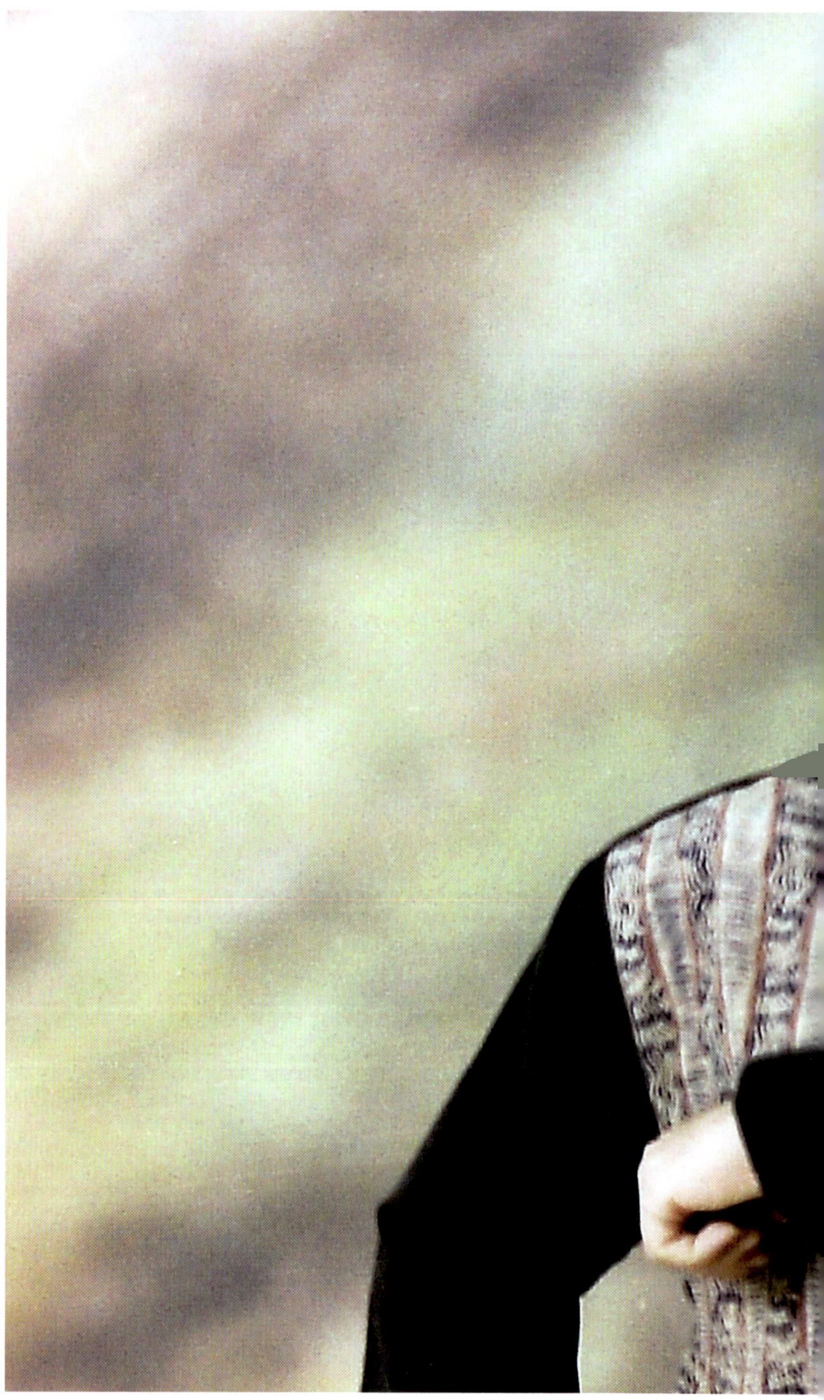

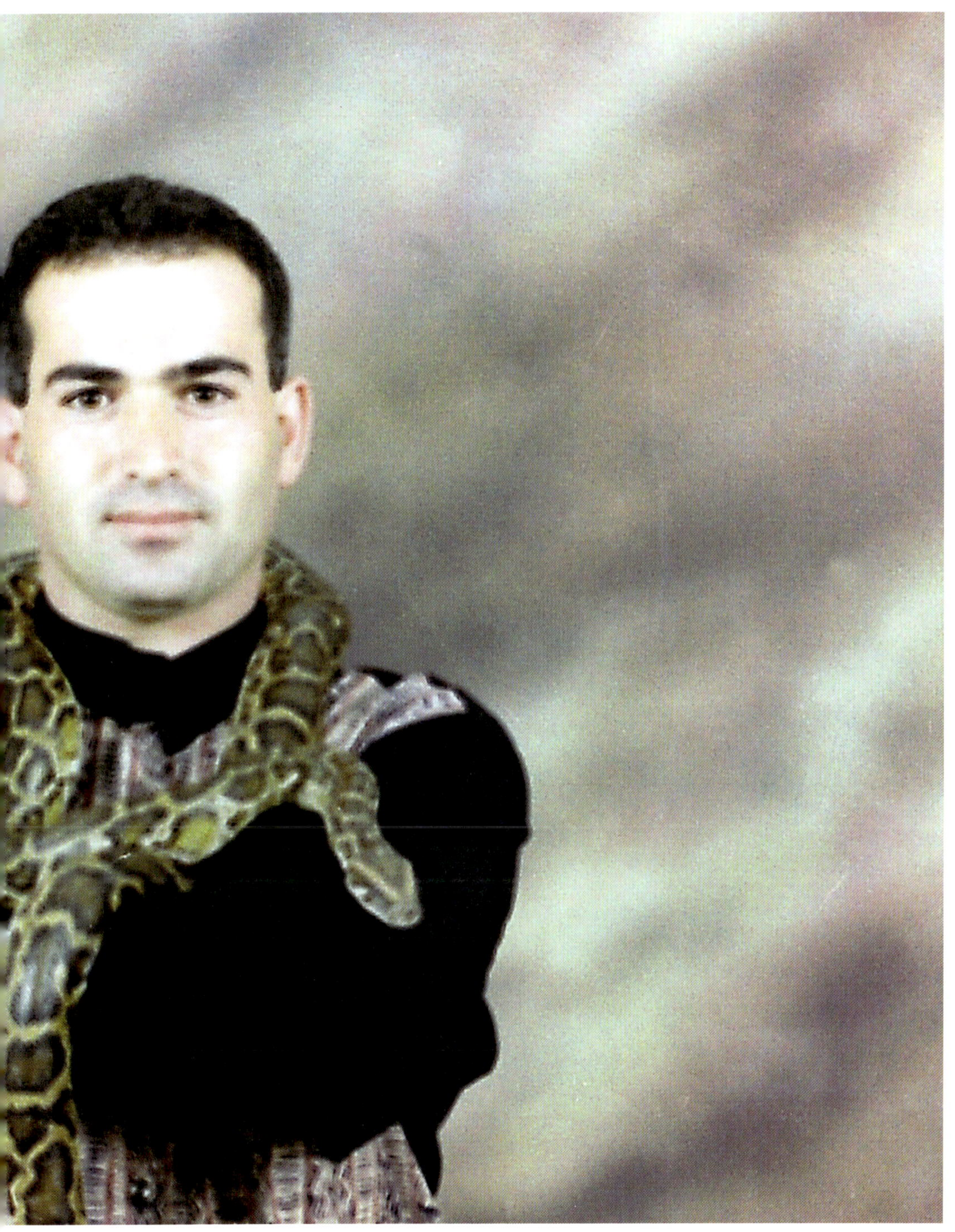

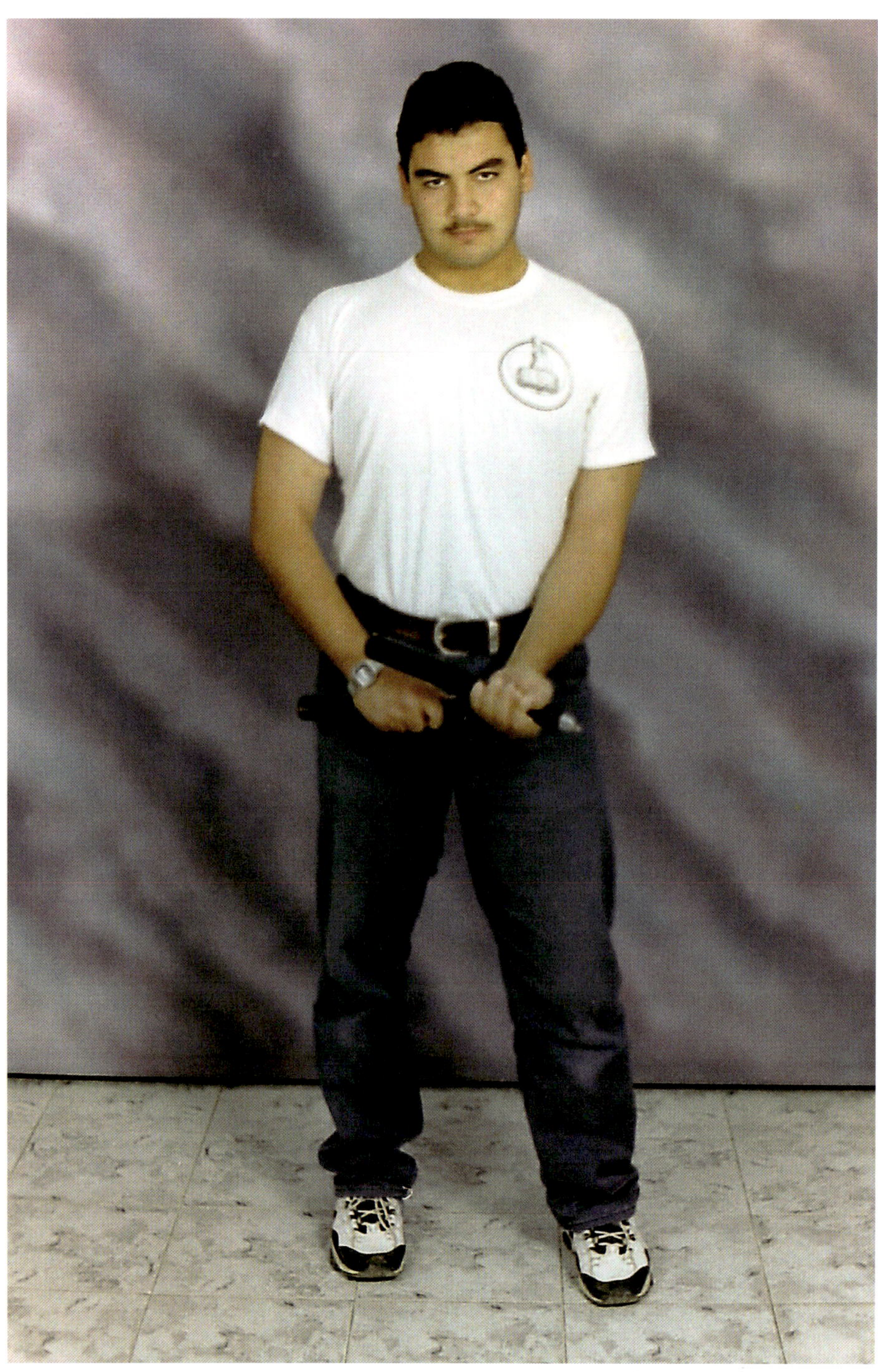

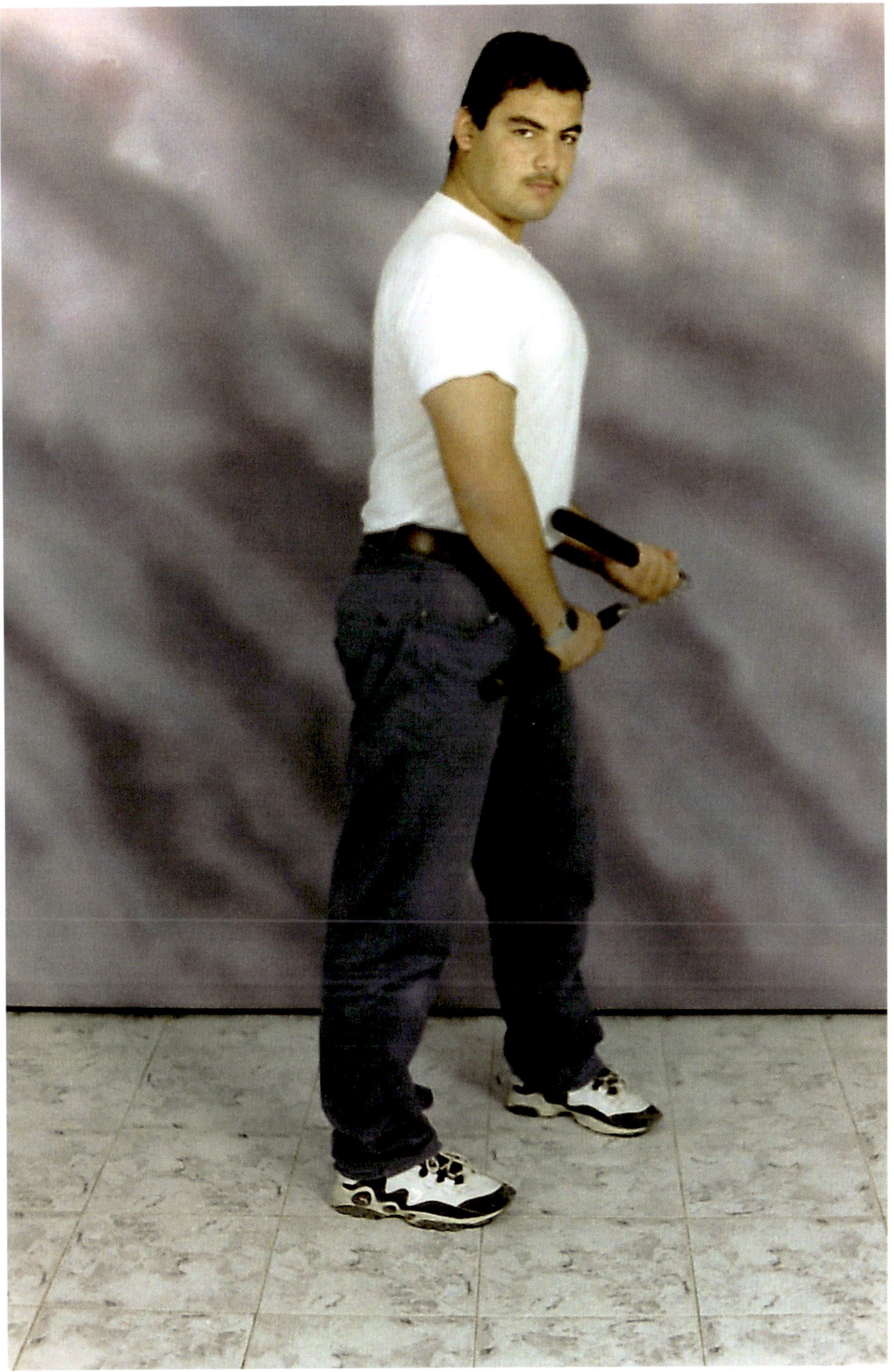

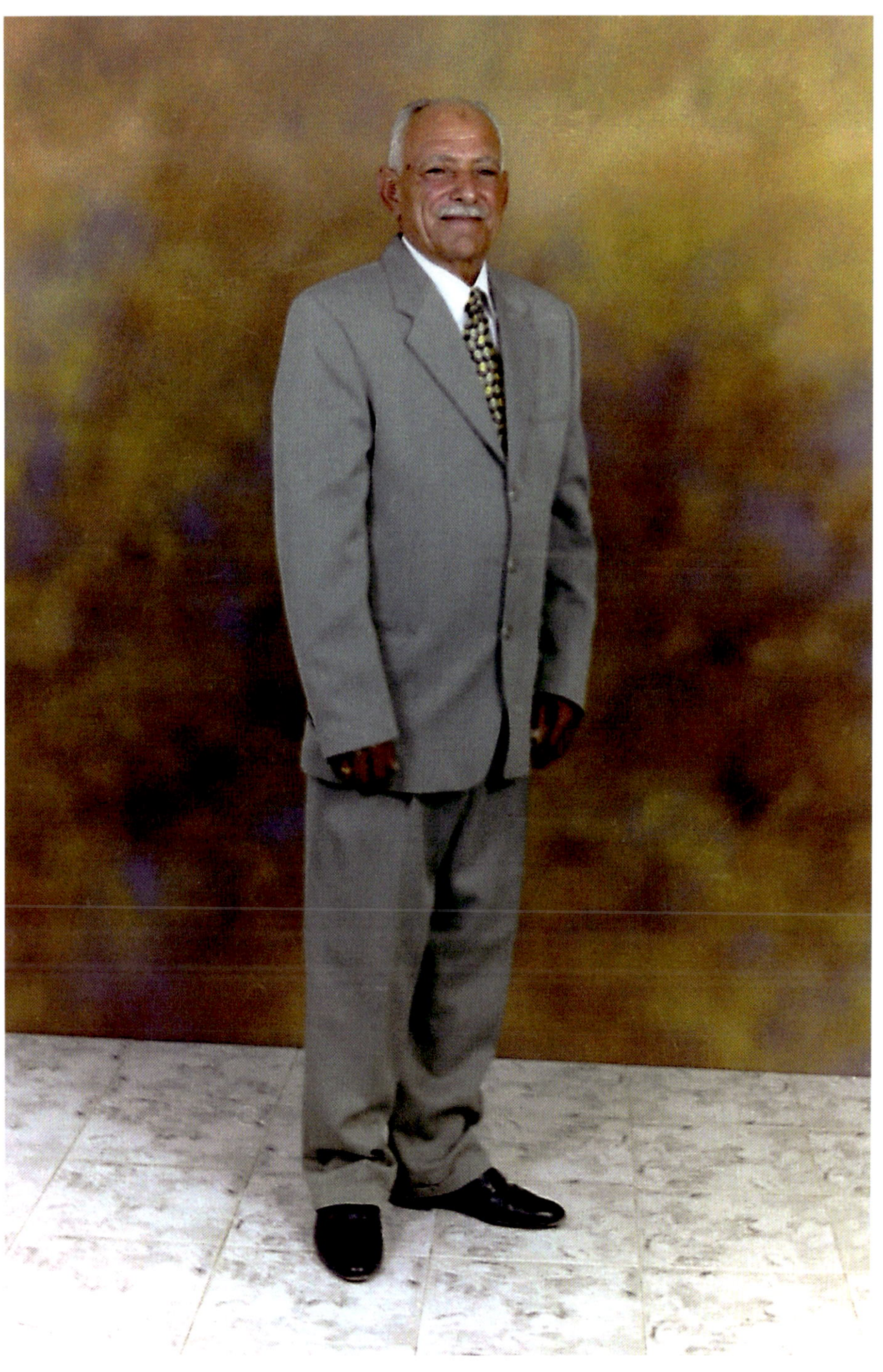

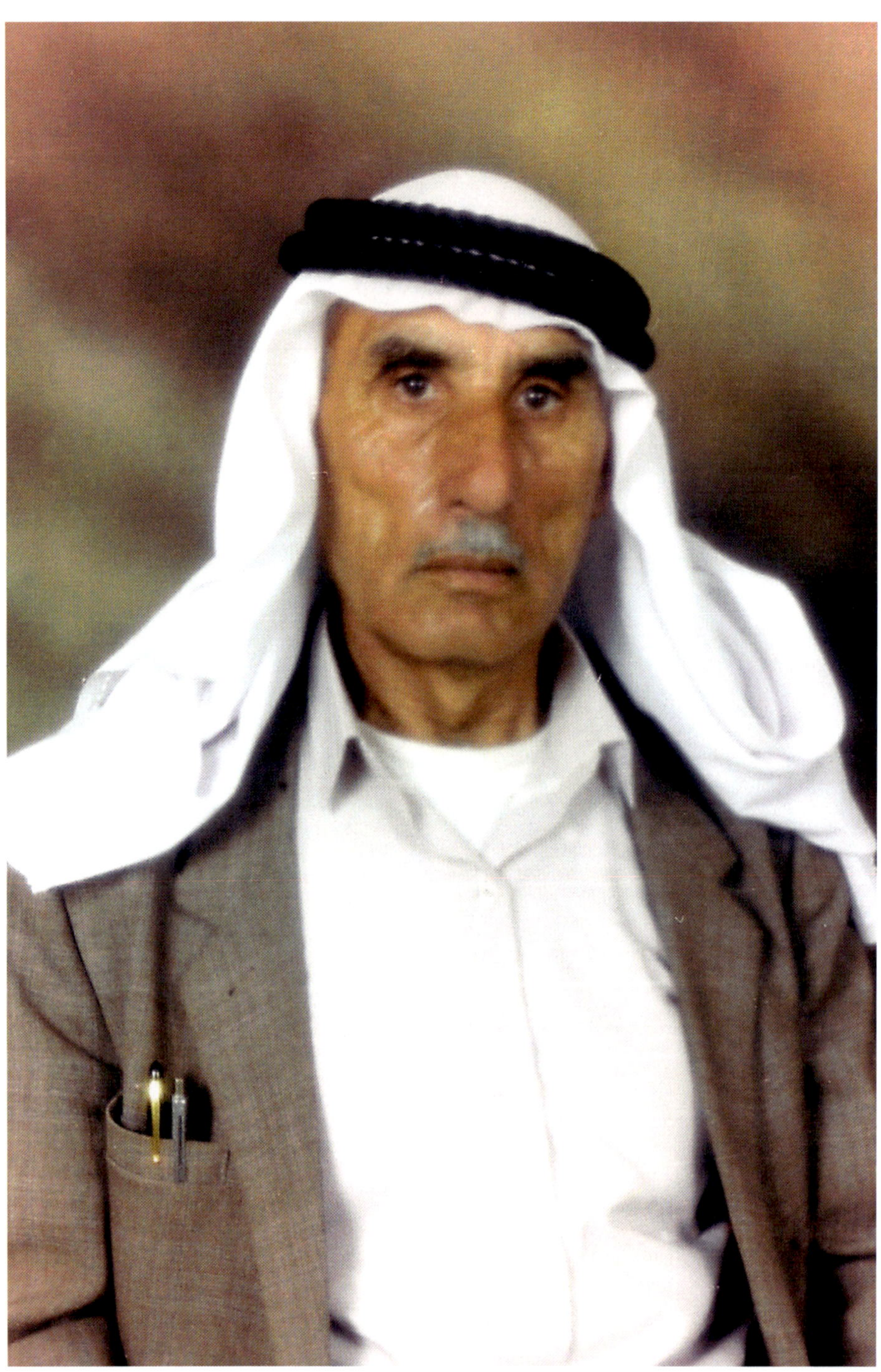

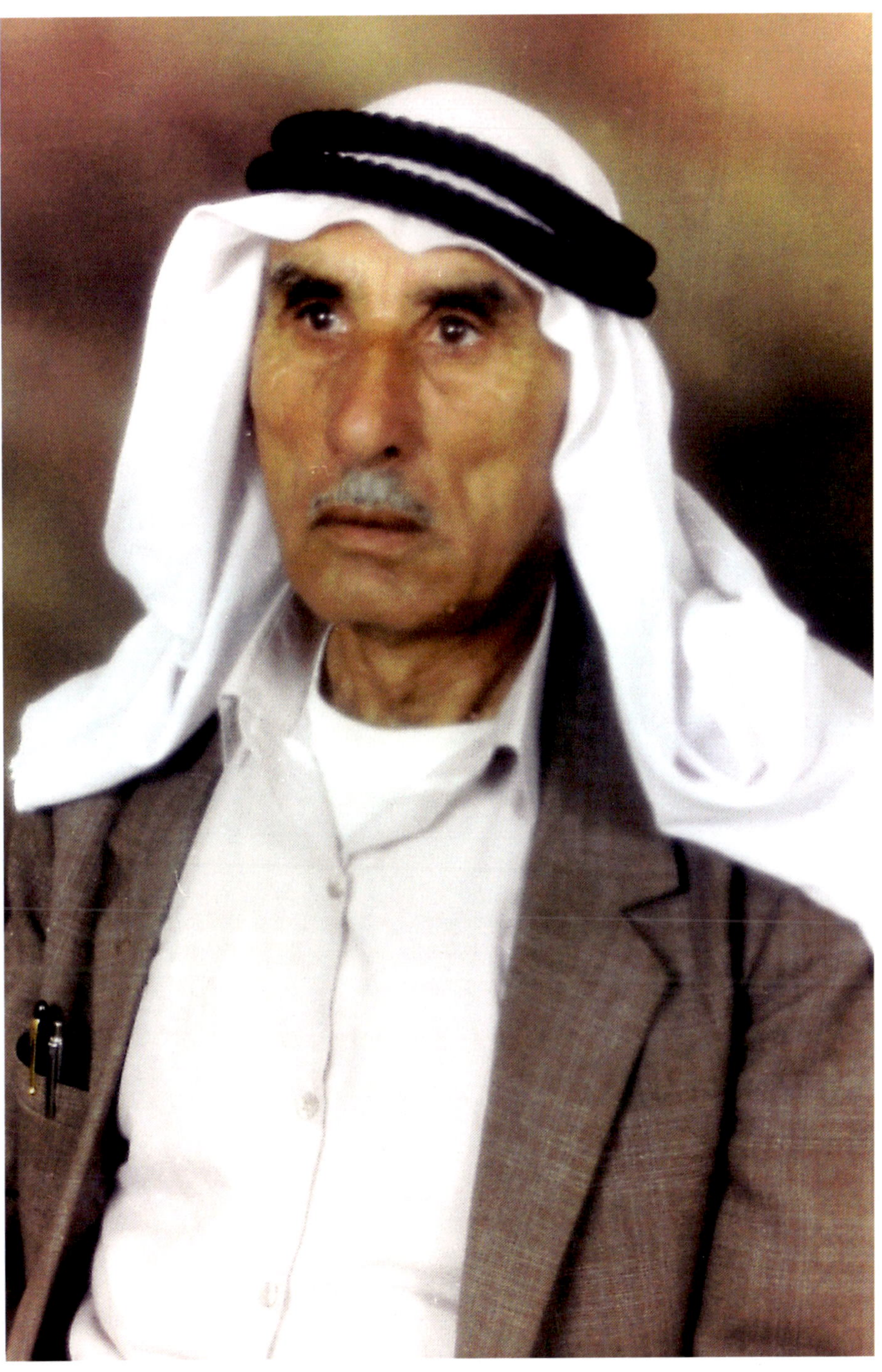

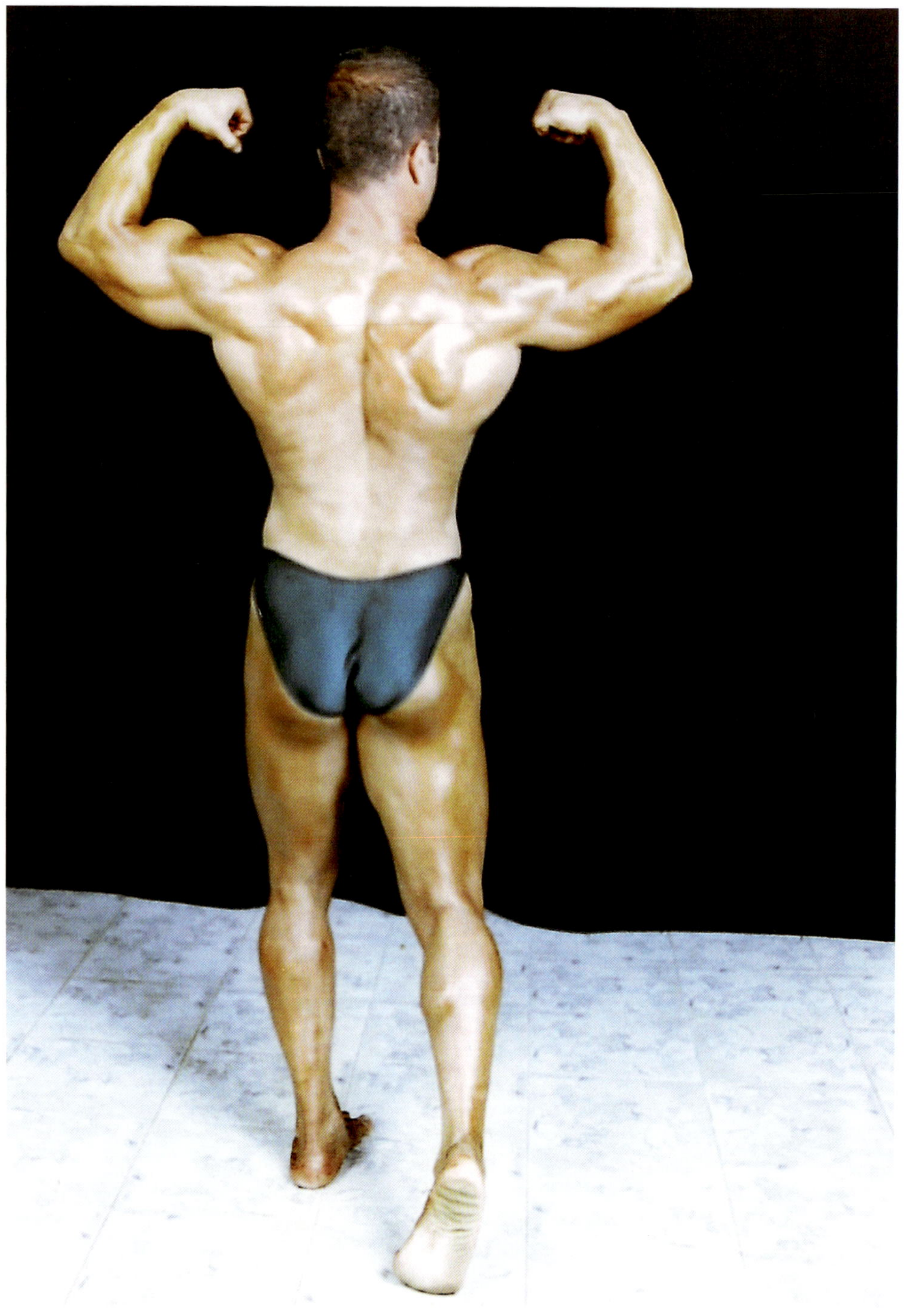

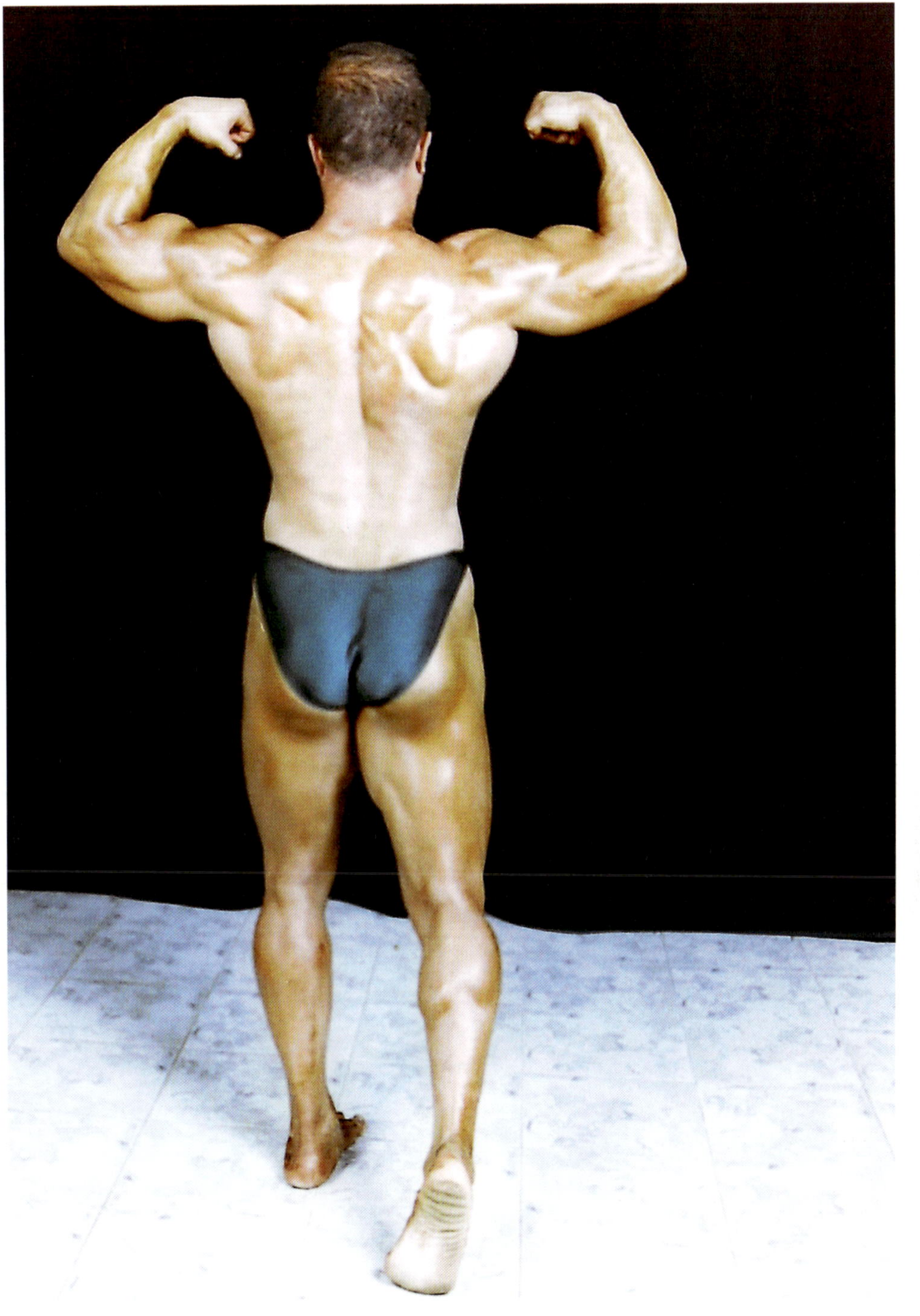

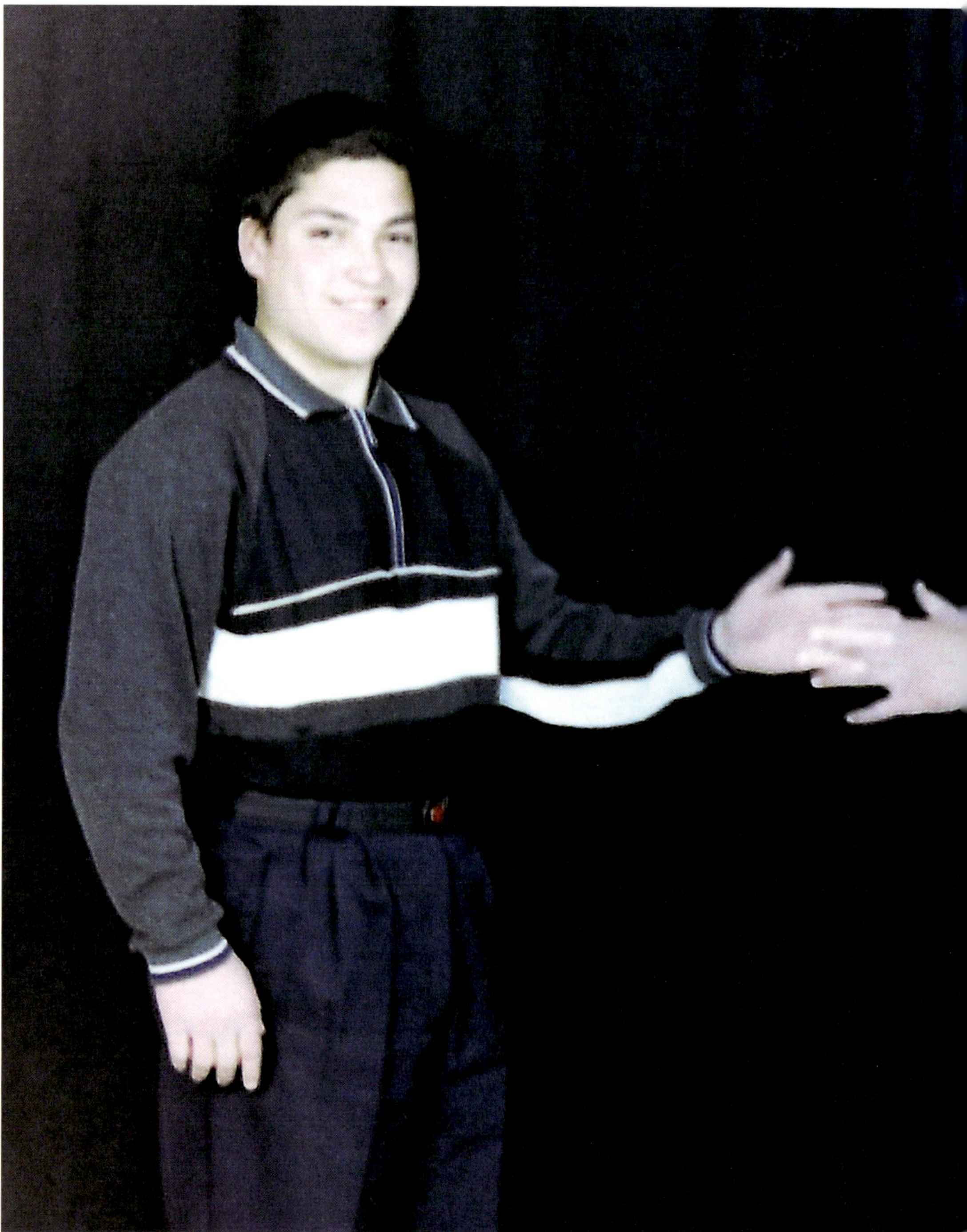

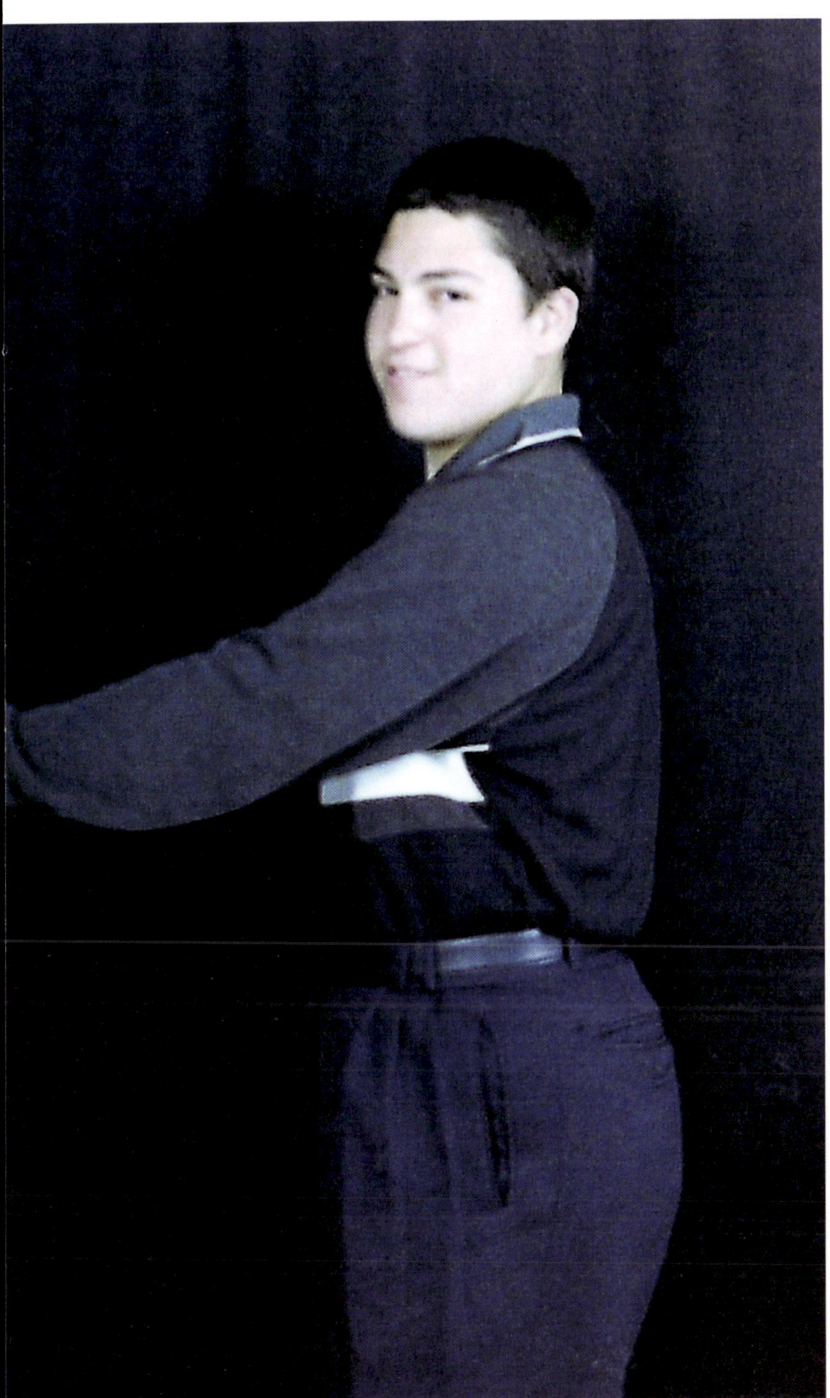

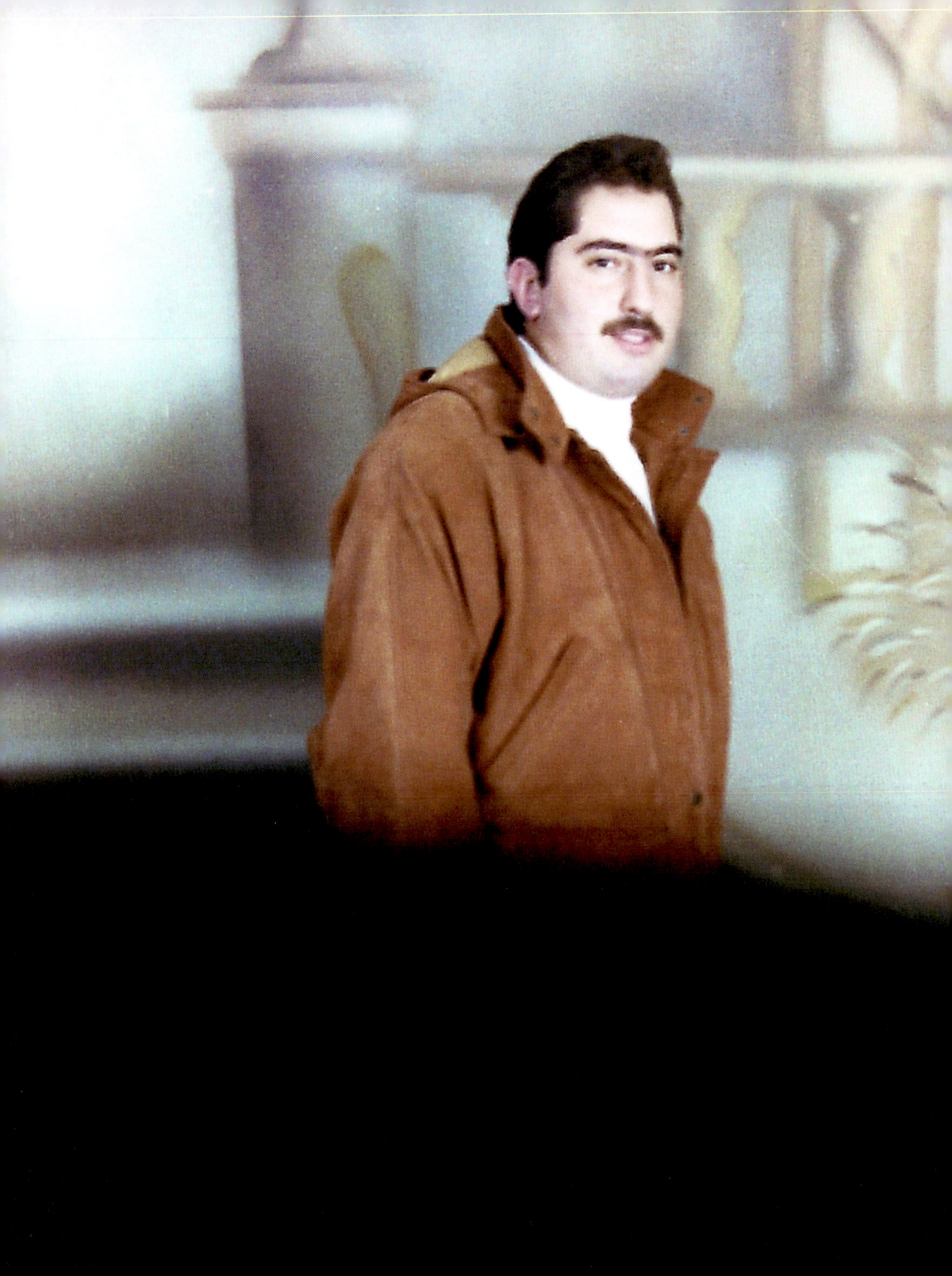

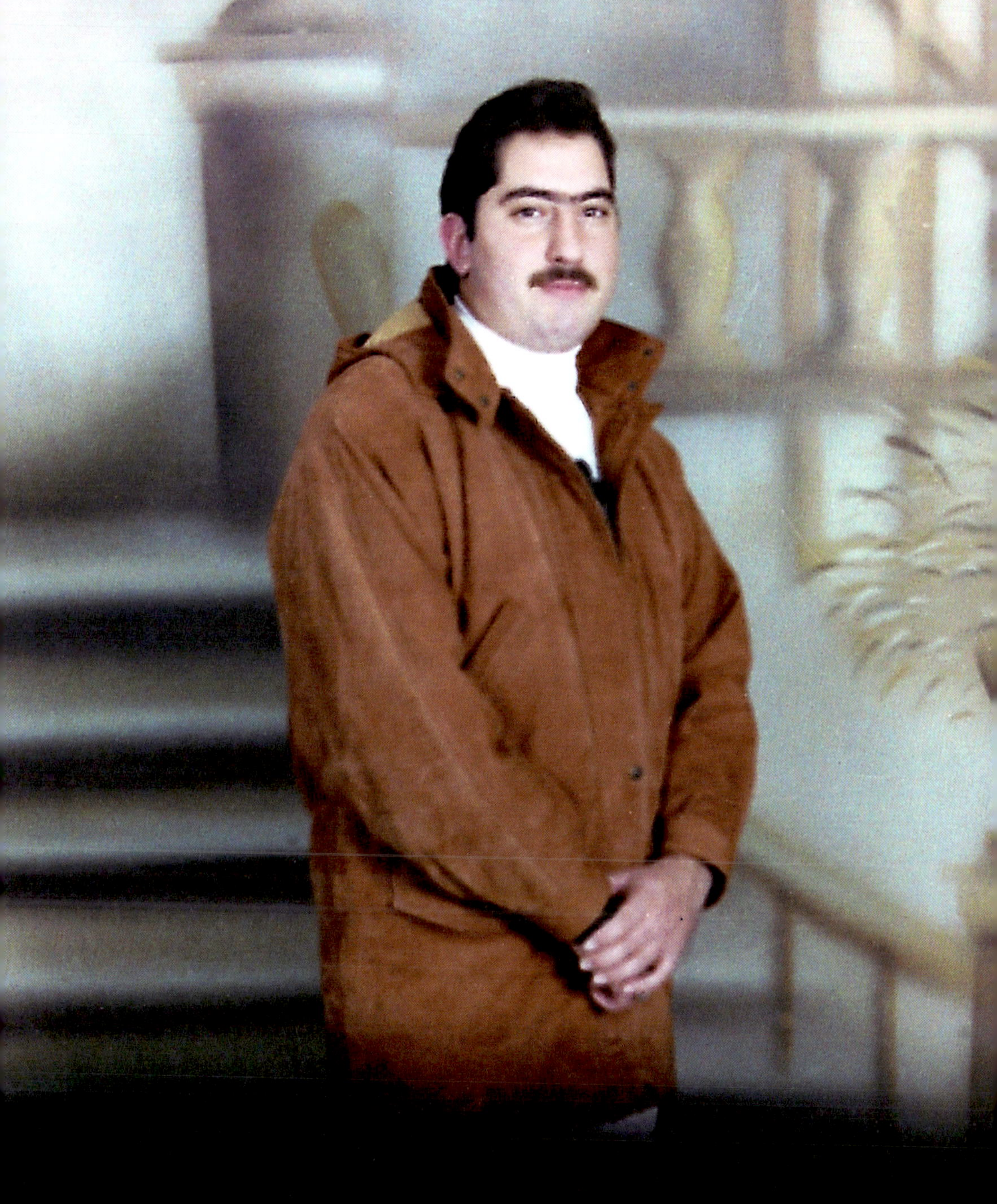

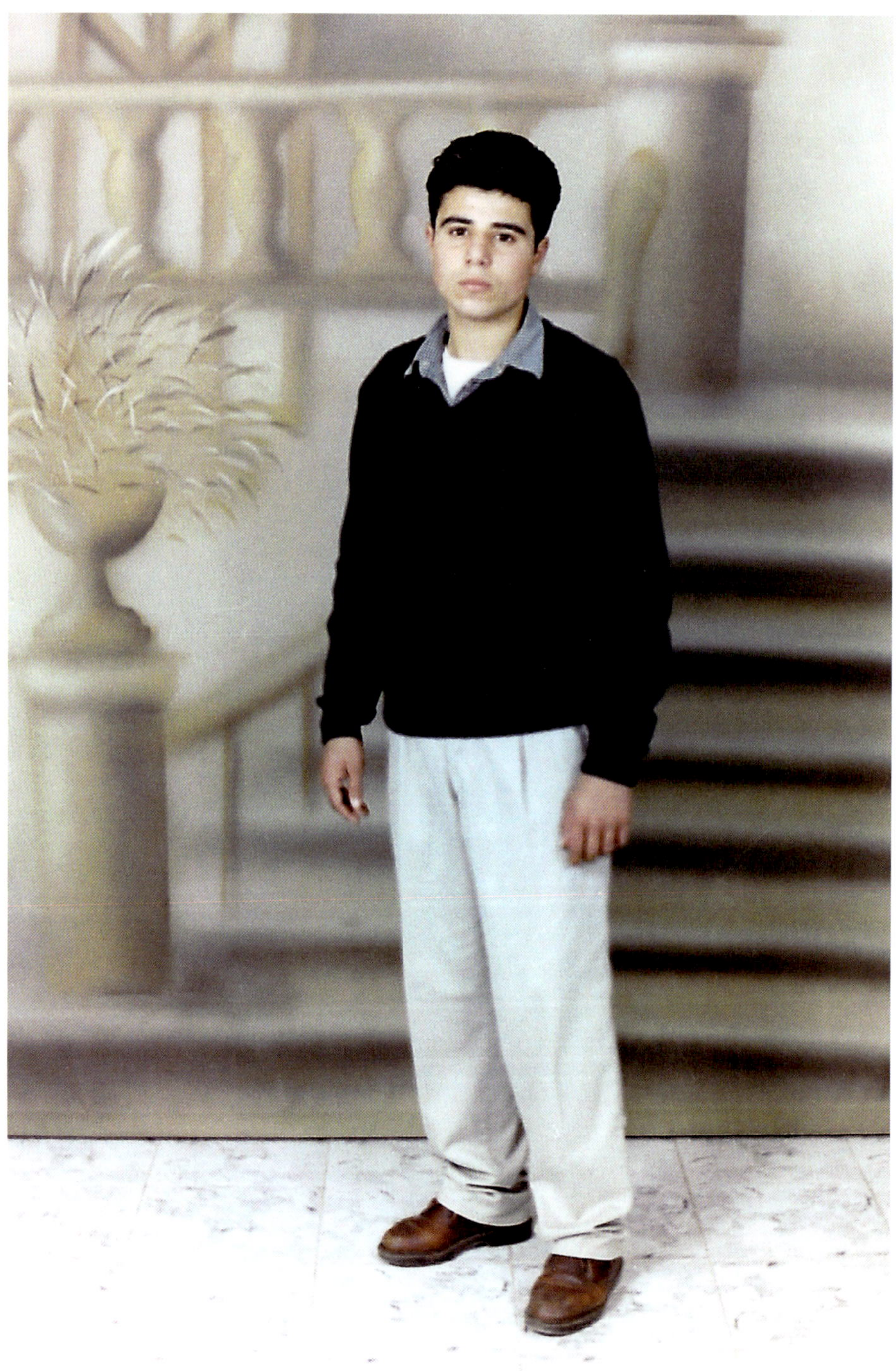

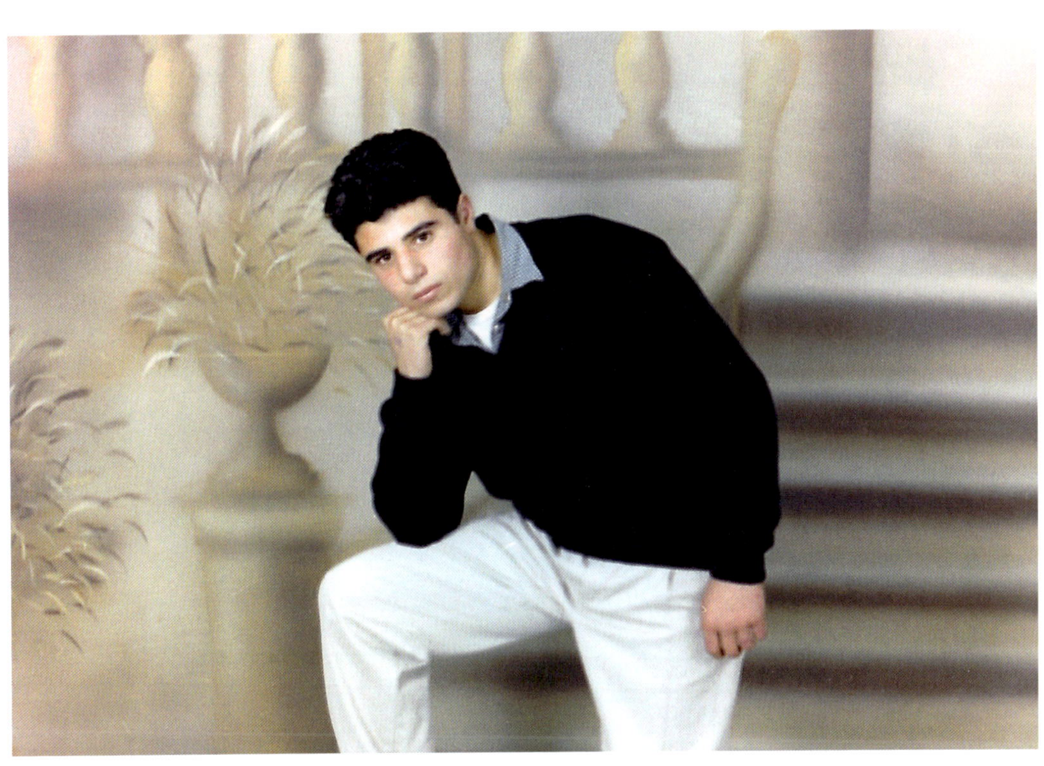

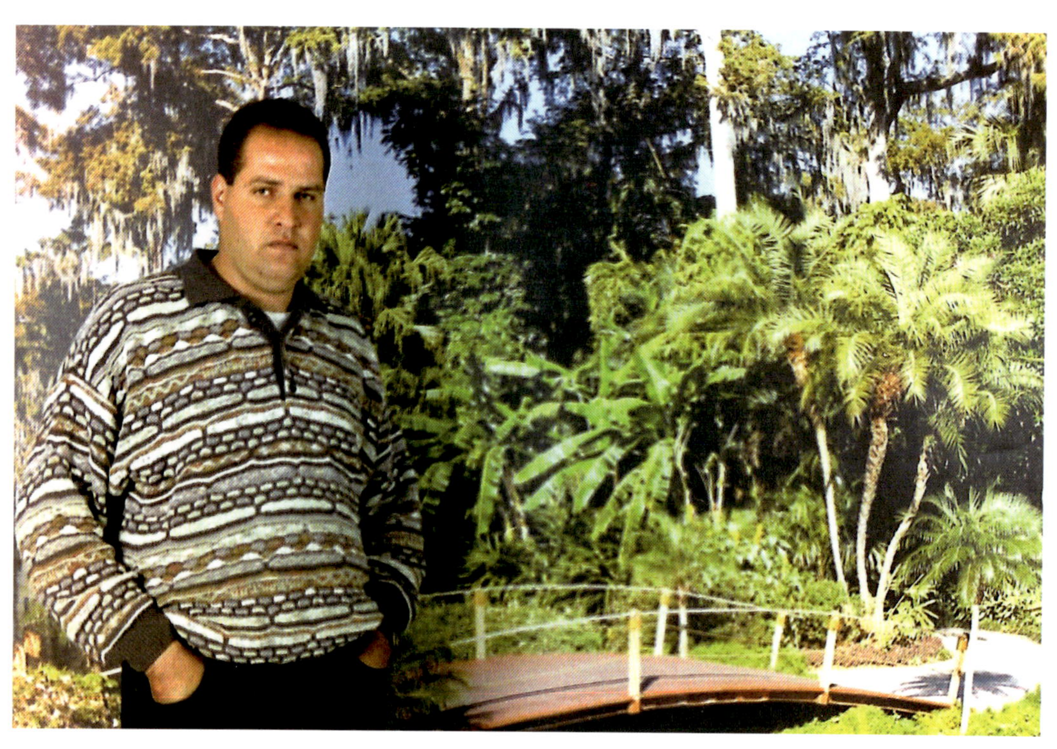

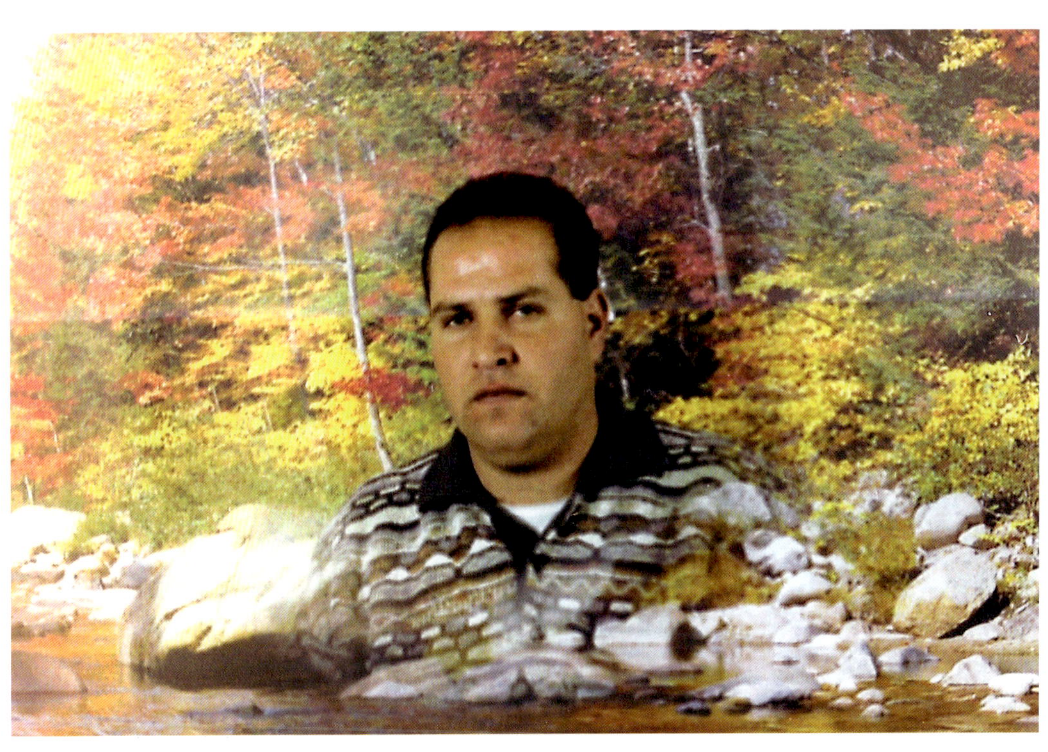

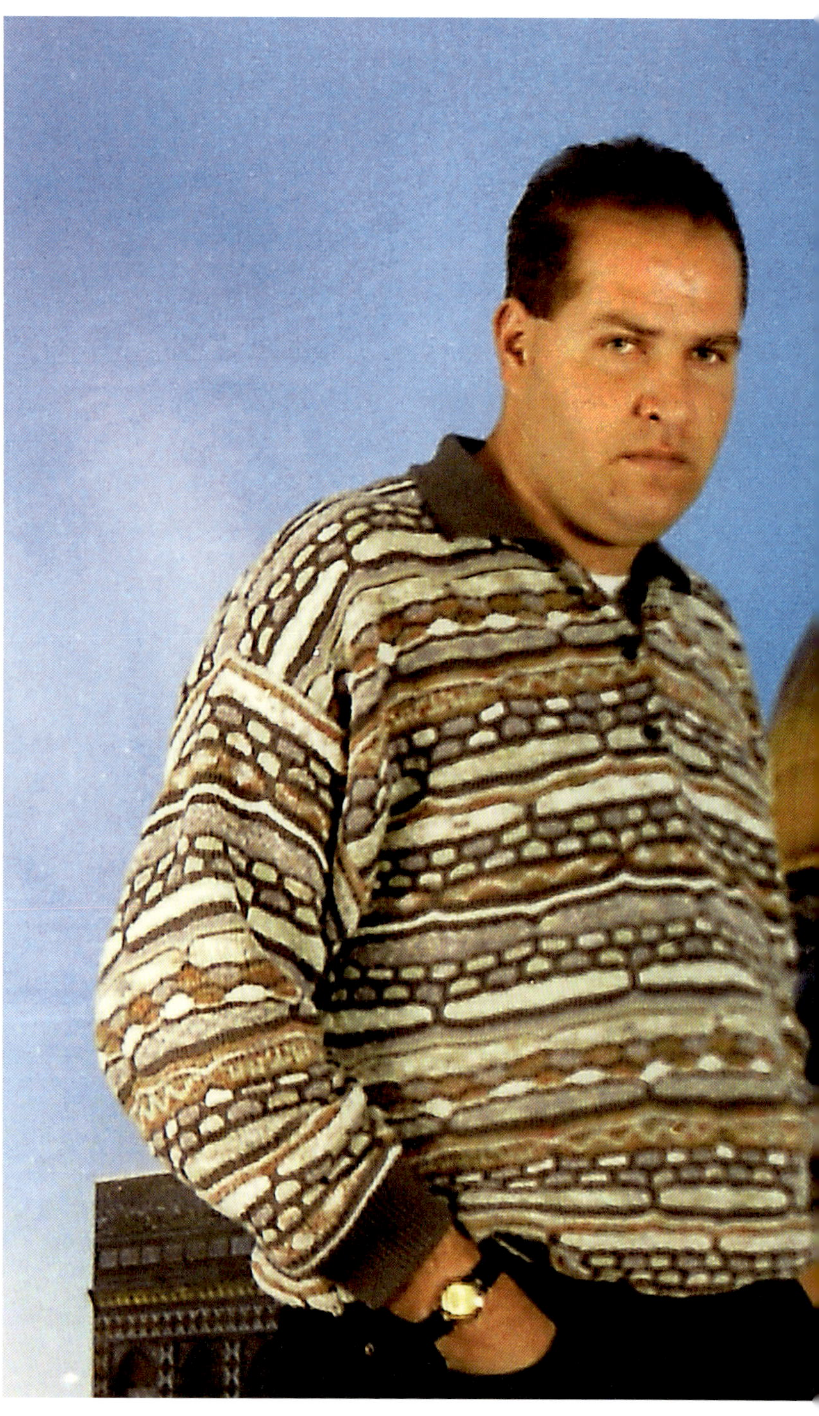

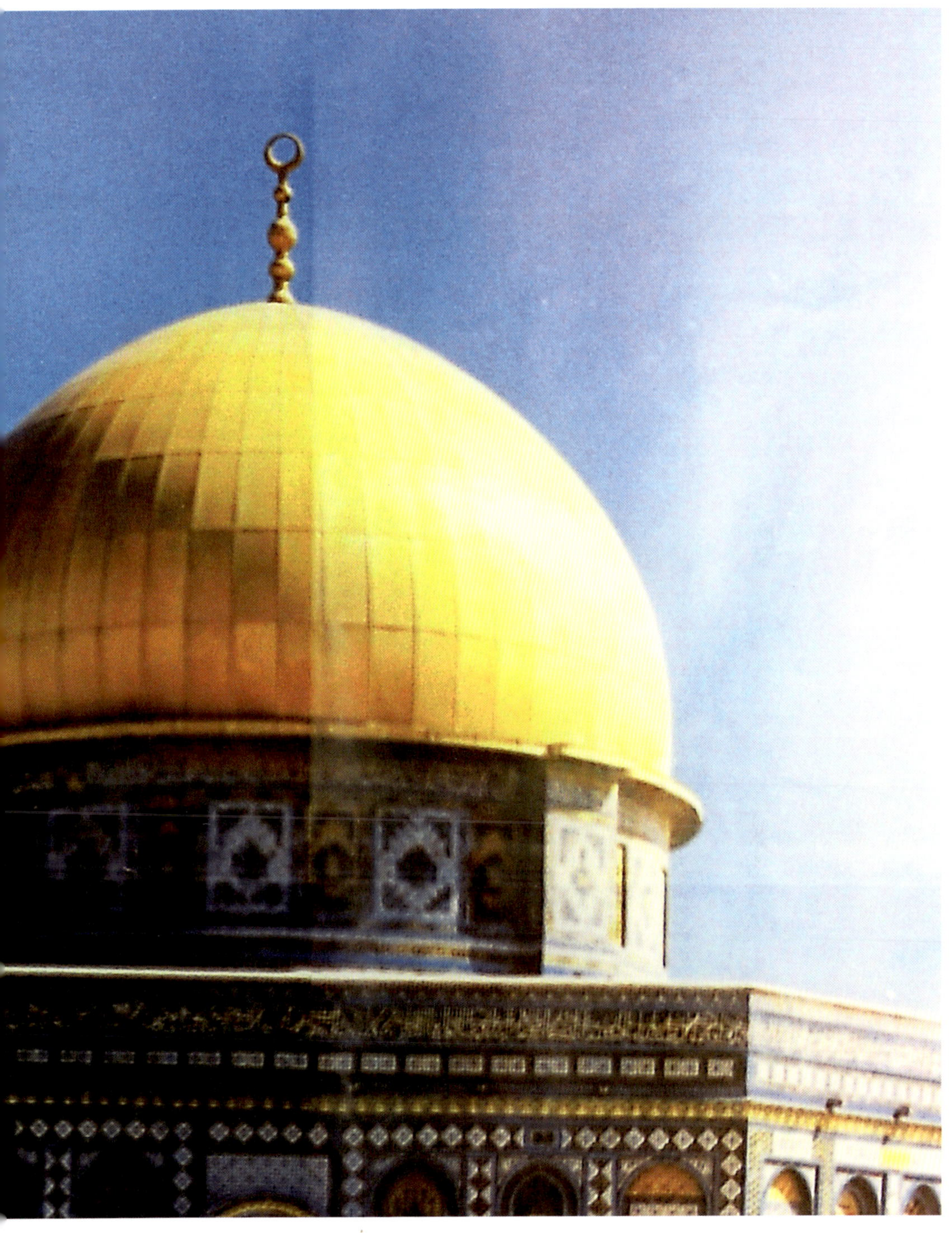

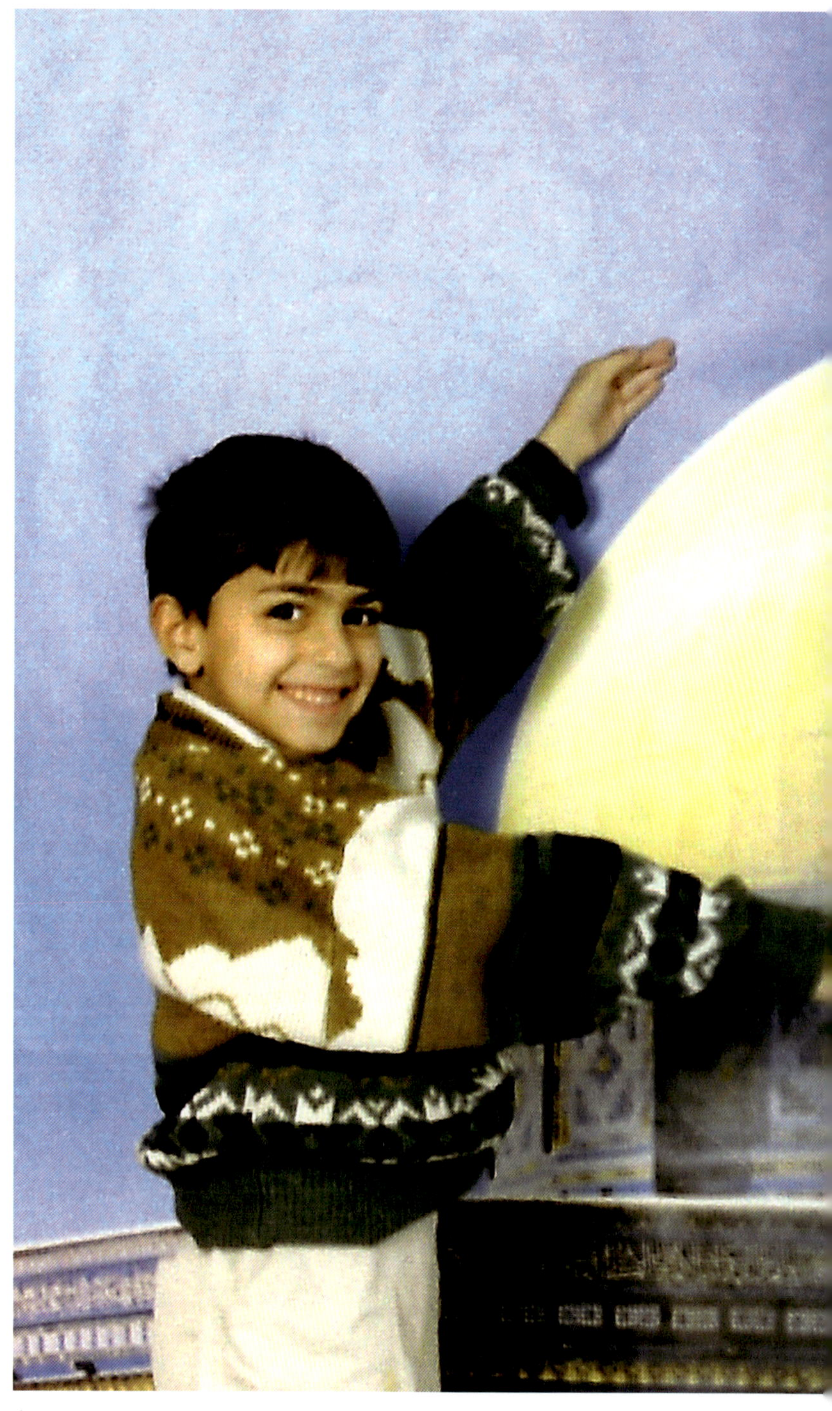

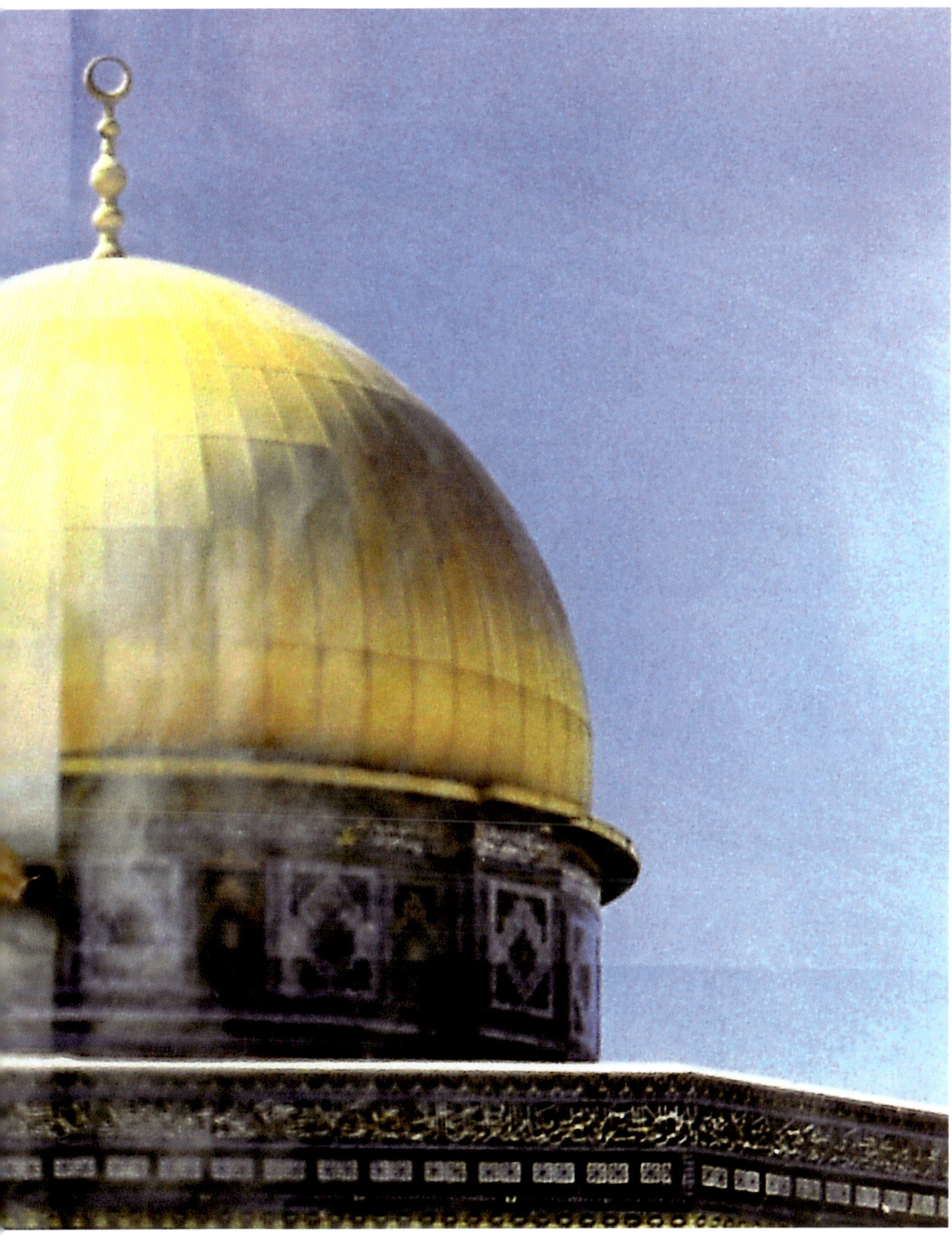

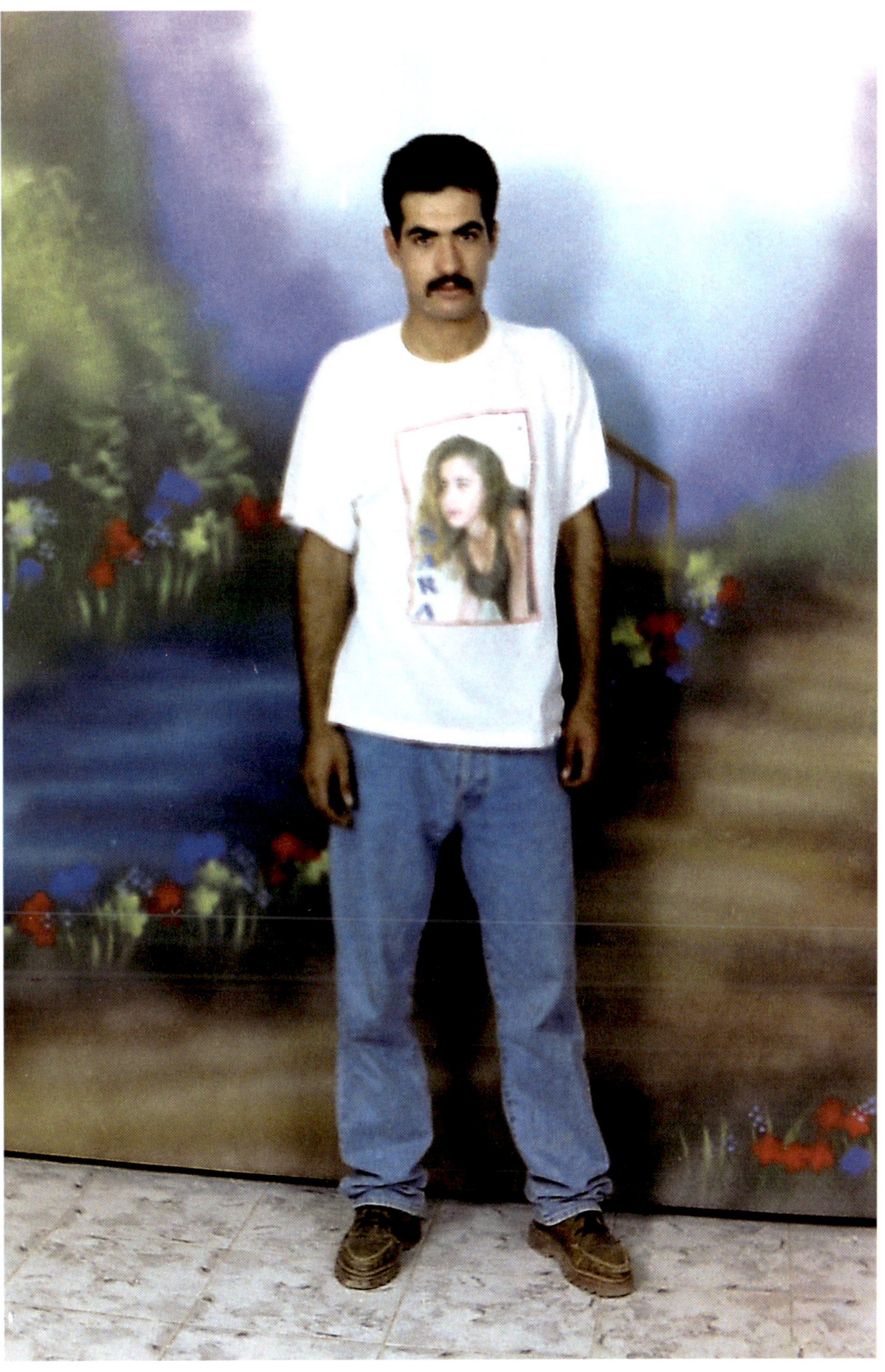

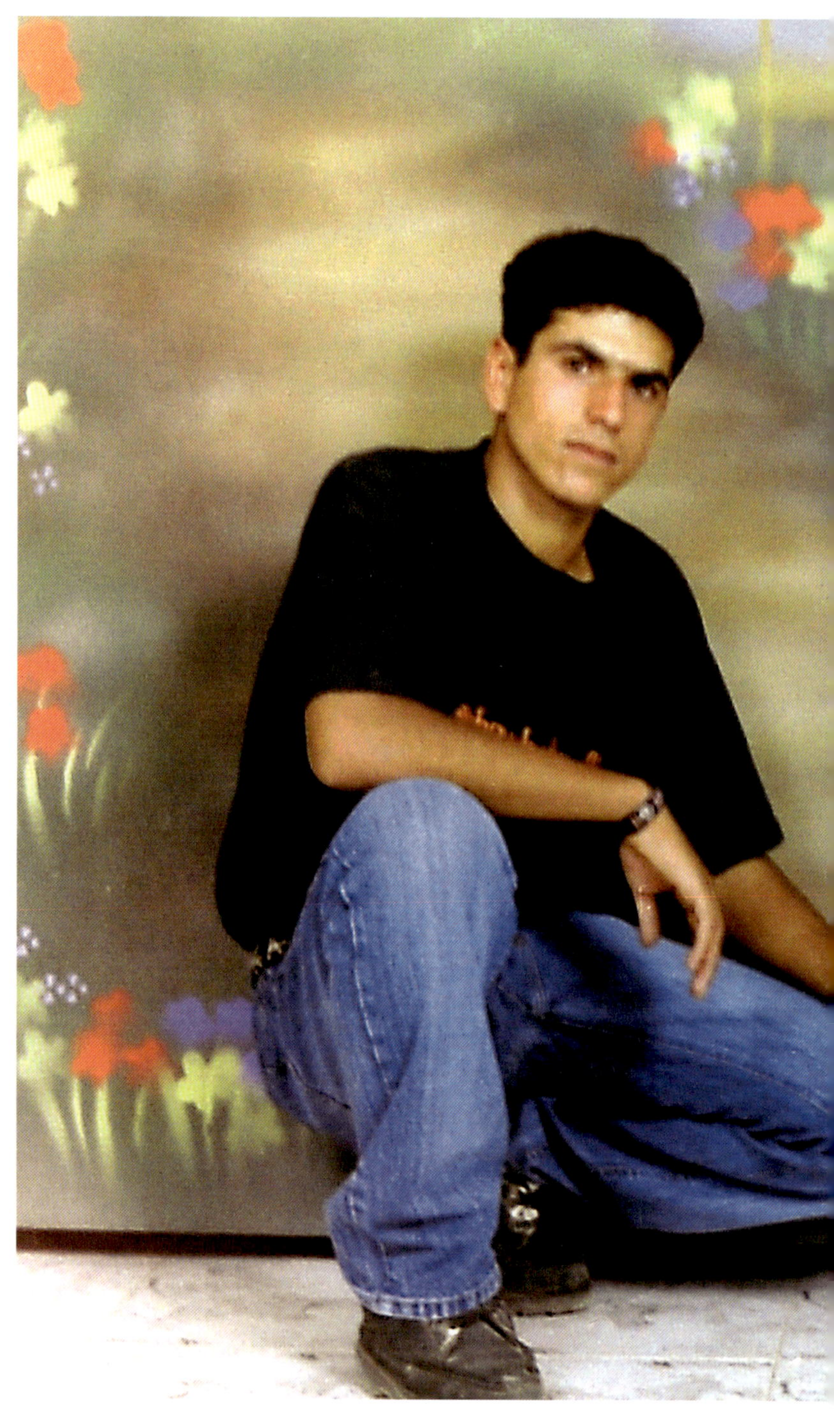

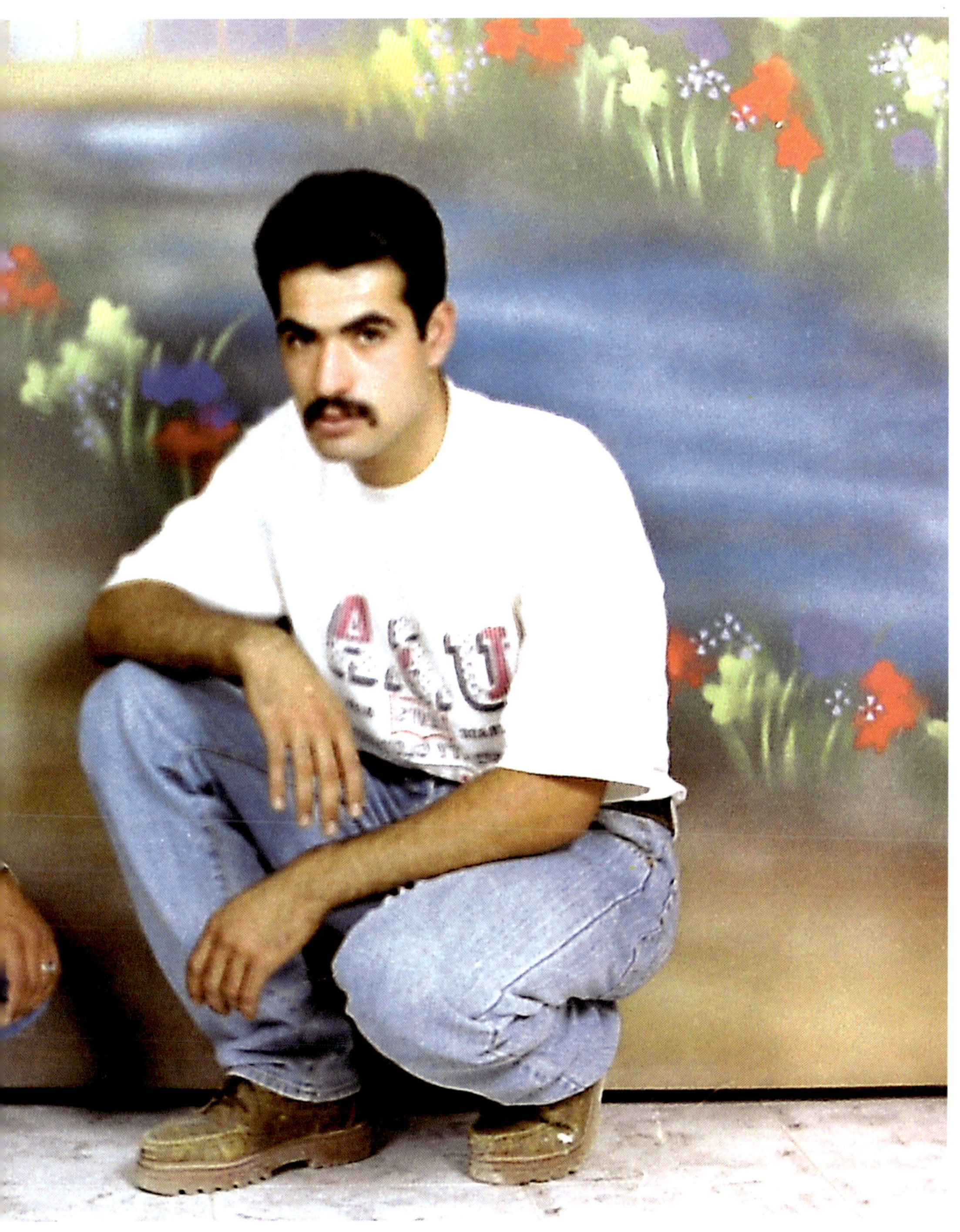

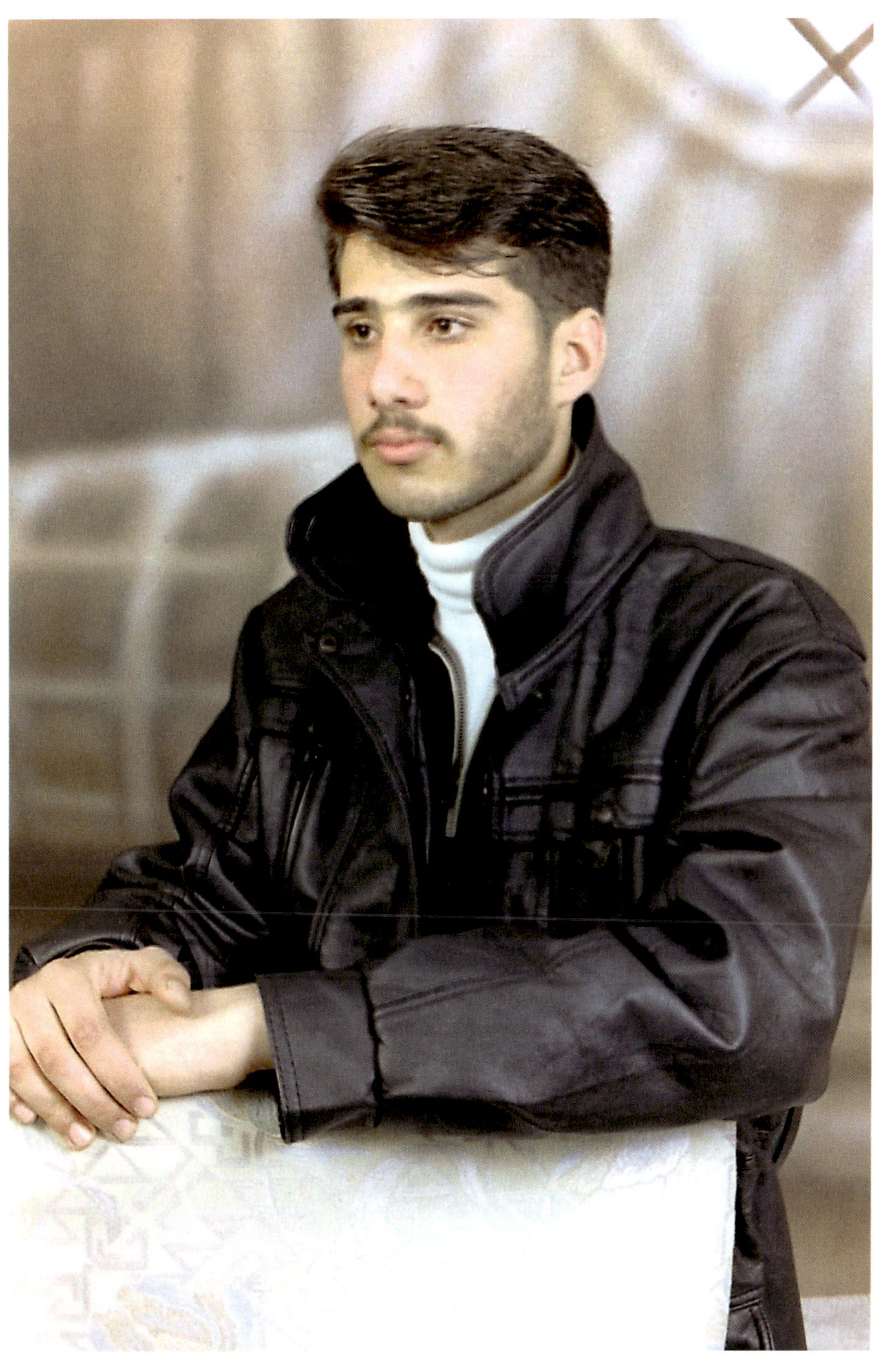

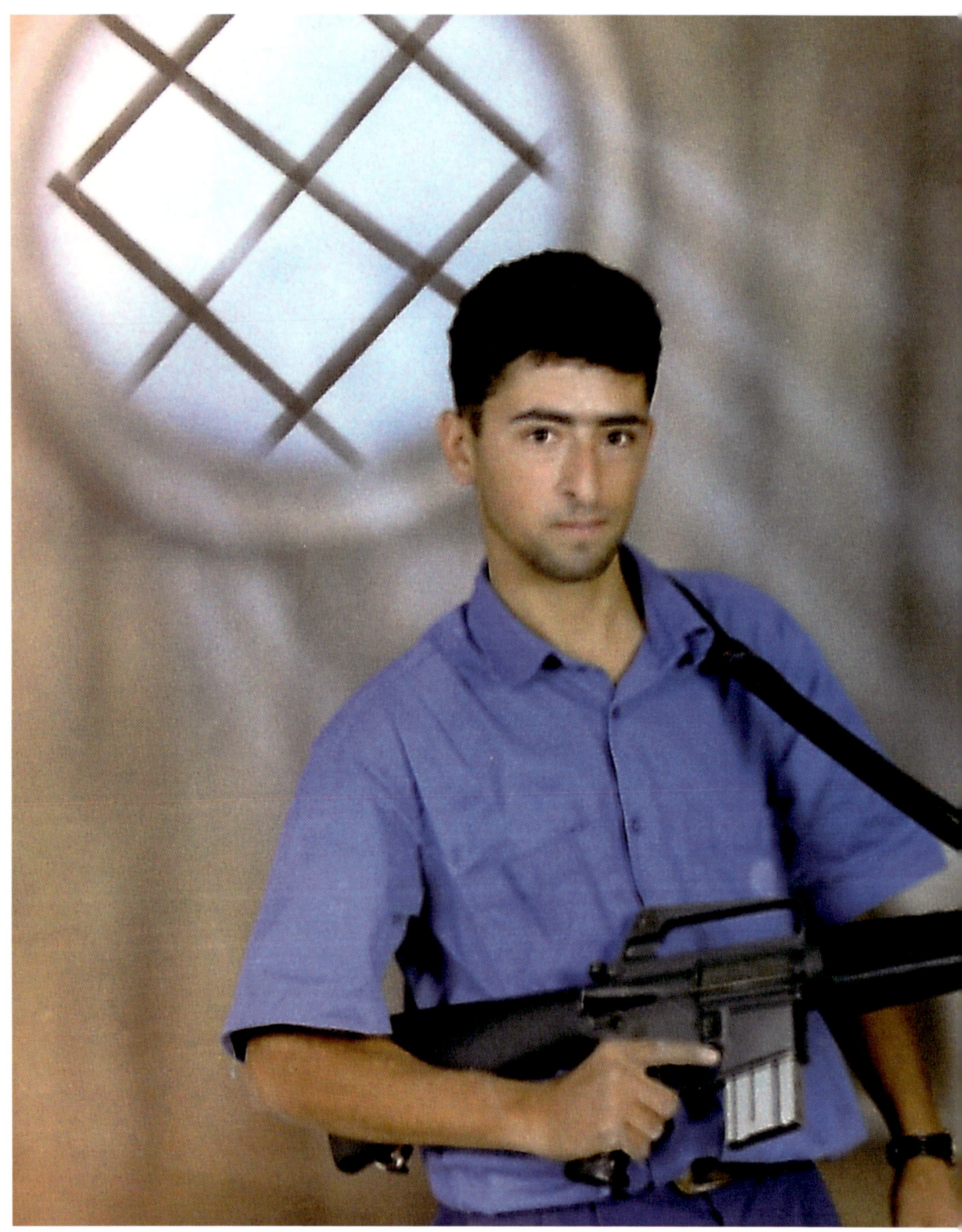

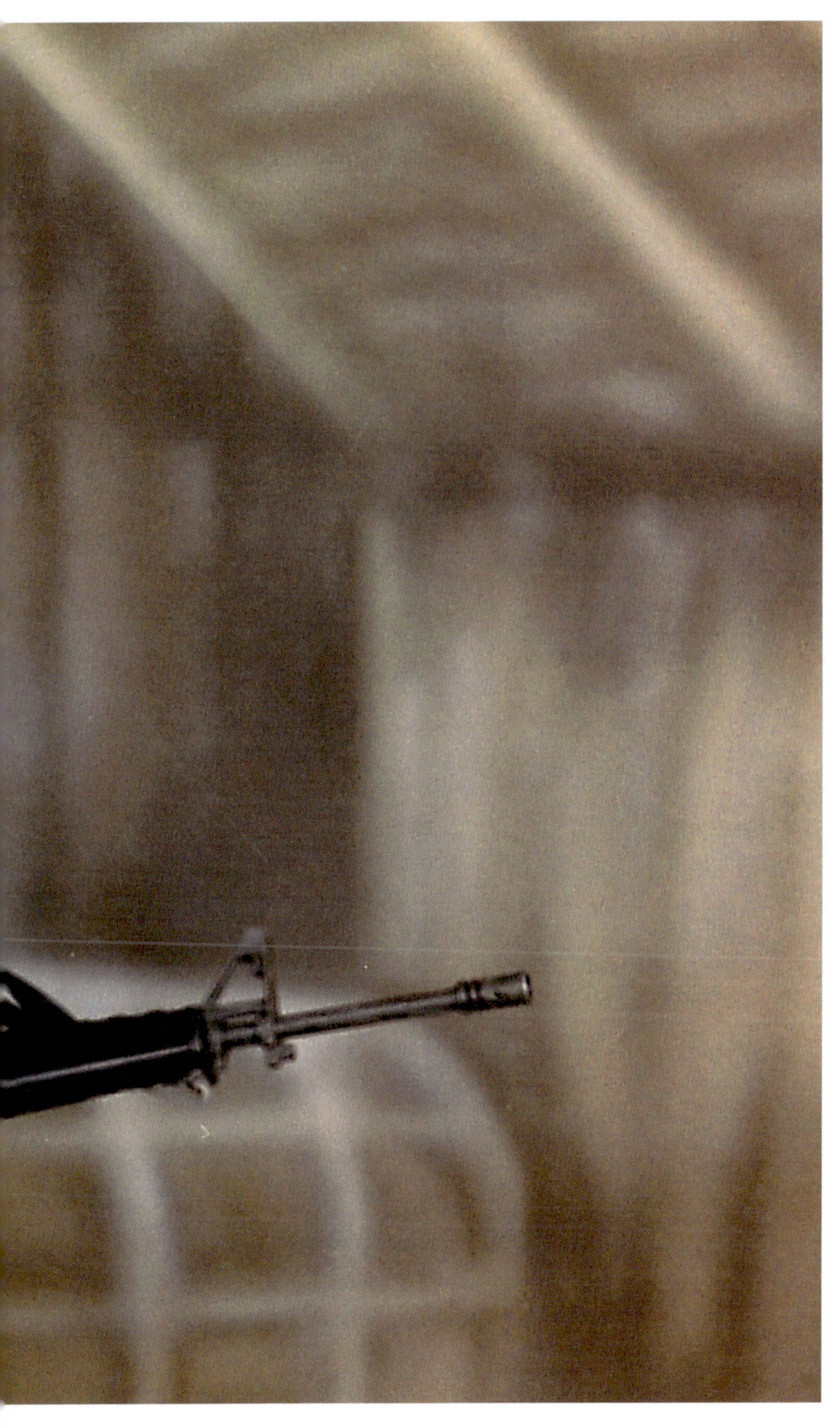

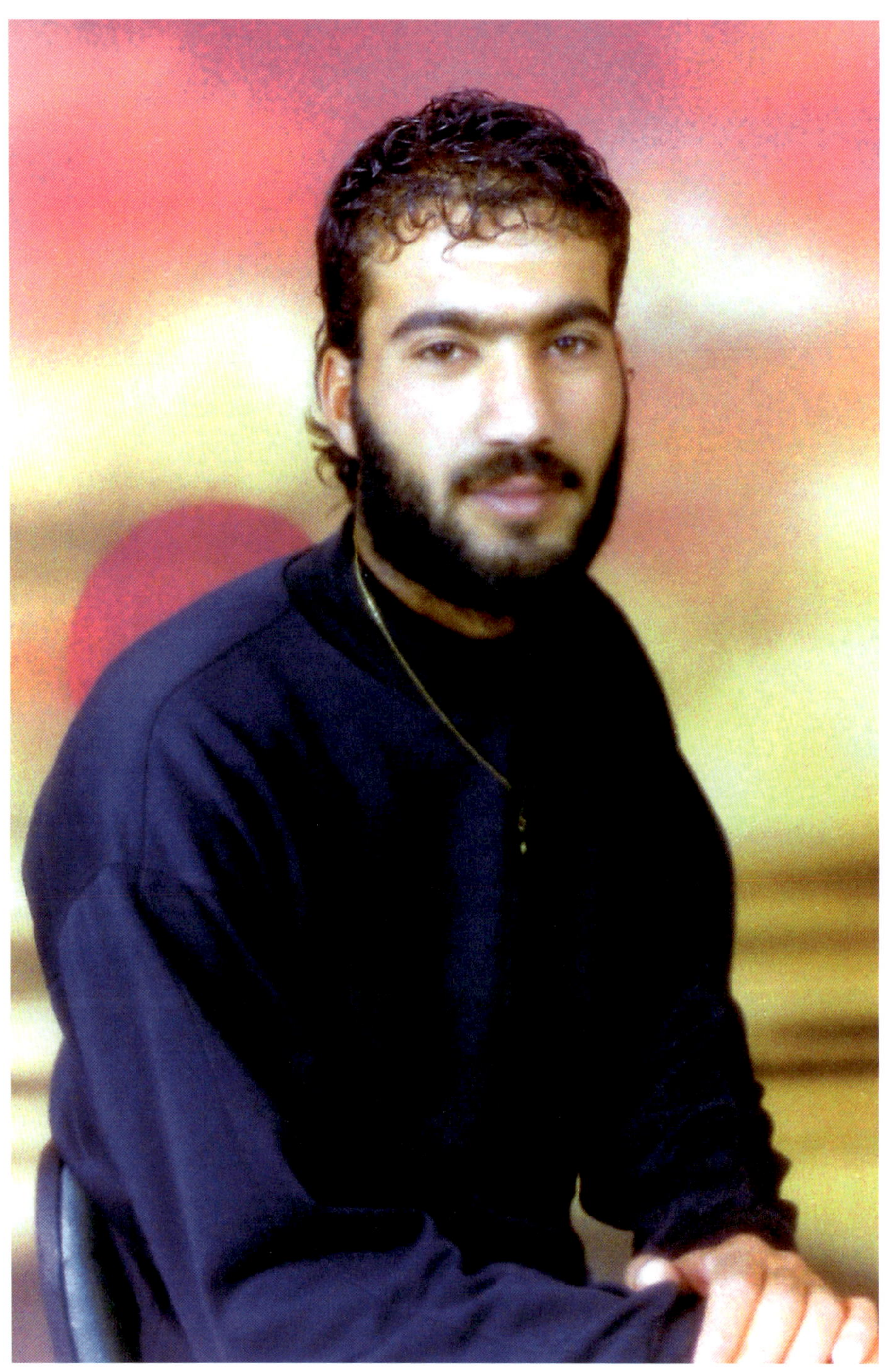

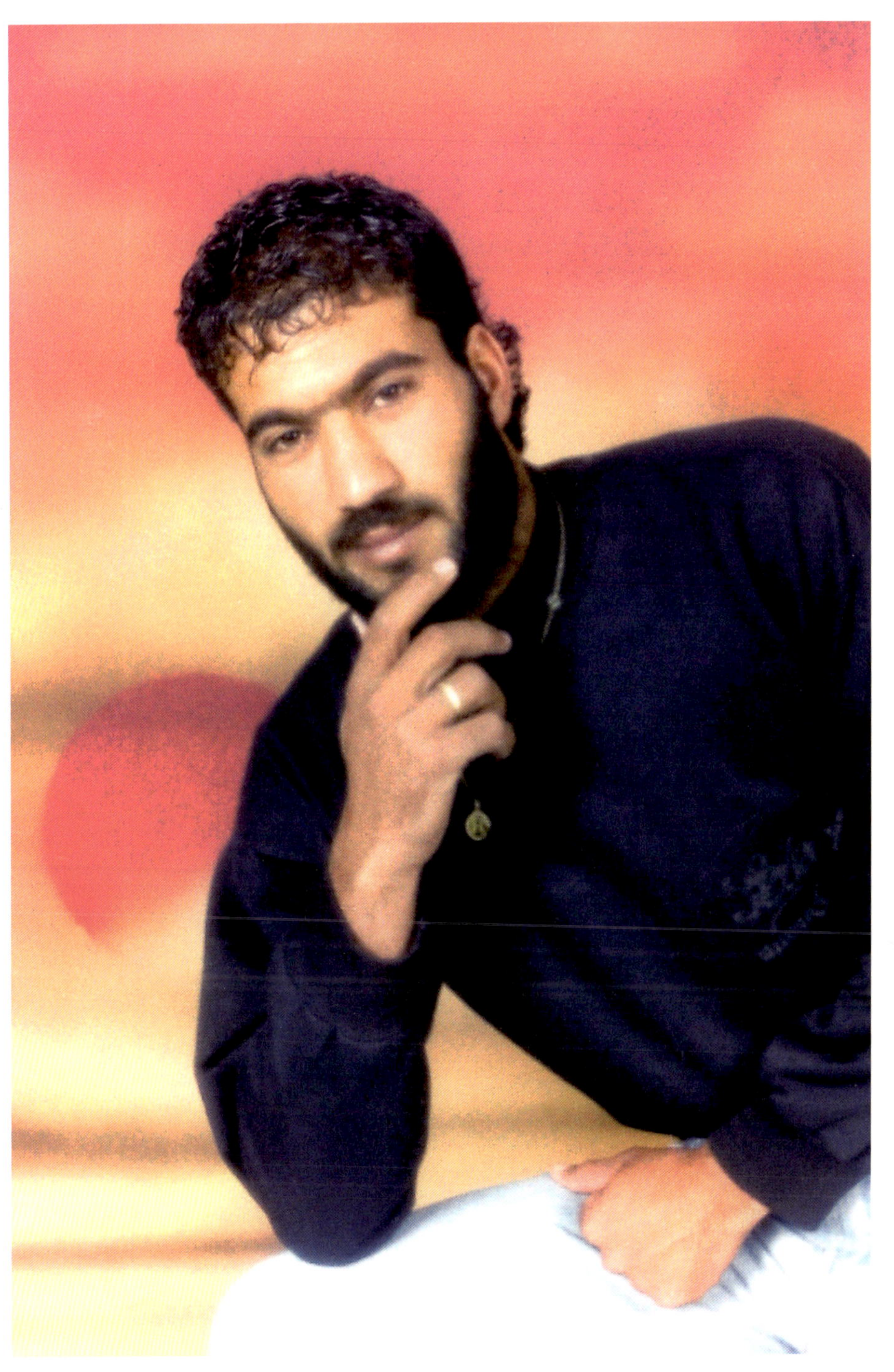

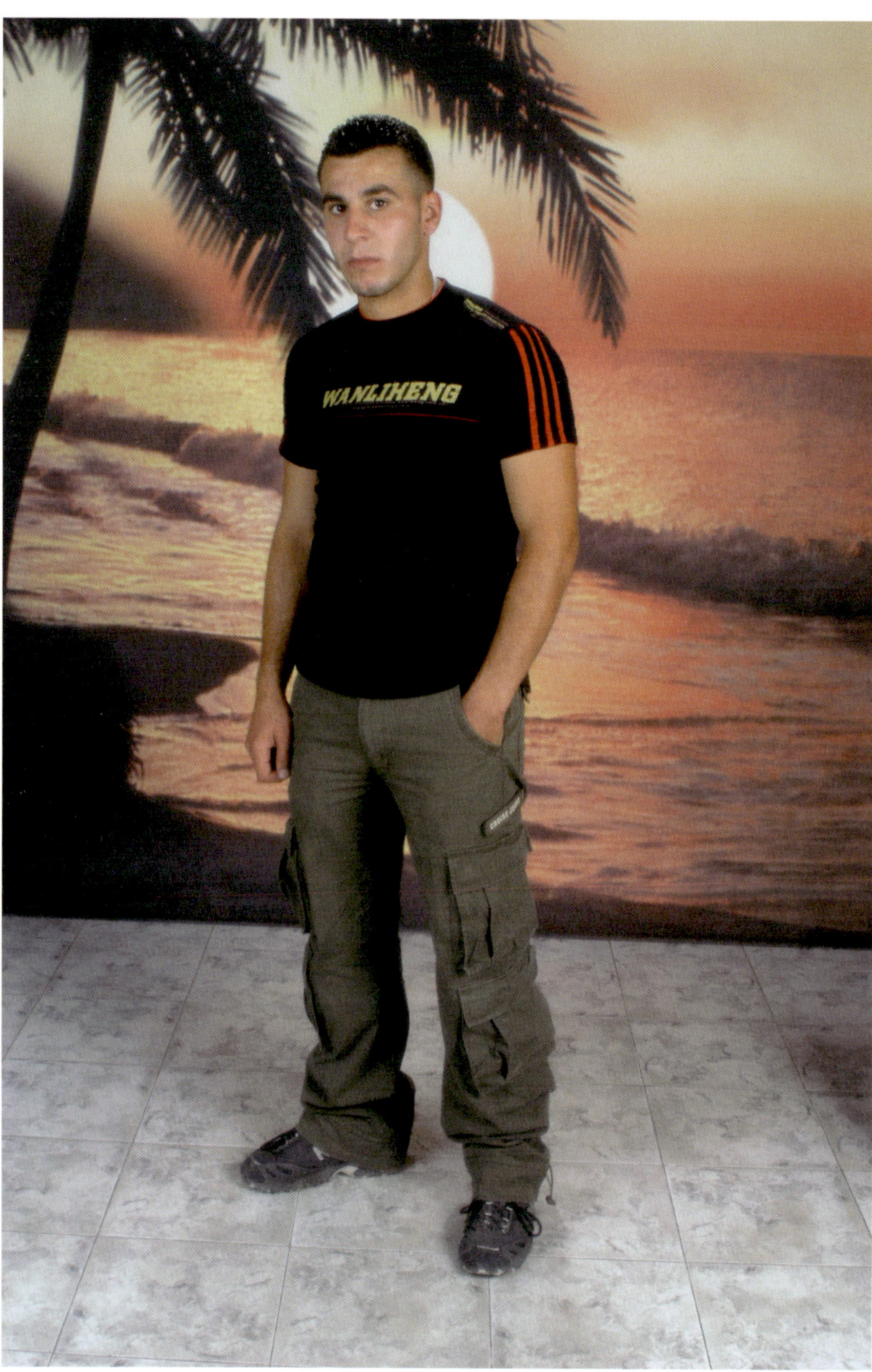
WANLIHENG

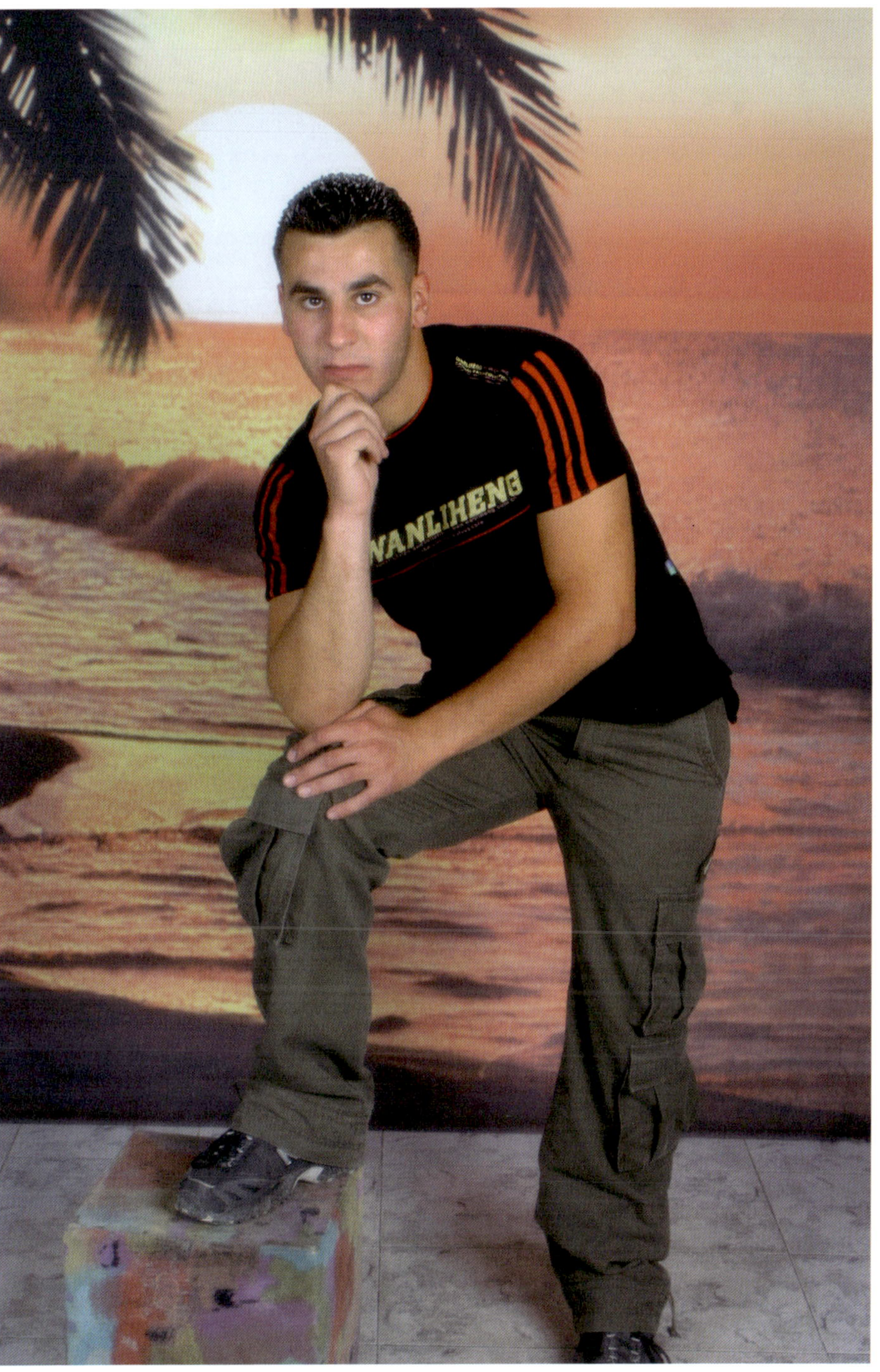

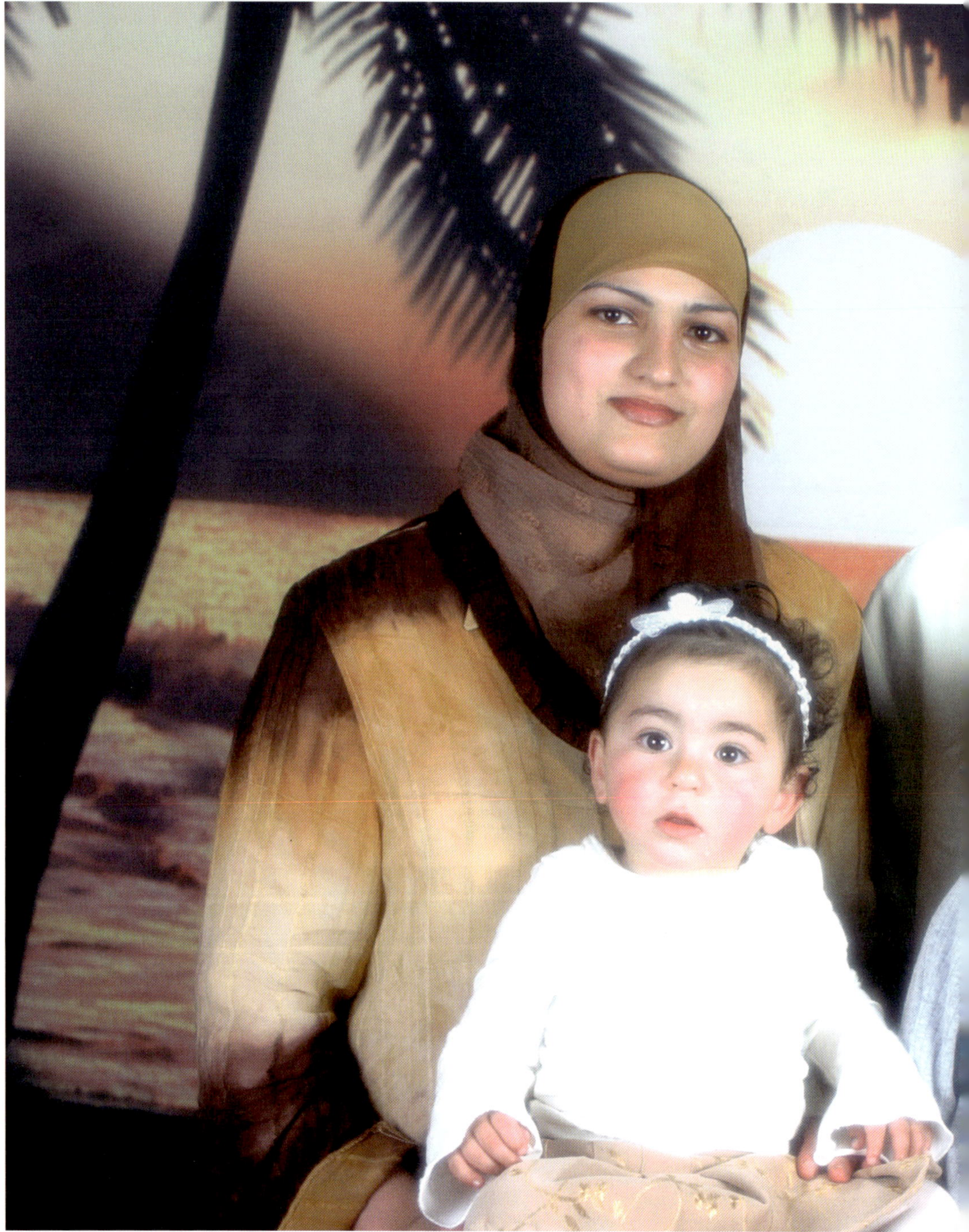

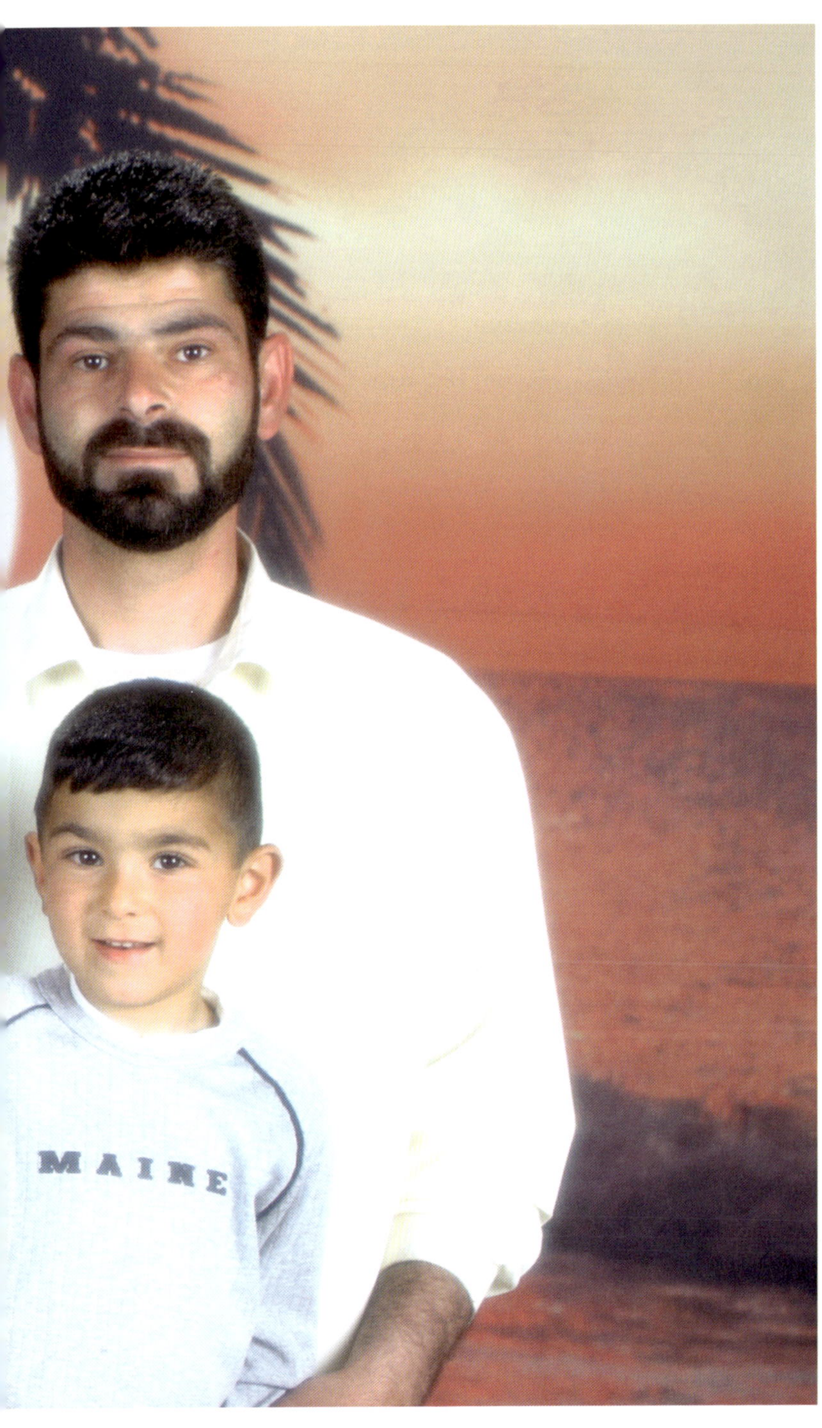

MAINE

The sign outside Studio Ahram on the outskirts of the Jenin refugee camp indicates that it was established in 1949, one year after the 'Nakba' (catastrophe) in which over 700,000 Palestinians were expelled from their homes by the advancing Israeli army. Abed Al Fateh Jarah, like most of the residents of the refugee camp, was expelled from his home in Haifa in 1948. When he established the studio the following year, he did so under the assumption that he would be there temporarily before being allowed to return home.

Like garages, butchers, laundries and grocery stores, Photography studios comprise part of the Jenin camp's economy for its 13,000 displaced inhabitants. Before the advent of digital processes, portraiture photography was rooted within the studio, where shooting, developing, printing and framing would occur. An invasion of the Jenin refugee camp by the Israel army in 2002 saw much of the camp destroyed. During this time, Studio Ahram was occupied by the IDF and used as a strategic military outpost at the edge of the camp. The soldiers destroyed most of the studio's archive, which on top of studio portraits contained thousands of negatives and historic glass plates produced in Jenin.

By 1949, Palestinian society had already played a pivotal role in the development of the medium of photography. It was taken up as a new craft by Palestine's local population as early as the 1860s when the Armenian Patriarch Issay Garabedian established a photographic workshop in Jerusalem to train young Armenian photographers.[1] Simultaneously, hordes of European photographers began obsessively documenting the region's sites of biblical and archaeological interest. The constant sunshine of the Middle East made the region the perfect place to experiment with the new light sensitive medium.

Photographers involved in such endeavours were, in most cases, proponents of the European expansionist agenda that sought to colonise the Middle East in the latter years of the Ottoman Empire. As such, images generated by them tended to prioritise images of Palestine as empty and devoid of human presence in such a way that complimented the early mobilising phrase of Zionism We are a people without a land going to a land without a people'.[2]

Two of Palestine's most prominent native photographers, Garabed Krikorian and Khalili Raad each had photography studios on Jaffa Street in the old city of Jerusalem in the early years of the 20th century. The two studios split the growing demand for photography between its two main concerns, with Krikorians studio dedicated to studio portraiture while Raad photographed daily life, current events and archeological sites in Palestine. Each output catered to the market for biblical and orientalist imagery generated by earlier photographic endeavours in the region.[3]

Jaffa Street was captured by the advancing Zionist armies in 1948 and both studios were expelled. Khalili Raad's archive only exists today because an Italian friend daringly crossed the Green Line during the night to rescue his thousands of glass plates and negatives.[4]

[1] BADR AL-HAJJ, "KHALIL RAAD - JERUSALEM PHOTOGRAPHER", JERUSALEM QUARTERLY (WINTER 2001) P.11-12 / [2] EDWARD SAID, 'THE QUESTION OF PALESTINE',1979, P.9 / [3] STEPHEN SHEEHI - 'THE ARAB IMAGO', CHAPTER 5 , 'PORTRAIT PATHS', 2016 , P.109 / [4] B.AL-HAJJ , 'KHALIL RAAD - JERUSALEM PHOTOGRAPHER', P.10

Studio Havana was established in Ramallah by O'hannes Shanlikian in 1970. Originally from Jaffa his family had also been expelled as a result of the Nakba' of 1948. A map of pre 1948 Palestine is sellotaped to the door of his darkroom. He trained in photography from the age of 14 in various studios around the city before establishing Studio Havana which he ran up until his death in 2012. The studio is now run by his three children.

A significant part of the body of work produced by O'hannes (which can be seen on the preceding pages) is in monochrome. The portraits are the product of a negotiation dictated by the lens between the subject's physical presence in the space and the lighting within it, whereby desirable features can be accentuated, and others obfuscated from sight. The hand tinting of photographs, which Shanlikian also specialised in, was a post-production technique that further augmented the appearance of subjects. Textures of complexion and bone structure could be accentuated or stylistically embellished with a loud colourful hue.

Azzam Al Shweiki set up Studio Chaplin in Ramallah in 1995. By this stage colour 35mm film was the default amongst amateur and professional photographers across the world. The advent of colour photography catalysed a greater emphasis on the backgrounds within portraits. The shadows surrounding the face were suddenly pushed back and the question became what the subject wished to be photographed against. As opposed to monochromes dependence on shadows or edges of the frame, the new standard of 35mm colour film pursued the

bright, busy and iconic. The backdrops simulate a collapse in geographical space. Blown up stock images of beaches, forests and city skylines are popular choices in photography studios throughout the world. The use of such backdrops in the context of the West Bank draw attention to more complex notions of spatial justice, national identity and citizenship.

Backdrops depicting the sea, allow subjects and their families to be photographed at the beach which, despite being a short distance away, is a physically out of bounds for most Palestinians living in the West Bank. 2.3 million Palestinians living in the West Bank are not permitted to go to the Mediterranean coast which is close by.[5] The coastline is visible from both Ramallah and Nablus on a clear day, yet most of the populations of these cities have never been able to access it.

Depictions of cityscapes such as New York or San Francisco, also attest to a geography that is out of reach. But on a more fundamental level they visualise an urban reality uncharacterised by rubble or unpackaged building materials found everywhere throughout the West Bank. This is due to Israeli urban planning restrictions and house demolitions by the Israeli army. Both strip the Palestinians of the autonomy to cultivate a cityscape that corresponds to their own desires, whilst rendering any potential of a state in the future unviable. Palestinians are not allowed to construct or build anything in most of the West Bank without a permit issued by the Israeli Military.[6] As of November 2017, the Civil Administration has drafted and approved plans for only

*5 LÉOPOLD LAMBERT, "WATER IN PALESTINE: SEGREGATED SEA ACCESS AND RUNNING WATER IN THE ISRAELI APARTHEID", THE FUNAMBULIST ,MAY 2018 /
*6 SALEM THAWABA, "BUILDING AND PLANNING REGULATIONS UNDER ISRAELI COLONIAL POWER: A CRITICAL STUDY FROM PALESTINE, PLANNING PERSPECTIVES, 34:1, 133-146, 2019

16 of the 180 communities who applied for such permits.[7] Since 1967, 48,000 Palestinian homes have been destroyed by the Israeli Army.[8]

The golden dome of Al - Aqsa mosque in Jerusalem, one of the holiest sites in Islam, features prominently in the backdrops of Azzam's photographs. The iconic structure is rarely seen by Palestinians in the West Bank without a specific ID card and almost never seen by those under siege in Gaza. The dome's status as a symbol of both religious and national identity is significant, in fact the second Intifada is said to have started in response to Ariel Sharon's provocative visit to the site in 2000.

Business ground to a halt during the second Intifada for Studio Chaplin when the surrounding area was sealed off by the Israeli military. During this time, clientele largely consisted of young men having their portraits taken holding weapons that they had borrowed from policemen that could subsequently be used in the martyr iconography.

Studios in the West Bank ran into increasing difficulty to obtain photographic materials and chemicals as the Israeli apartheid barrier was constructed in 2008. Movement between the West Bank, Gaza and the rest of the country became increasingly impossible to navigate due to a matrix of restrictions, fences, roadblocks and checkpoints. The likes of backdrops, frames, paper and chemicals were, in most cases, more easily obtained from China than they were in Tel Aviv. Studio Chaplin bought in plain blue backgrounds to meet the demand for identity card portraits

that became mandatory for Palestinians to travel through any checkpoint.

Around this time the medium saw itself shifting towards digital processes. Such technological advancements instigated a decline in photography studios, where the craftsmanship once reserved by studio practitioners was steadily unbound from the confines of both professional expertise and the site of the studio itself. Although all of the studio practitioners that I spoke to adopted digital technology within their practices, most claimed that it subsequently became unfulfilling. Studio Garo in East Jerusalem equated it with 'making falafel', repetitive, impersonal and quick whereby subjects would immediately want to see their photograph after it was taken. The practice of studio portraiture is largely becoming obsolete.

*7 B'TSELEM "PLANNING POLICY IN THE WEST BANK", 2019 / *8 THE ISRAELI COMMITTEE AGAINST HOME DEMOLITIONS , "A HISTORY OF ICAHD UK 2003-2019

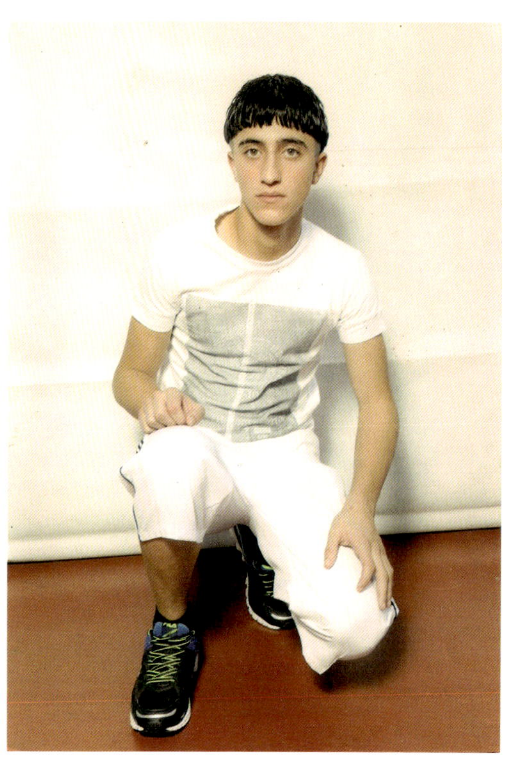 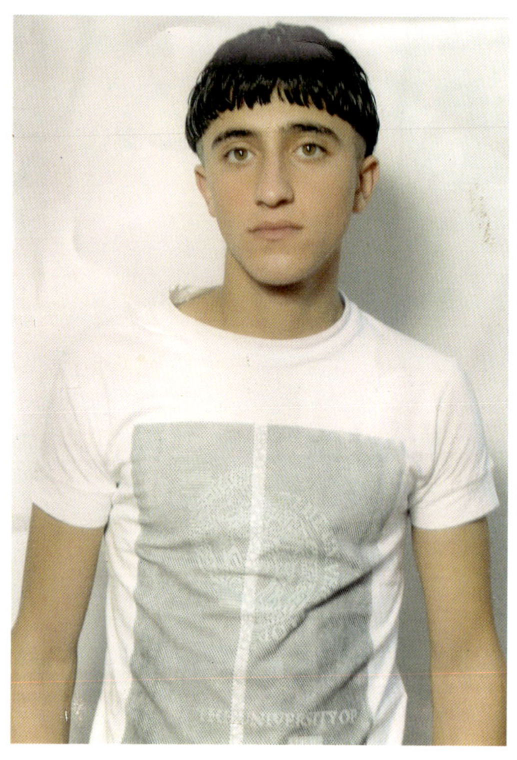

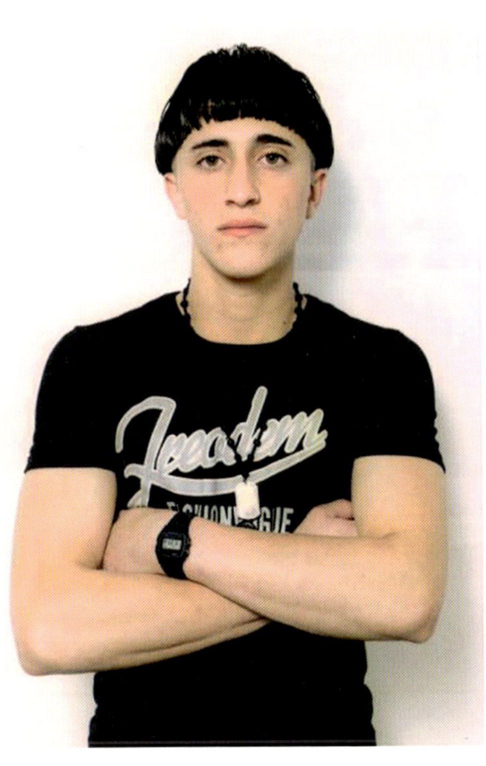
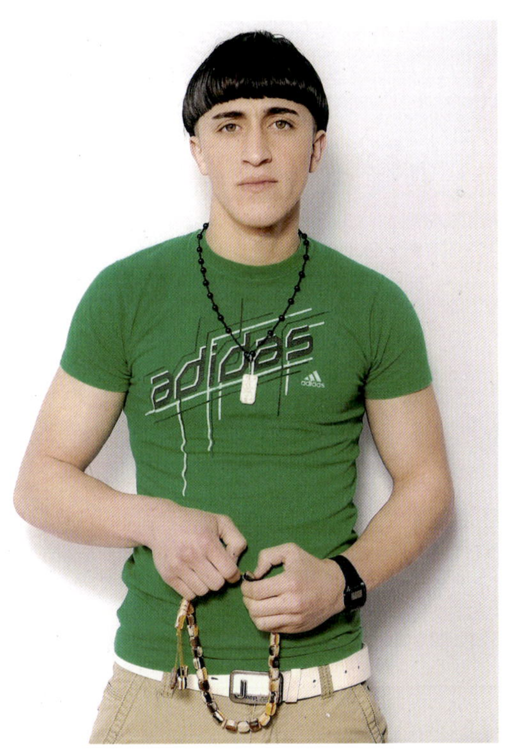

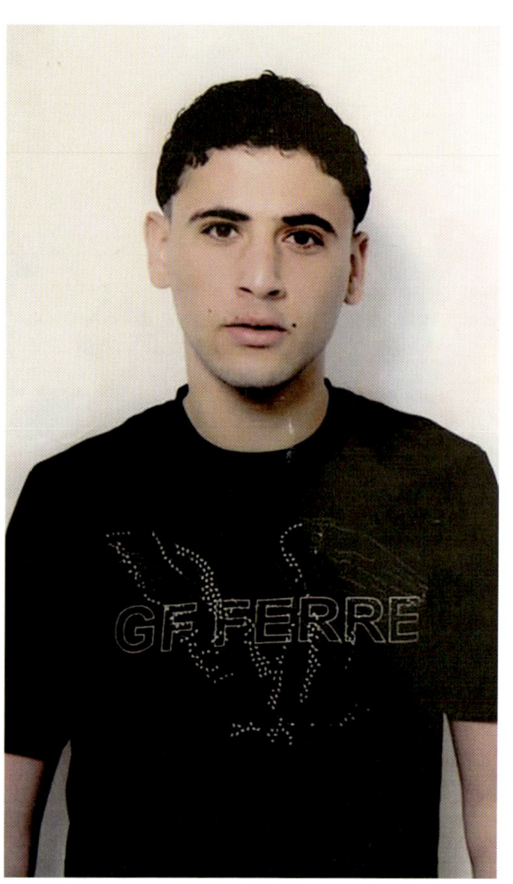
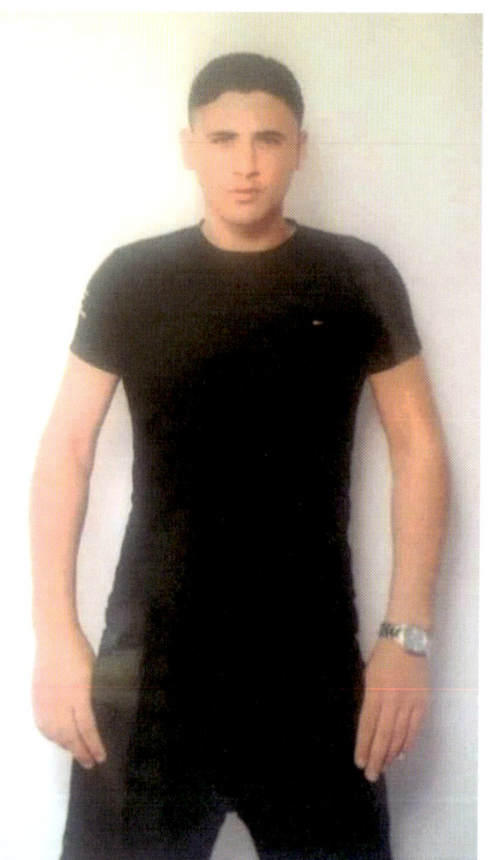

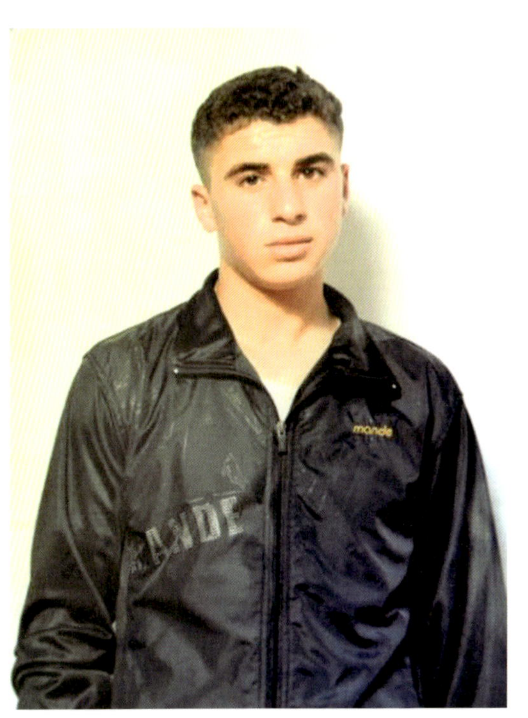
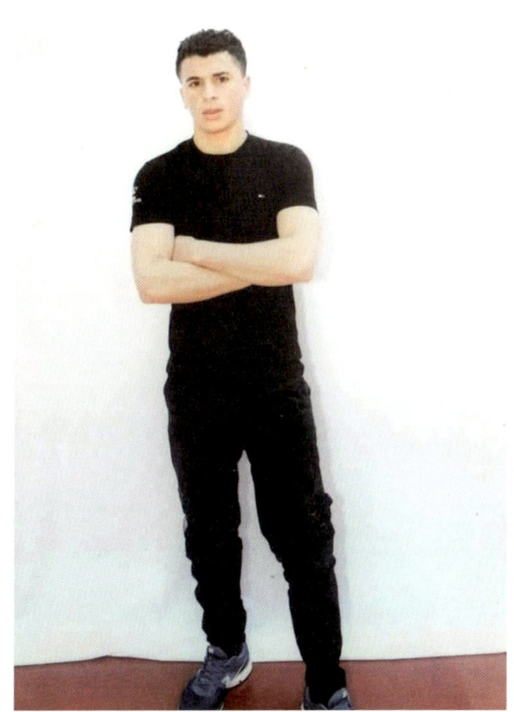

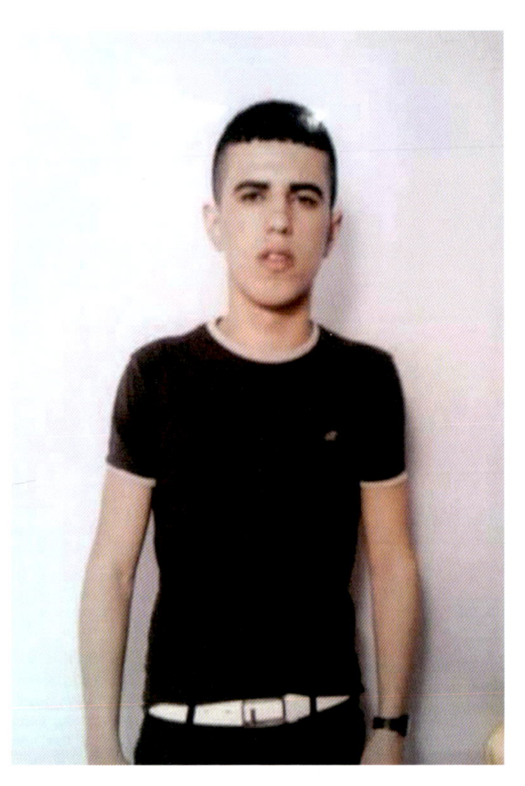
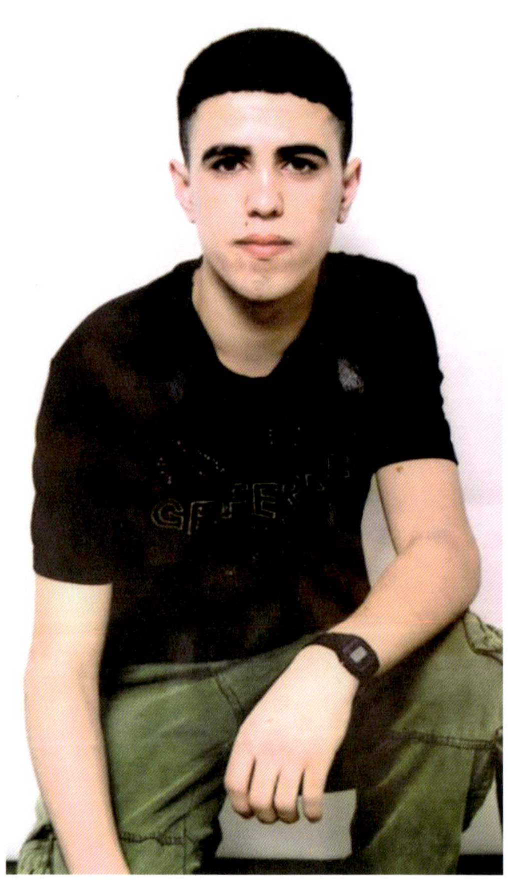

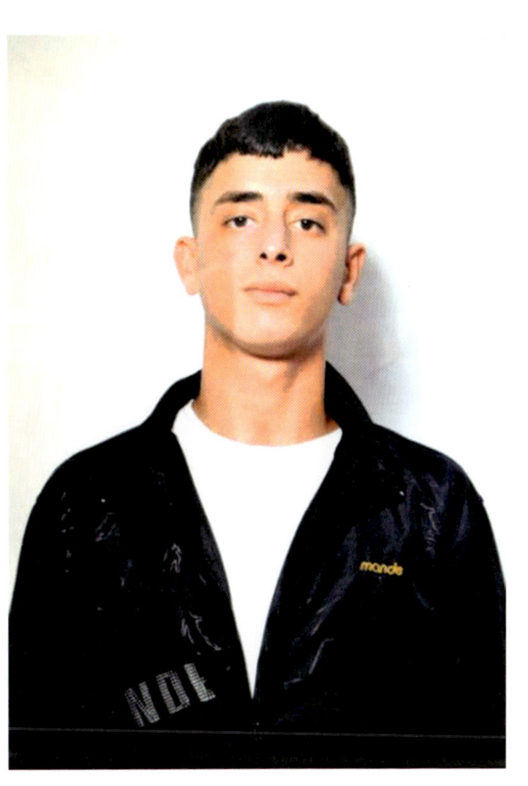
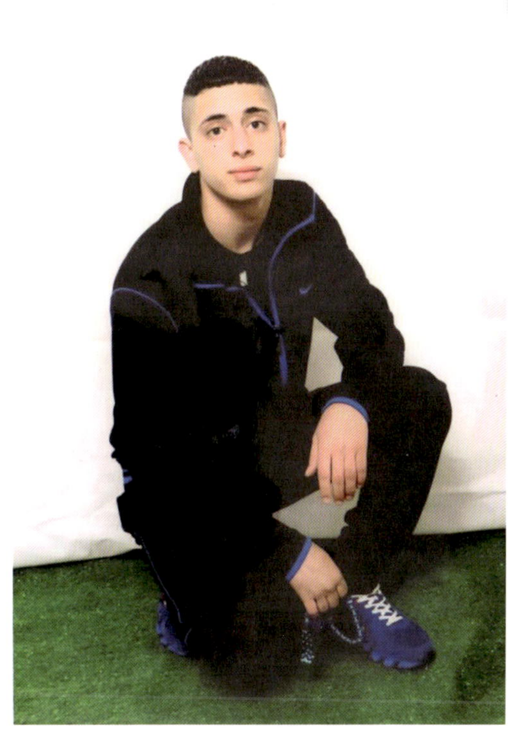

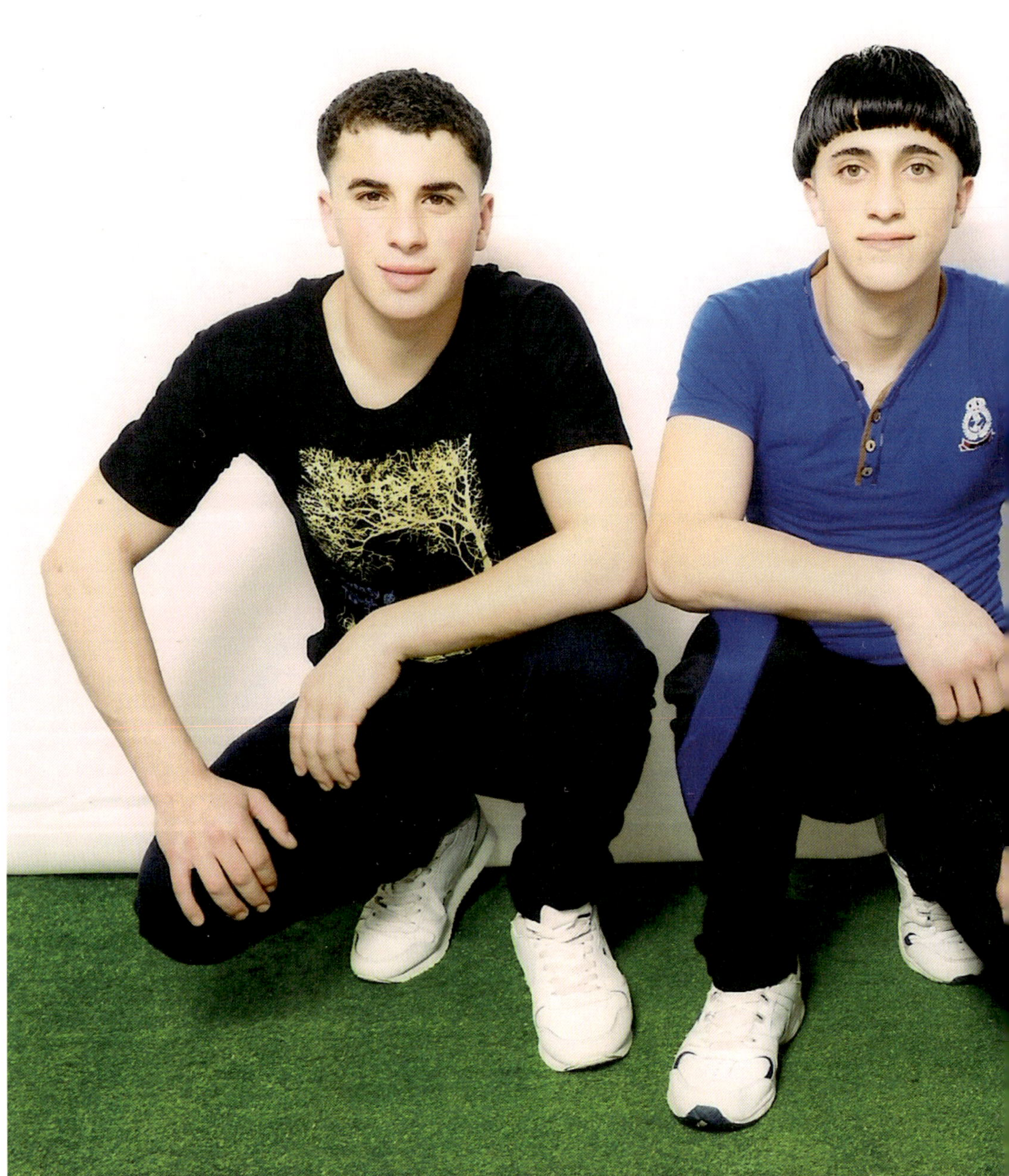

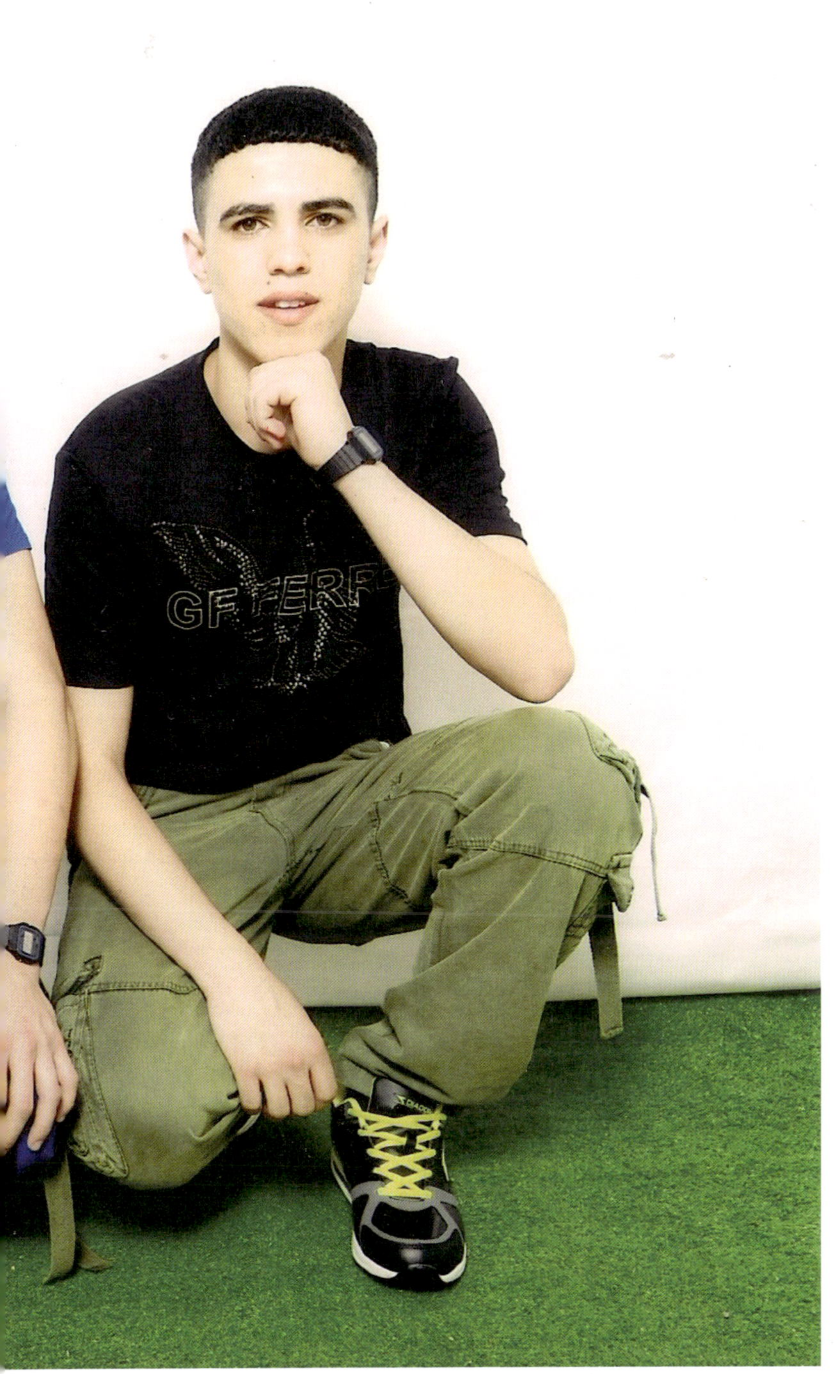

Since the beginning of the Israeli occupation in 1967, Israel forces have imprisoned more than 800,000 Palestinians which constitutes 20% of the population of the occupied territories. It is therefore rare to meet anybody in the West Bank who does not bear direct kinship with somebody who has been a political prisoner at some stage in their lives. The most common form of detention is the use of Administrative Detention, a practice stemming from the British Mandate in Palestine that allows for anybody to be imprisoned indefinitely without charge or trial. This law can be used on anybody from the age of twelve upwards. In April 2016, the world's youngest female prisoner, Dima al-Wawi aged 12, was released after spending 75 days in prison.[1]

In cases where Palestinians are charged with a crime, such convictions are made in the context of an Israeli military court system in which the judge, prosecutor, clerks and translators are active duty Israeli soldiers and military personnel. Palestinians are forced to plead guilty to be eligible for plea bargains and limited sentences within a system that has a 99% conviction rate against them.[2] Forced confessions, lack of adequate legal counsel, torture and solitary confinement are also routine.

Photographic acts charter this process on both sides of the bars. In an odd replication of the dynamic of studio portraiture, each year that a detainee is incarcerated is marked by the production of a studio portrait within the prison itself. These photographs are taken by the IDF on an annual basis and are sent to the detainees families and communities; reducing their relationship with them to one with a photographic object. The white backdrop, unchanging from year to year, presents the spatial and social limitations imposed on the subject's experience over indefinite, endlessly extendable periods of time.

The images on the preceding pages show the Hares boys; 5 young men who, at the age of 15, were each sentenced with 20 counts of attempted murder by an Israeli military court despite an overwhelming lack of evidence against them. Their 'confessions' were procured under conditions of torture after each teenager was left in solitary confinement for two weeks without access to legal representation. They will remain in prison until they are at least 41 years old.[3]

In some instances, the event of these portraits facilitate a brief perforation of the prison dynamic itself. If a prisoner's parents are both over the age of 60, they are granted permission to pass through the bars to appear in the portrait alongside their children. This is the only instance where an inmate will physically be allowed in the same room and have the opportunity to touch their parents, undivided by glass or bars, in the entirety of their time as a political prisoner.

Whereas the production of a studio portrait is, largely speaking, a private collaboration between photographer and subject, there are two occasions in which that very same photograph may be reproduced and disseminated throughout the public sphere for all to see; In

*1 PALESTINE CHRONICLE, "ISRAEL RELEASES 12-YEAR-OLD PALESTINIAN GIRL, DIMA AL-WAWI", APRIL 2016 / *2 WAR ON WANT , "MILITARY COURTS" / *3 PALSOLIDARITY, "ONE YEAR ON: THE HARES BOYS "18TH MARCH 2014 / *4 KERSTIN SCHANKWEILER AND VERENA STRÄUB,"SHAHEED" , 2016

the event of political imprisonment (Administrative Detention) or in Martyrdom, a term used unanimously to describe the fatalities caused by the Israeli Army.

شهيد (Shaheed) is the Arabic term for Martyr, somebody who's death is a result of religious or political conditions. It shares the same etymological root as Martyr in the English language which is that of 'martys', the Greek word for 'witness'.[4] ملثم (Molatham) on the other hand, describes a person's participation in resistance to the occupation and their simultaneous need to remain anonymous whilst doing so. A masked subject participating in resistance (Molatham) turned martyr or 'witness' (Shaheed) will exist as such in relation to the visual conditions dictated by the occupation.

The removal of bodies by the Israeli military is met with a drive to make them visible. This is achieved through the use of iconography which is plastered throughout the streets of the West Bank, functioning as an 'unmasking' of the subject and establishing their physical presence throughout the urban landscape. The most recent or readily available photograph of the subject (often a studio portrait) will be replicated countless times as it becomes the centre piece to layers of information within posters, placards, banners and other printed paraphernalia.

Posters hung at eye level are plastered one after another forming a row of faces that insist upon the collective experience of their individual subjects.

In his essay on 'Visual Representations of Martyrdom in Palestine', Mahmoud Abu Hashash points out that many of the sites in which posters are hung are not always strictly public. Shopfronts and even vehicles are utilised because 'martyrs are public figures through which the process of legitimisation takes place and which allows the makers and hangers of posters to act on behalf of the public with unchallenged authority'[5]

In many cases, the proportions laid out by the backdrops of studio-based photographs define the layout of the poster itself, with the background images of ocean scenery forming the political horizon not of its individual subjects but for all who witness it. The photography studios themselves can thus be located squarely within the social fabric of Palestine, their private interiors fusing with the public exterior. The subjects represented within them are never bruised, bloodied or violated. The violence inflicted upon their bodies is not presented to emphasise the emotional tone of their death or incarceration, instead we see them looking directly into the lens, confronting the viewer in health and dignity, in the same way they wished to represent themselves through the conditions inherent to those of the photography studio.[6] As such, they continue to be represented as active, resisting agents within political struggle, not as victims of it. Nor do they ever appear as faceless or masked.

As well as being dispersed throughout public spaces, such images are also carried physically by family members and local communities on vigils and

[5] MAHMOUD ABU HASHASH , "ON THE VISUAL REPRESENTATION OF MARTYRDOM IN PALESTINE", THIRD TEXT VOLUME 20, 2006 - ISSUE 3-4: THE CONFLICT AND CONTEMPORARY VISUAL CULTURE IN PALESTINE & ISRAEL. / [6] LORI A ALLEN, "MARTYR BODIES IN THE MEDIA: HUMAN RIGHTS, AESTHETICS, AND THE POLITICS OF IMMEDIATION IN THE PALESTINIAN INTIFADA", AMERICAN ETHNOLOGIST VOLUME 36 NUMBER 1 , FEBRUARY 2009, P.165

demonstrations. The original master copy of the studio portrait can be traced back through these chains of reproduction to those who bear the most intimate link with its subject, usually their mothers, who will carry the original photograph to these same events. Some are made into permanent memorials that straddle the gap between buildings. Sometimes they are encased within marble or stone sculptures. For the most part however, the posters are plastered on top of one another throughout the public sphere of the West Bank. They are bleached by the sun and distorted through exposure to the wind and rain. Parts of posters peel off, revealing other posters underneath. Such exposure to the elements coupled with the ongoing struggle for exhibition space see the subjects of the portraits return once again to facelessness.

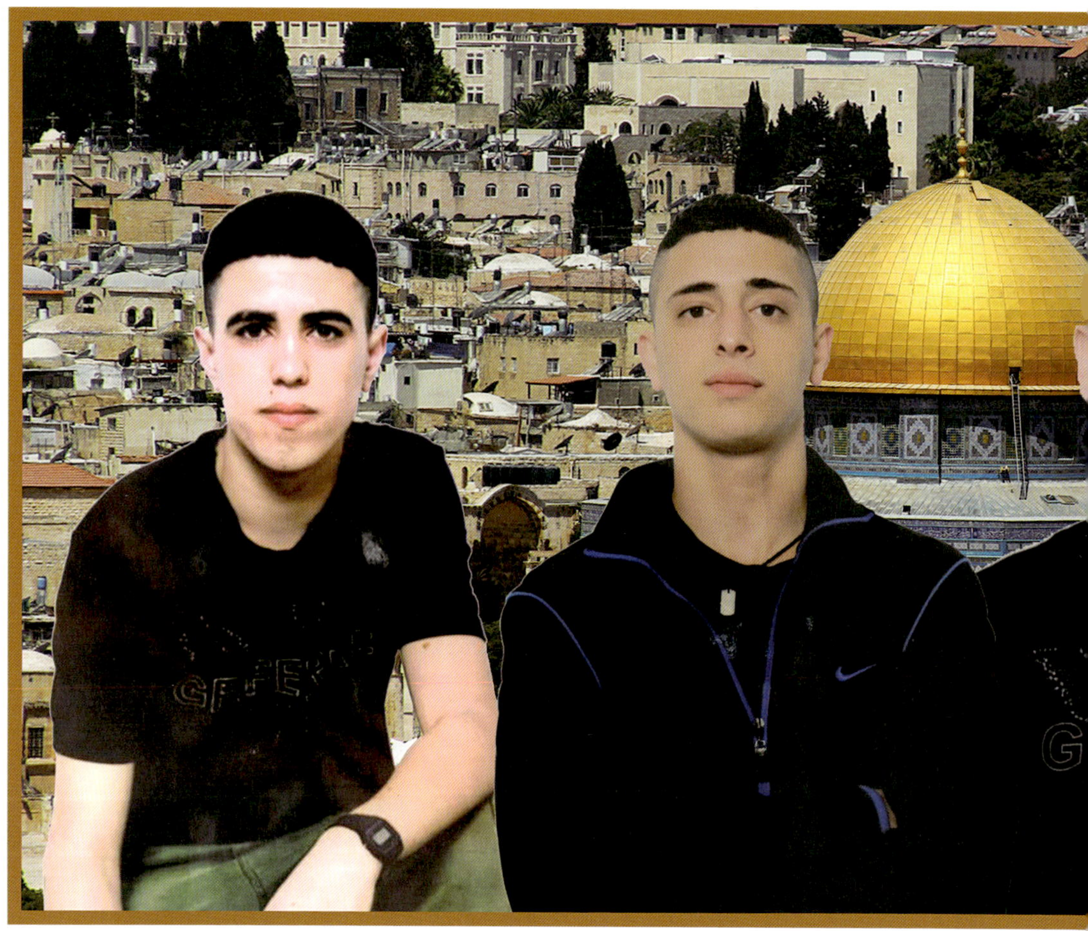

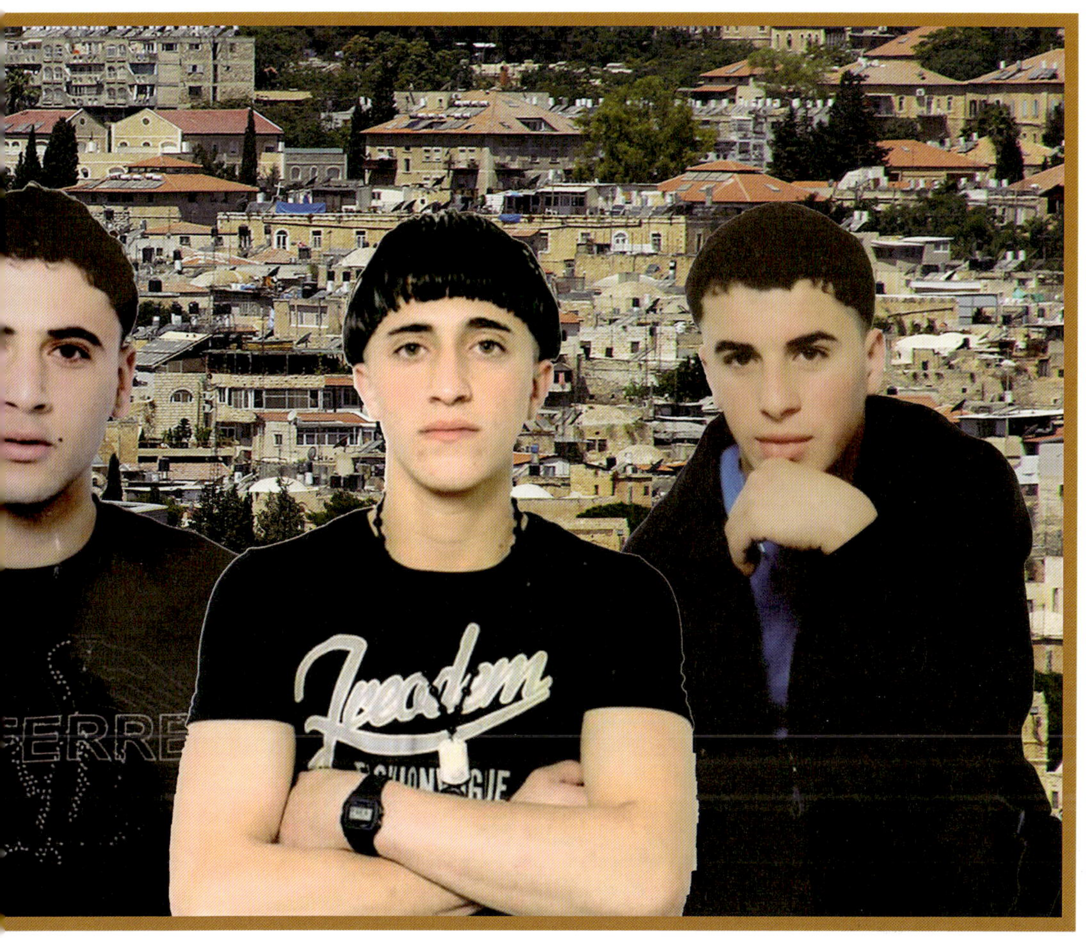

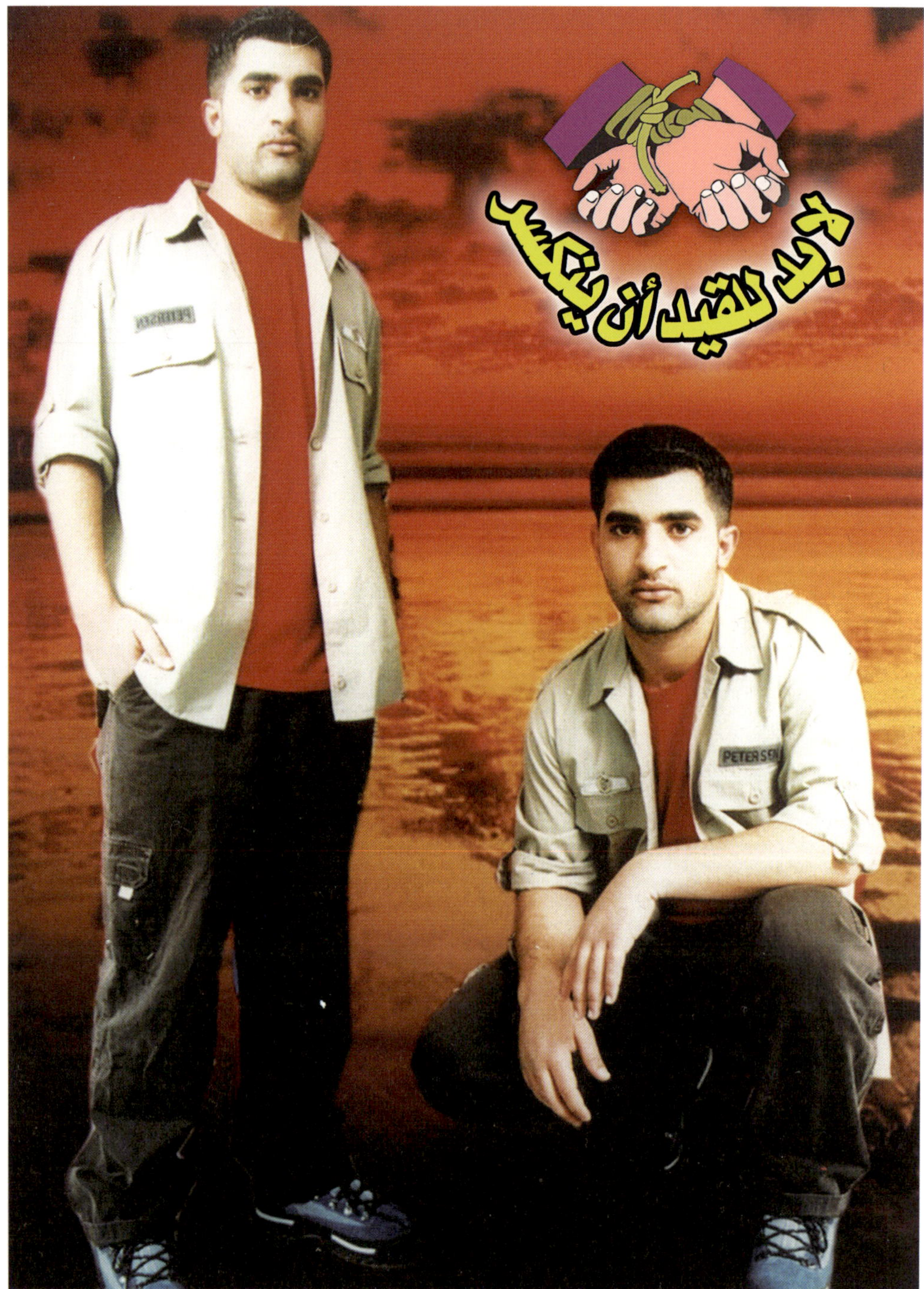

لا بد للقيد أن ينكسر

"THE CHAINS WILL EVENTUALLY BREAK" FROM A POEM BY ABU AL KASSEM AL SHABI

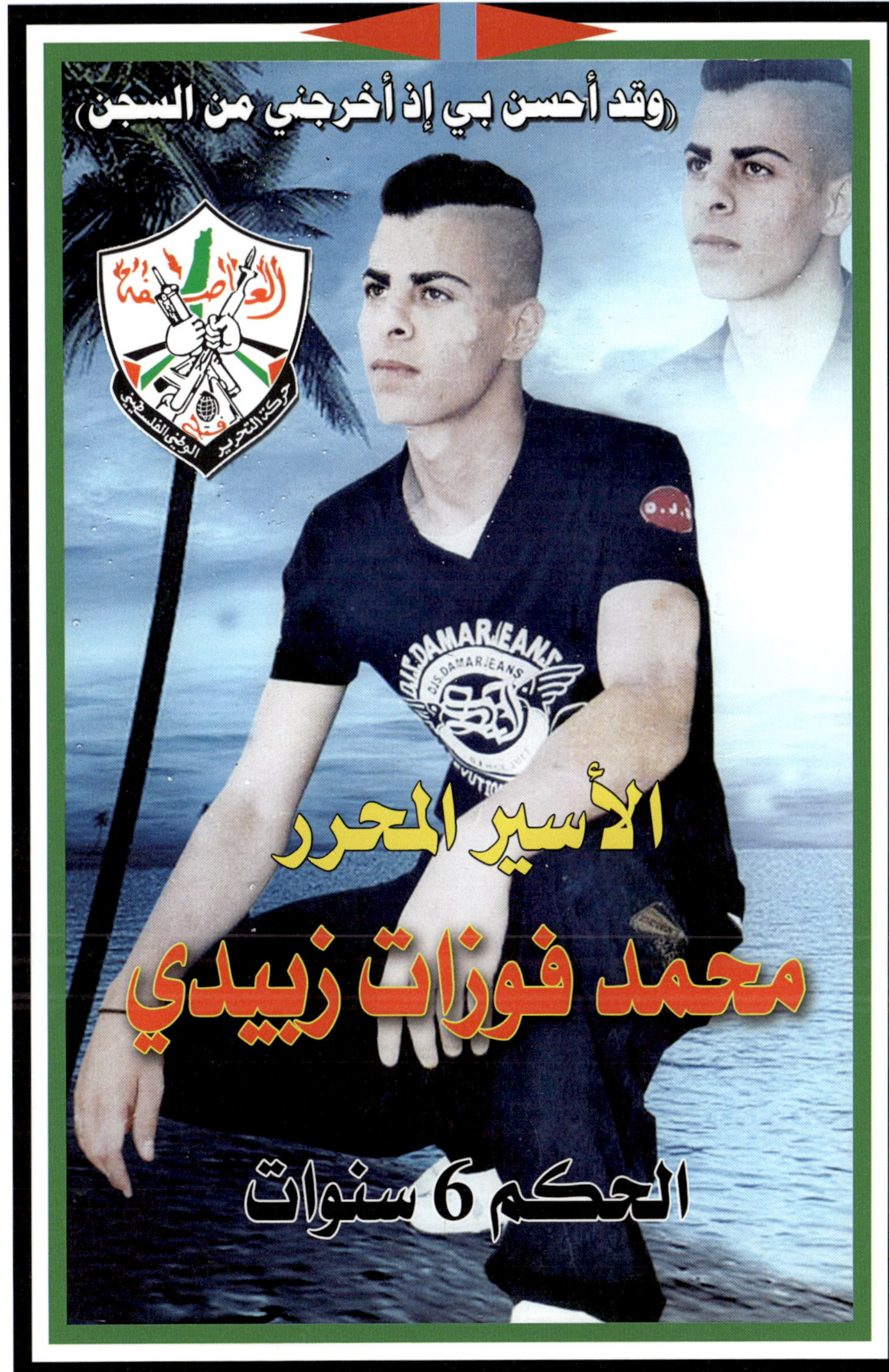

﴿وقد أحسن بي إذ أخرجني من السجن﴾
الأسير المحرر
محمد فوزات زيدي
الحكم 6 سنوات

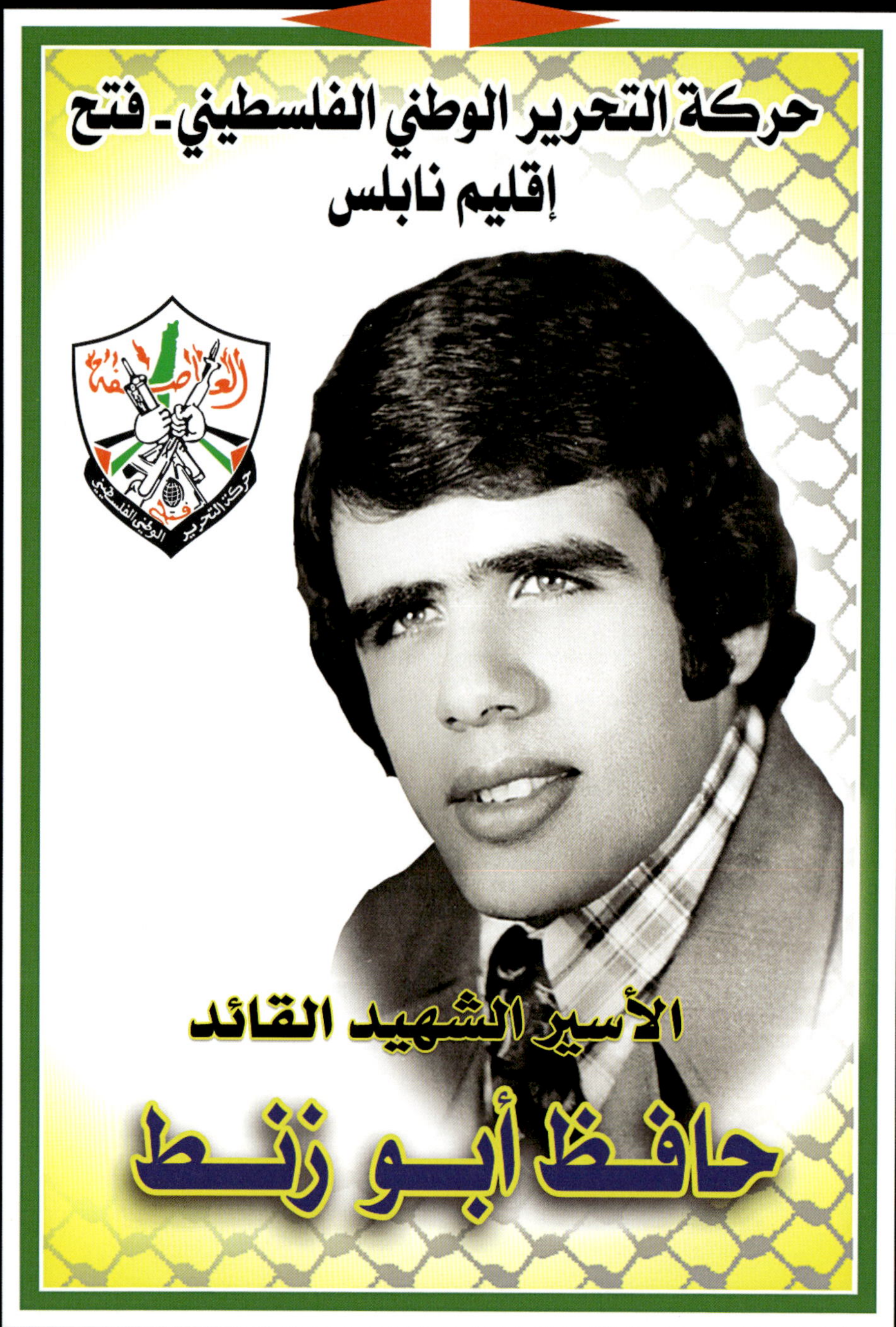

حركة التحرير الوطني الفلسطيني - فتح
إقليم نابلس
الأسير الشهيد القائد
حافظ أبو زنط

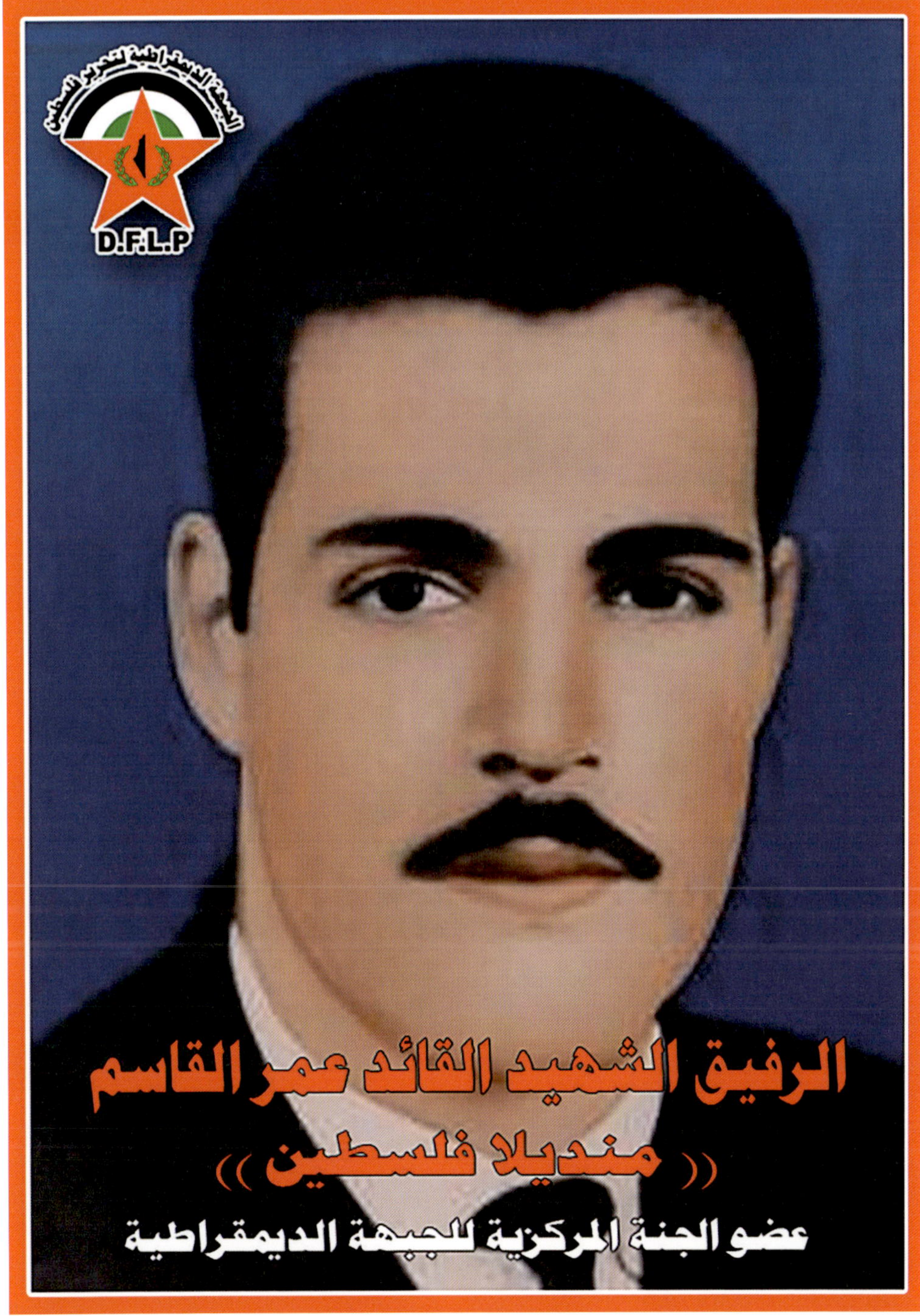

D.F.L.P
الرفيق الشهيد القائد عمر القاسم
((منديلا فلسطين))
عضو الجنة المركزية للجبهة الديمقراطية

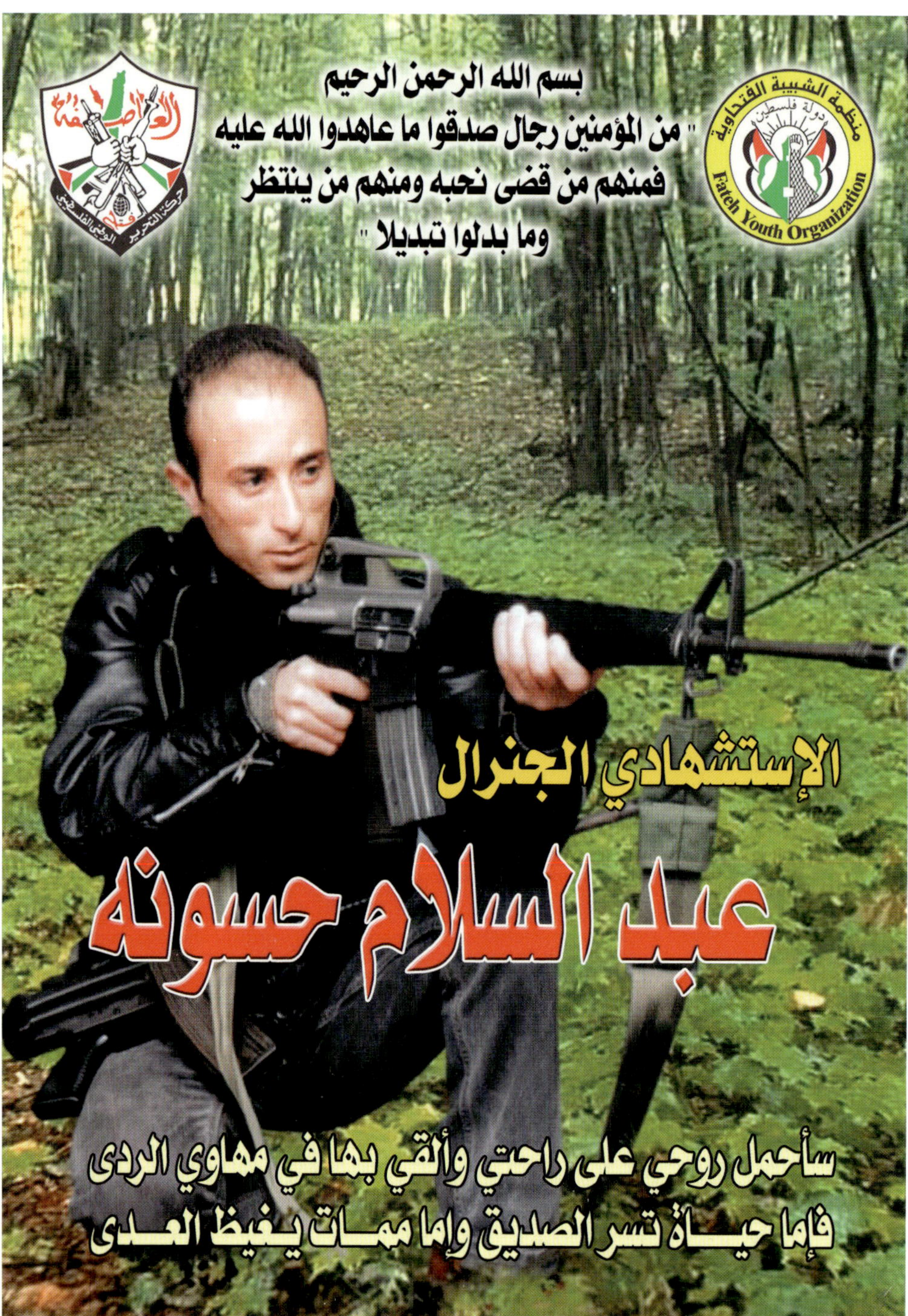
بسم الله الرحمن الرحيم
" من المؤمنين رجال صدقوا ما عاهدوا الله عليه
فمنهم من قضى نحبه ومنهم من ينتظر
وما بدلوا تبديلا "
Fateh Youth Organization
الإستشهادي الجنرال
عبد السلام حسونه
سأحمل روحي على راحتي وألقي بها في مهاوي الردى
فإما حياة تسر الصديق وإما ممات يغيظ العدى
"FATAH AND SHABEEBA MARTYR GENERAL ABED AL SALAM HASSONEH. I WILL CARRY MY SOUL IN MY HANDS. I WILL DROP IT IN THE VALLEYS"

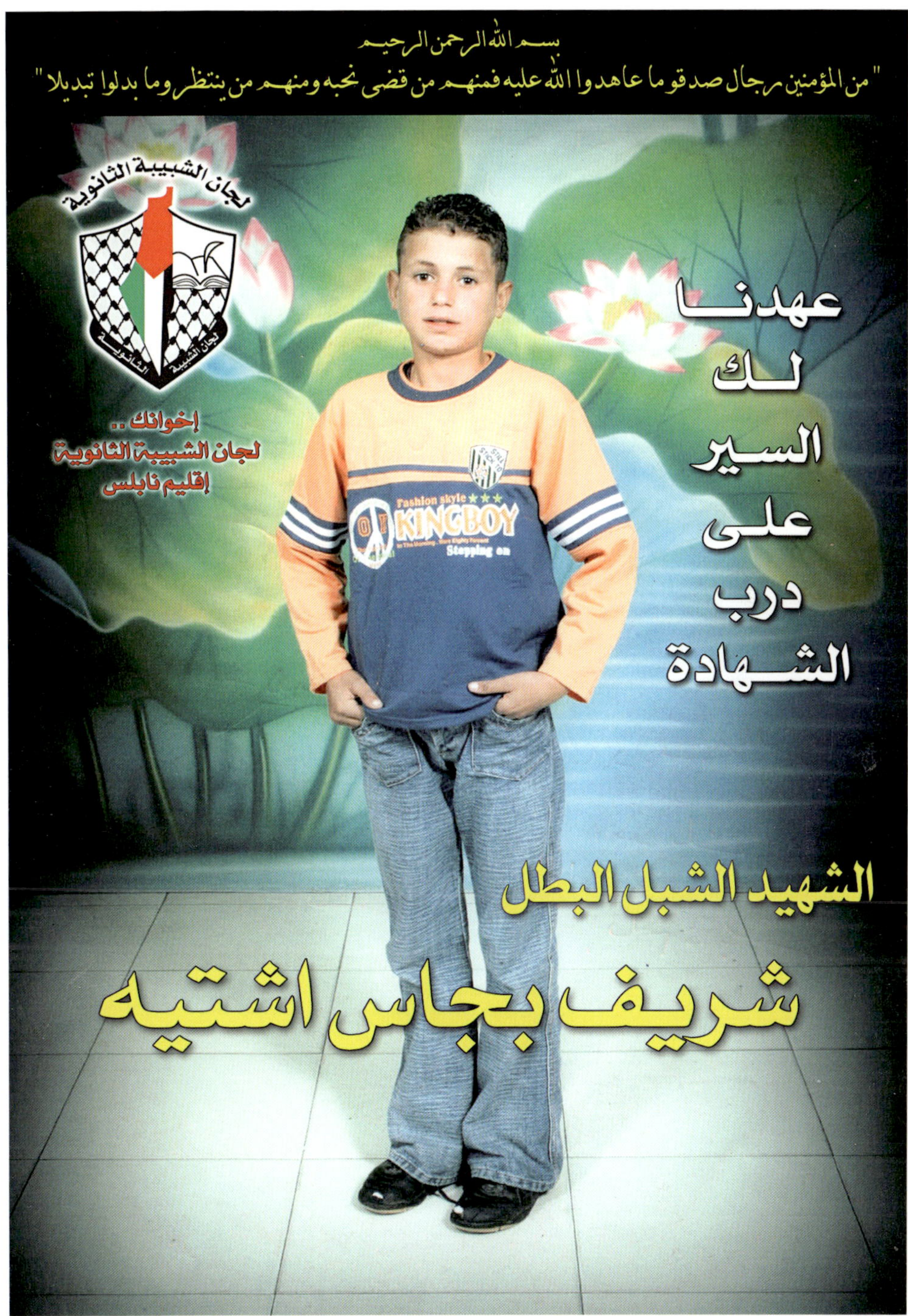

بسم الله الرحمن الرحيم
"من المؤمنين رجال صدقوا ما عاهدوا الله عليه فمنهم من قضى نحبه ومنهم من ينتظر وما بدلوا تبديلا"
إخوانك ..
لجان الشبيبة الثانوية
إقليم نابلس
عهدنا لك السير على درب الشهادة
الشهيد الشبل البطل
شريف بجاس اشتيه
"FATAH SCHOOL WING OUR OATH IS TO MARCH BEHIND YOU ON THE PATH TO MARTYR-DOM THE YOUNG MARTYR HERO FATAH SHAREEF SHATYEH"

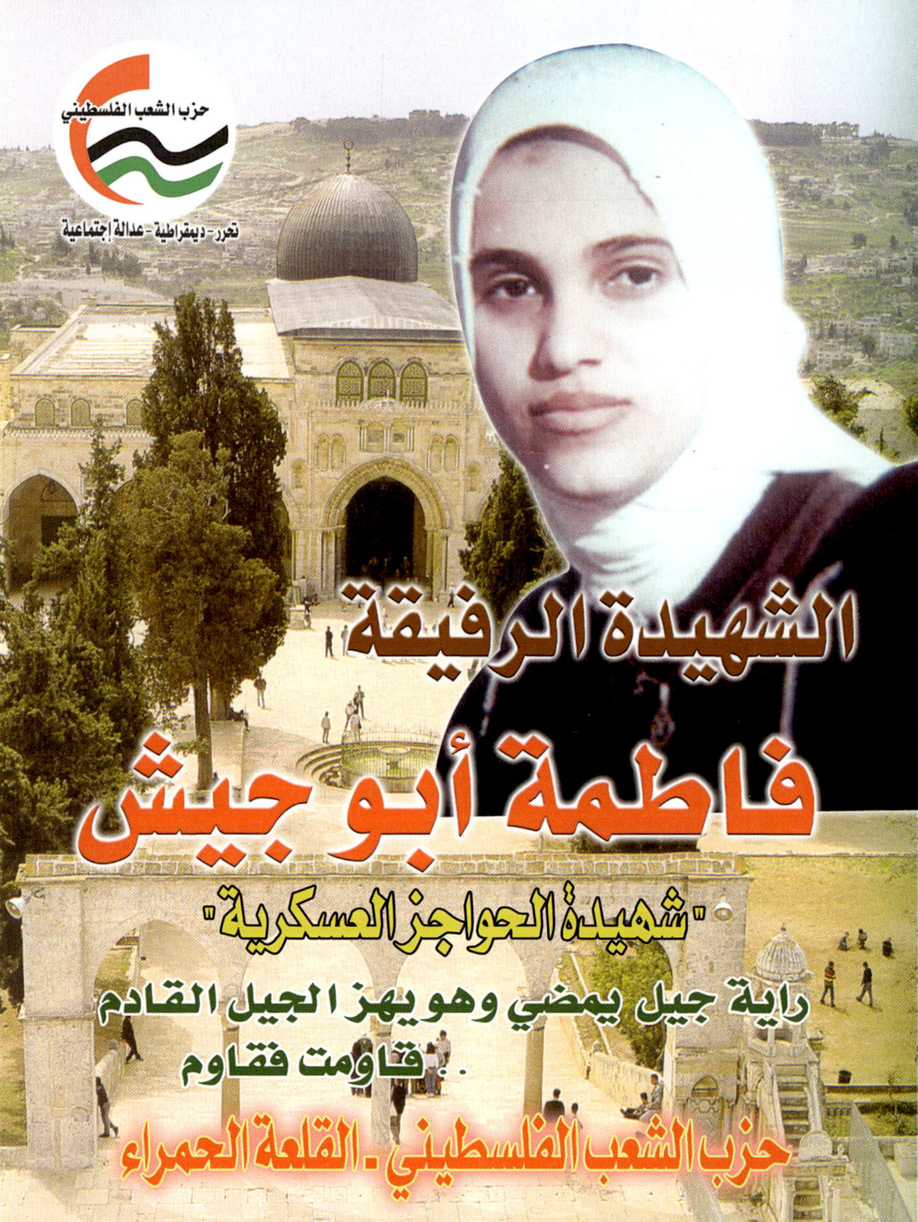

حزب الشعب الفلسطيني

تحرر - ديمقراطية - عدالة إجتماعية

الشهيدة الرفيقة

فاطمة أبو جيش

"شهيدة الحواجز العسكرية"

راية جيل يمضي وهو يهز الجيل القادم

.. قاومت فقاوم

حزب الشعب الفلسطيني ـ القلعة الحمراء

"THE MARTYR COMRADE FATMA ABU JEESH MARTYR OF THE CHECK-POINTS, SHE HAS RESISTED FOR THE FUTURE GENERATIONS"

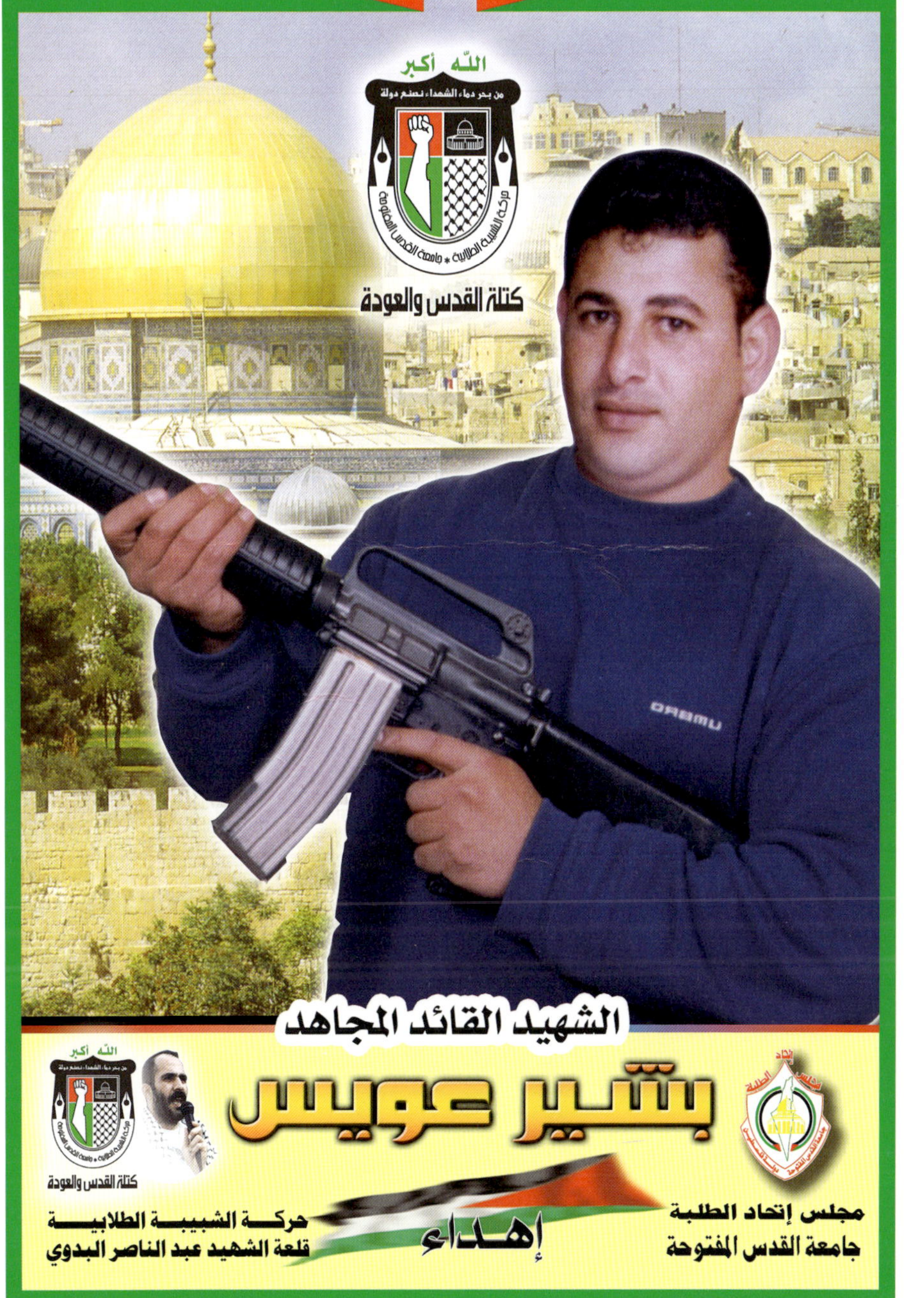

اللّه أكبر
من بحر دماء الشهداء نصنع دولة
كتلة القدس والعودة
الشهيد القائد المجاهد
بشير عويس
اللّه أكبر
من بحر دماء الشهداء نصنع دولة
كتلة القدس والعودة
مجلس إتحاد الطلبة
جامعة القدس المفتوحة
إهداء
حركة الشبيبة الطلابية
قلعة الشهيد عبد الناصر البدوي

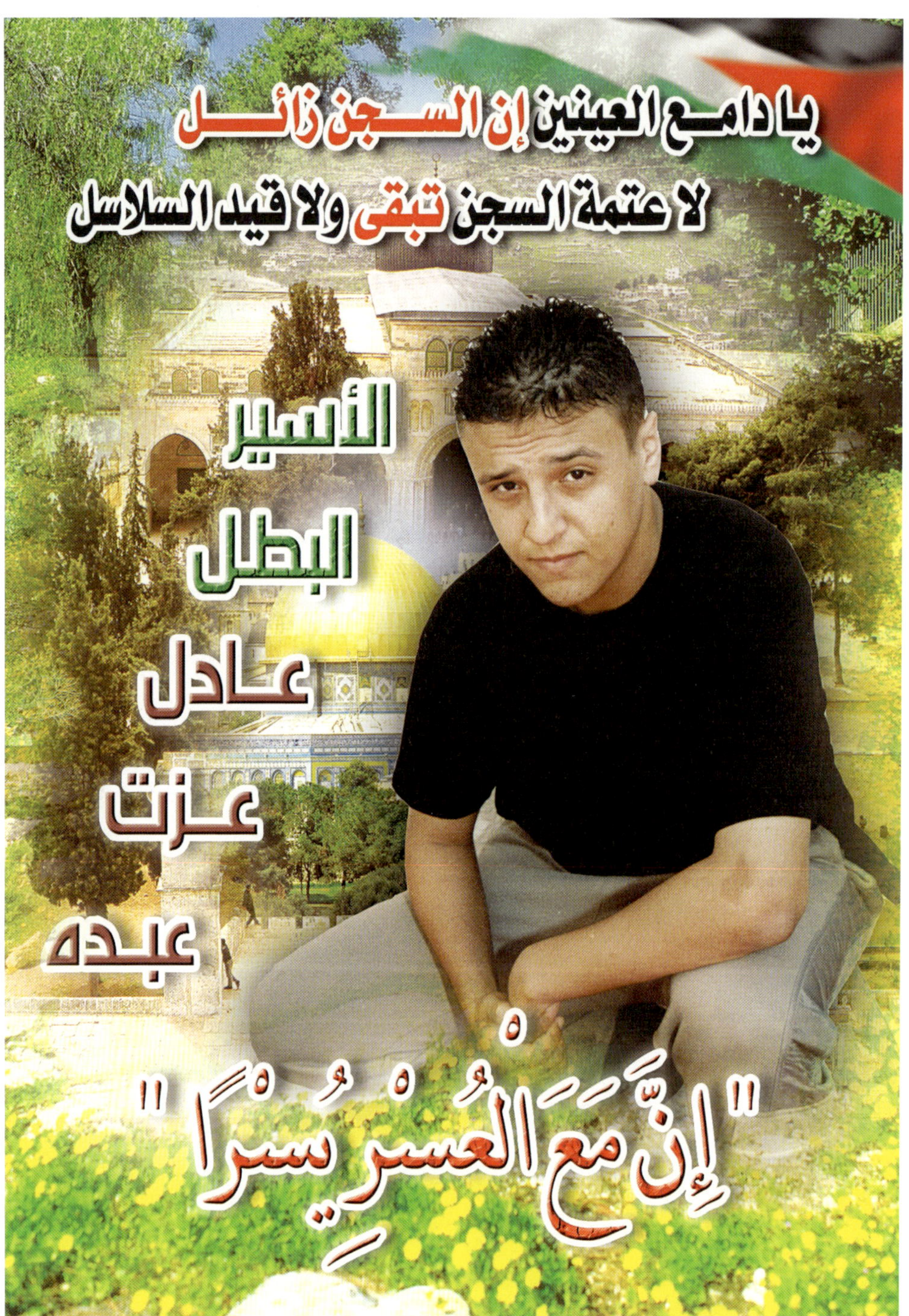
يا دامع العينين إن السجن زائل
لا عتمة السجن تبقى ولا قيد السلاسل
الأسير
البطل
عادل
عزت
عبده
"إن مع العسر يسرًا"
"YOU WITH THE TEARY EYES, THE PRISON WILL DISAPPEAR. THE DARKNESS AND CHAINS WILL NOT LAST" THE PRISONER HERO ADEL AZZAT ABDO

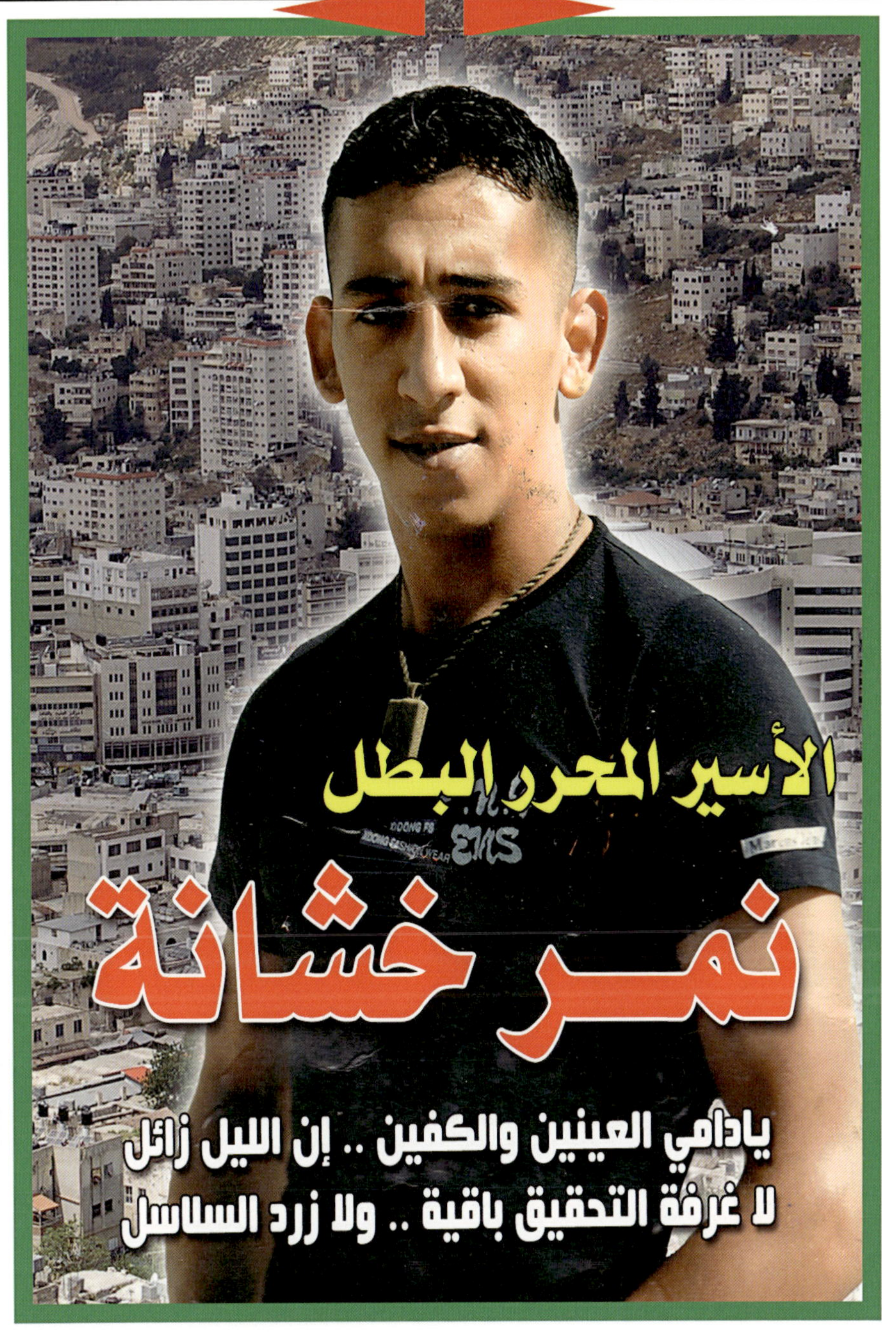

الأسير المحرر البطل
نمر خشانة
يادامي العينين والكفين .. إن الليل زائل
لا غرفة التحقيق باقية .. ولا زرد السلاسل

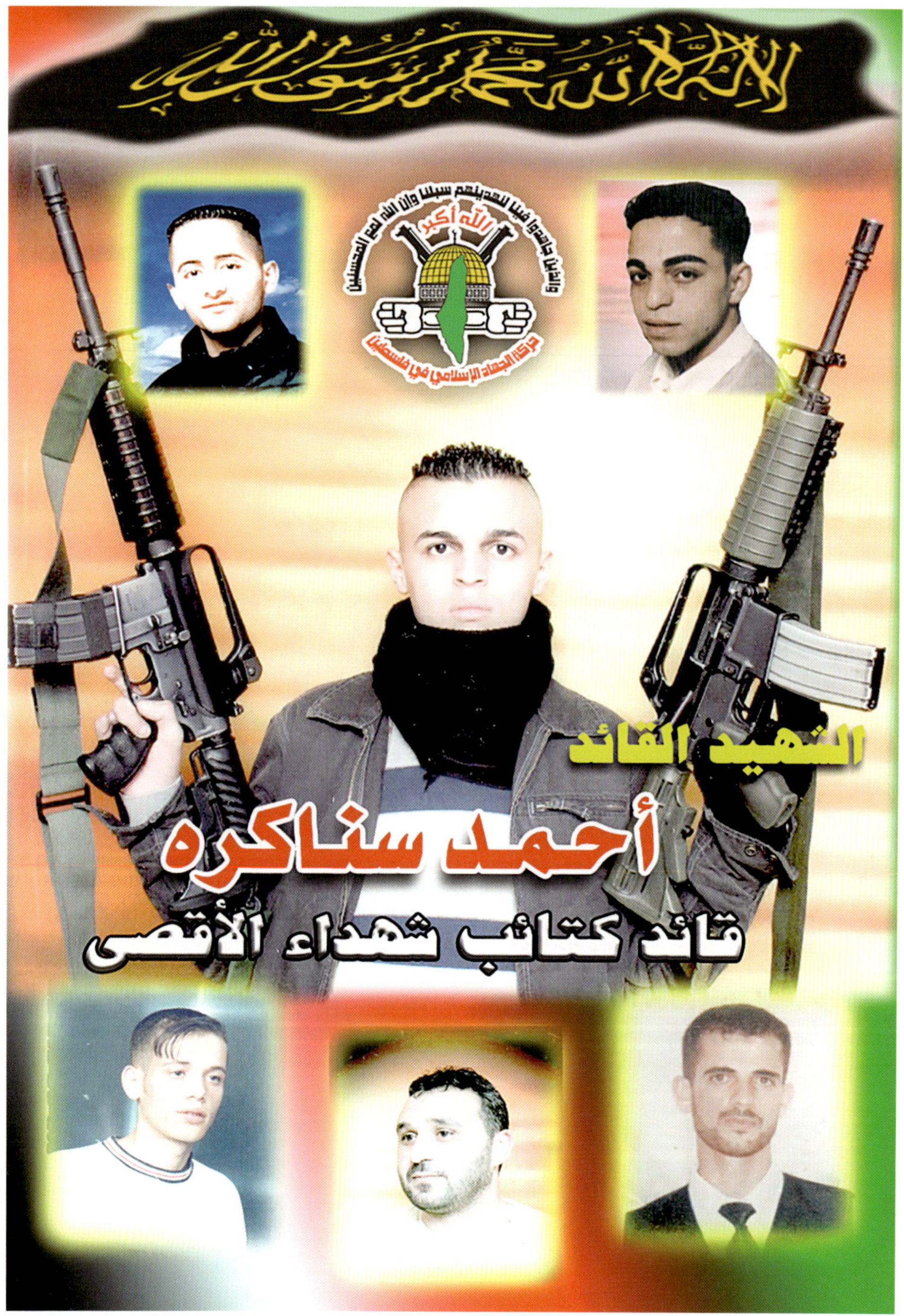

لا اله الا الله محمد رسول الله
الشهيد القائد
أحمد سناكره
قائد كتائب شهداء الأقصى
"ISLAMIC JIHAD THE MARTYR LEADER AHMED SANAKREH LEADER IN AL AQSA MARTYR BRIGADE"

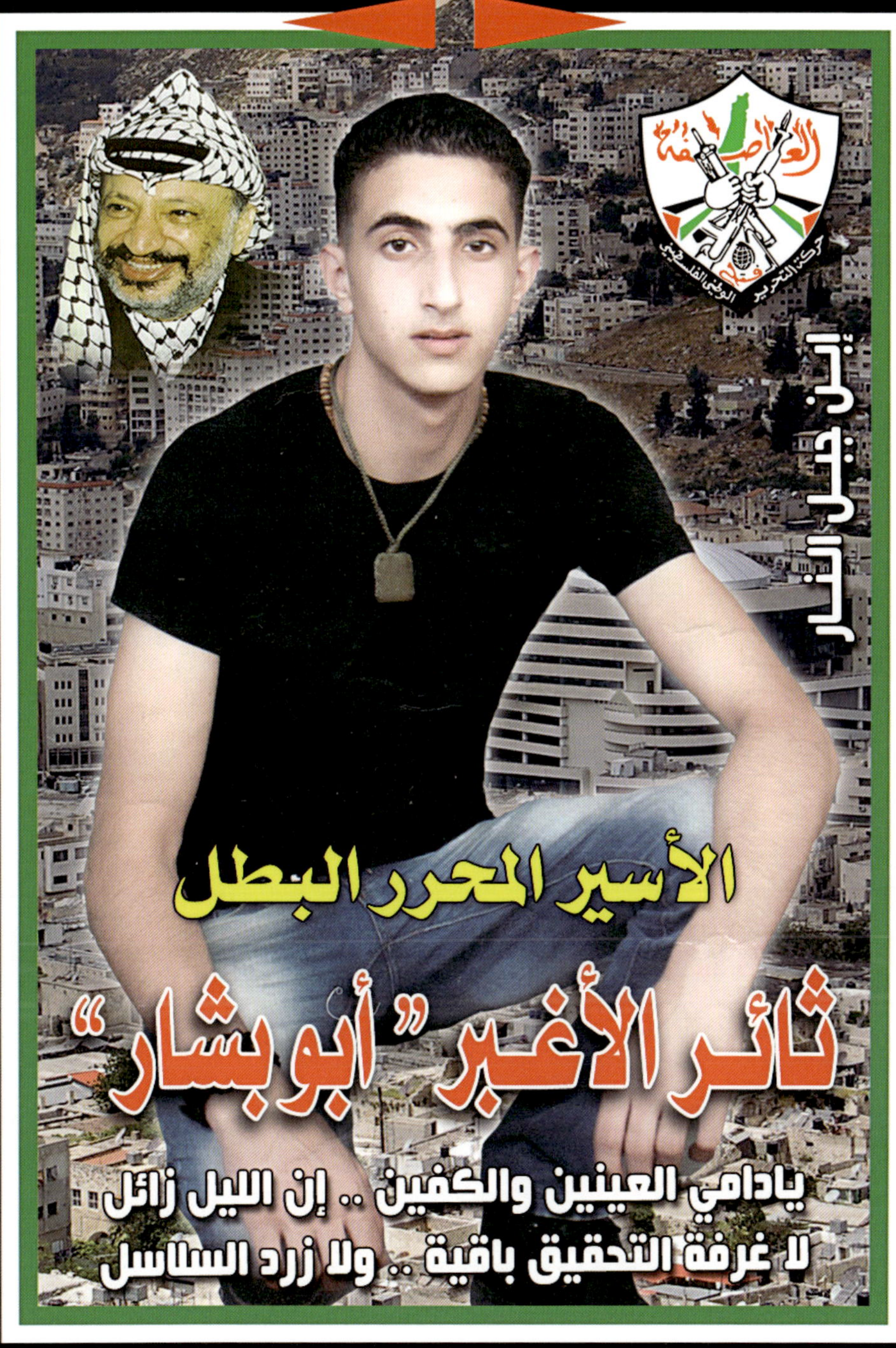
العاصفة
حركة التحرير الوطني الفلسطيني فتح
أبن جبل النار
الأسير المحرر البطل
ثائر الأغبر "أبو بشار"
يادامي العينين والكفين .. إن الليل زائل
لا غرفة التحقيق باقية .. ولا زرد السلاسل

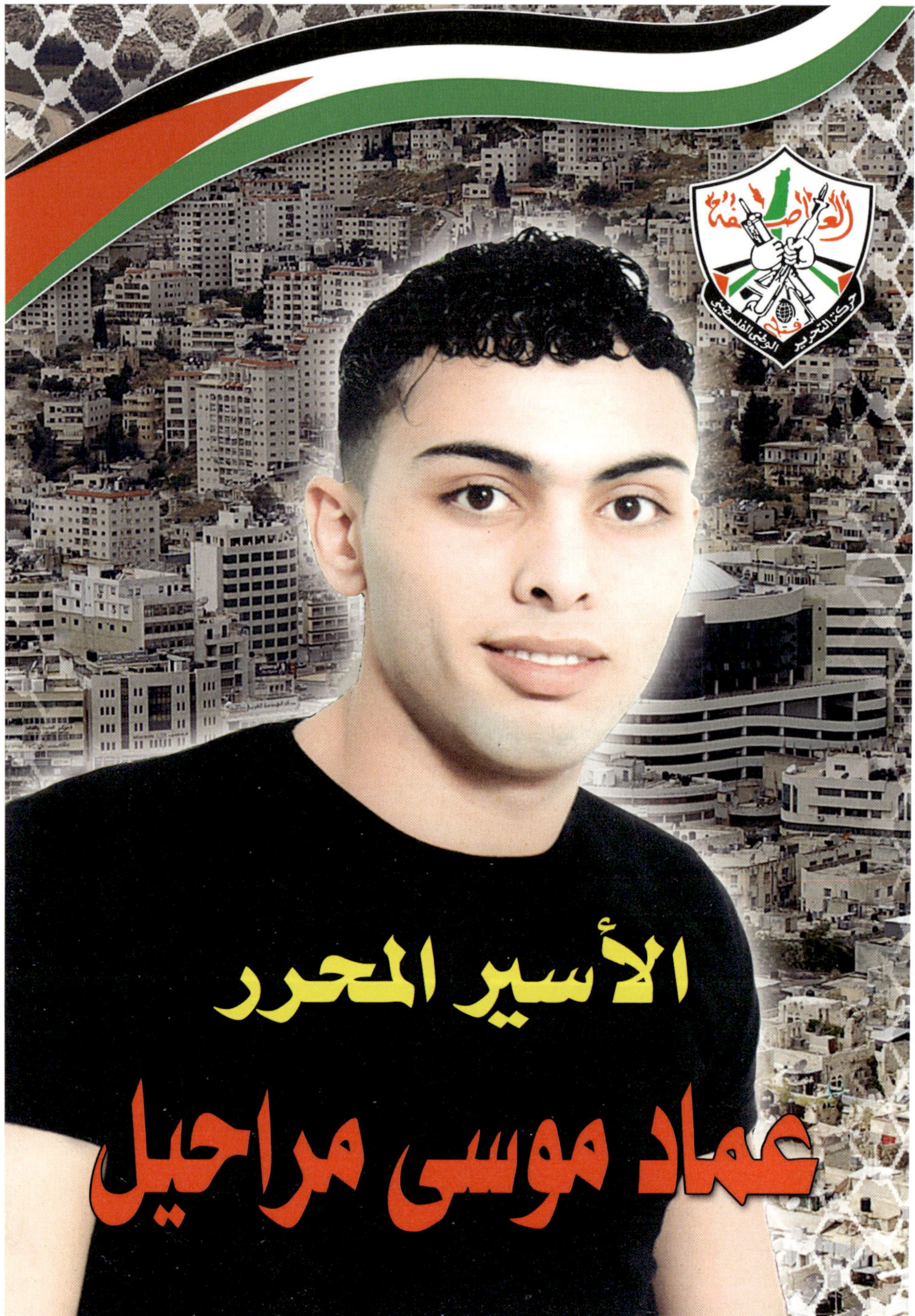

الأسير المحرر
عماد موسى مراحيل

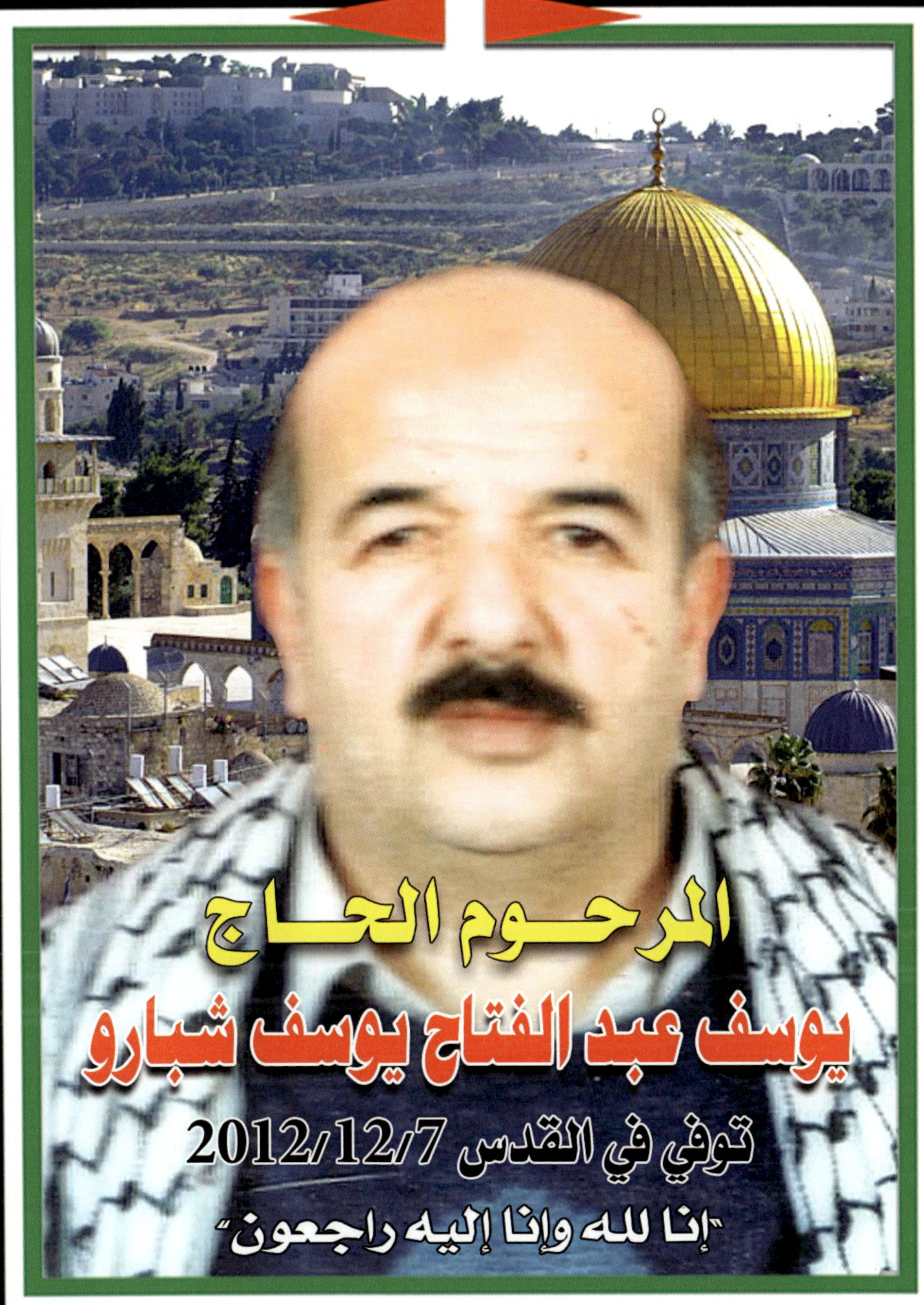
المرحـــوم الحـــاج
يوسف عبد الفتاح يوسف شبارو
توفي في القدس 2012/12/7
"إنا لله وإنا إليه راجعون"
"YUSEF ABDEL FATAH YUSEF SHABARO DIED FROM NATURAL CAUSES IN JERUSALEM"

The material gathered under this section is owed to a graphic designer in Nablus who wishes to remain anonymous. He has been creating martyr and prisoner iconography since the outbreak of the second intifada in 2001.

SCOTT Tell me how long you have been designing martyr and prisoner posters for?

ANON I started designing posters since the start of the second Intifada

S When designing the posters do you usually follow a brief? Or are you free to design the posters however you like?

A We make the design that fits with the current events depending on the conditions and also on the martyr's nature and belonging as well as the death circumstances

S I have noticed that photographs of beaches / paradise are a recurring theme in the posters, can you explain why?

A Paradise and beaches are carrying more than just one meaning, their most important signification is that they represent the symbol of the grandparents and parents' Palestinian lands that were occupied in 48, and they are also a mean to confirm the idea that the martyrs who fought and died, they defended the whole Palestinian territory. It is also to show how beautiful Palestine is as well as to express the meaning of comfort and reassurance.

S Have there been times in your career where you have had to design more posters than others?

A Surely there have been times where I have had to design more posters than other times like during the invasions or at national occasions.

S Where do you obtain peoples photographs to use on the posters?

A I obtain peoples' photographs either online or I get them from relatives and friends of the person who want to design.

S Are there posters that you have designed that you are particularly proud of?

A Yes I really feel proud and glad of this beautiful work

S When the posters are stuck up on the walls in the streets of Nablus, what sort of role do you think they play in daily life?

A Getting the posters stuck up on the walls in the streets of Nablus, makes people aware of what is happening around , create communication between them and remind them about these people's names who Sacrificed themselves for their homeland.

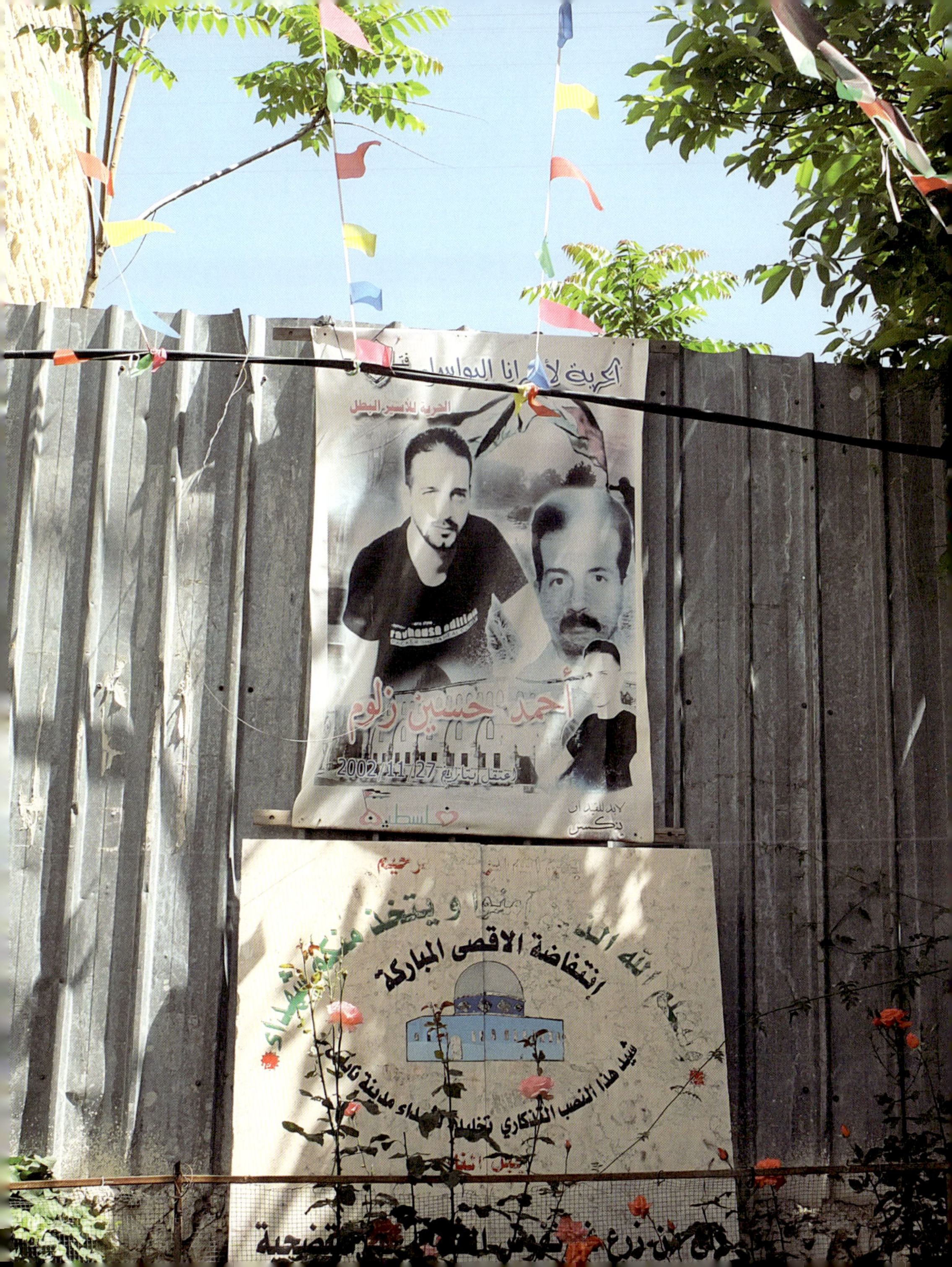
الحرية لأسرانا البواسل
الحرية للأسير البطل
أحمد حسين زلوم
2002/11/27
فلسطين
انتفاضة الأقصى المباركة

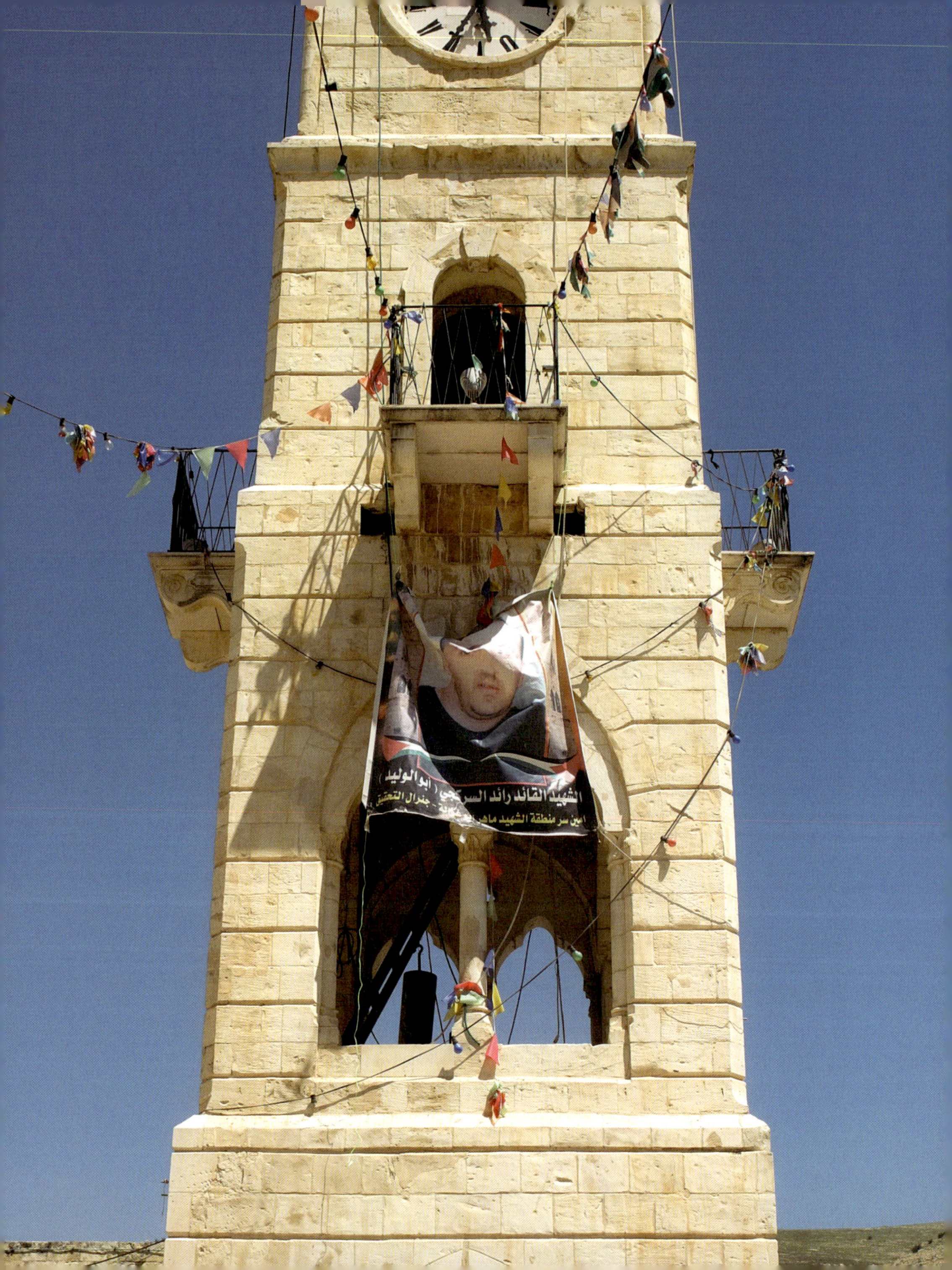
(أبو الوليد)
الشهيد القائد رائد السركجي - جنرال التعفيش
أمين سر منطقة الشهيد ماهر

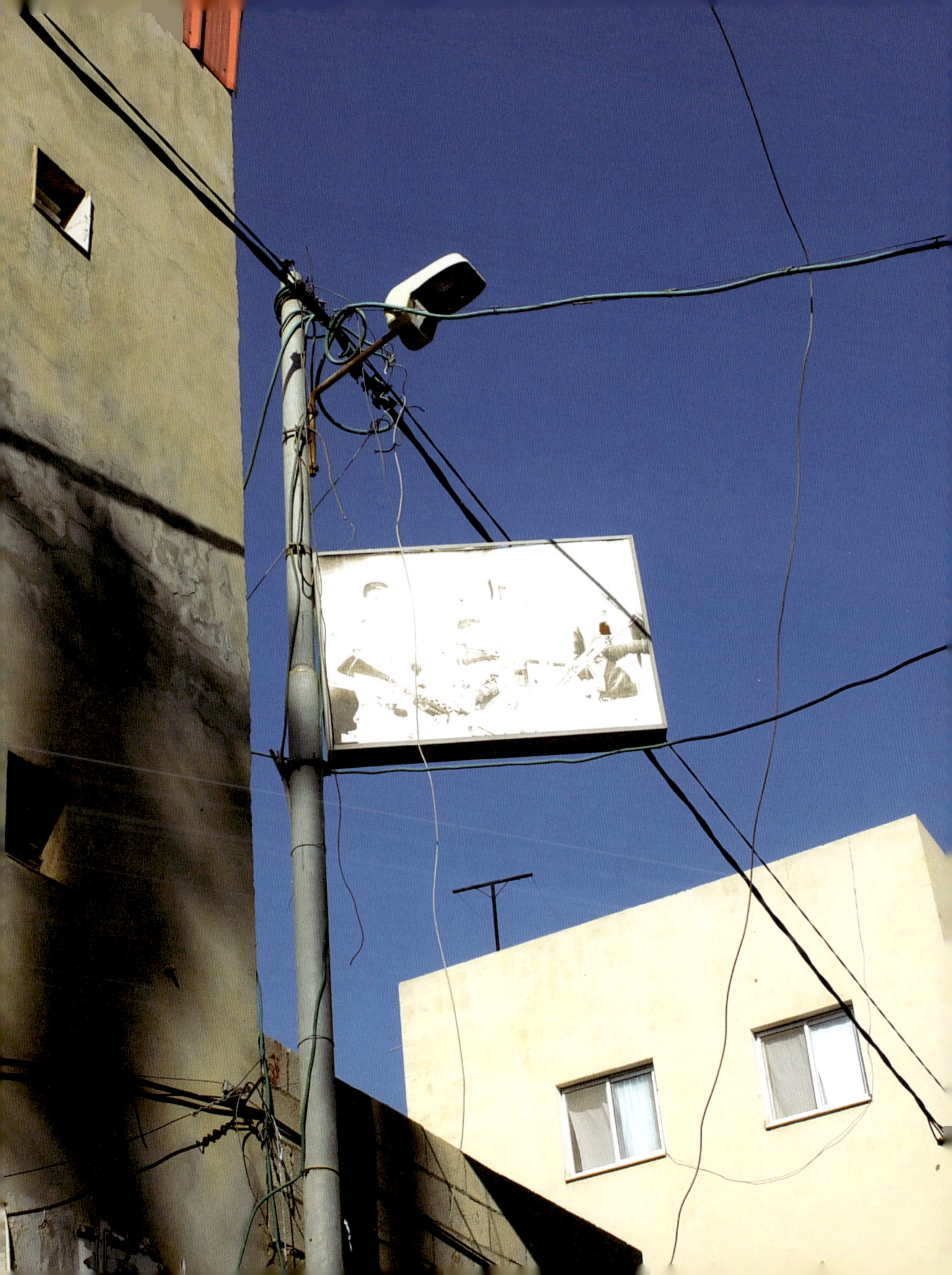

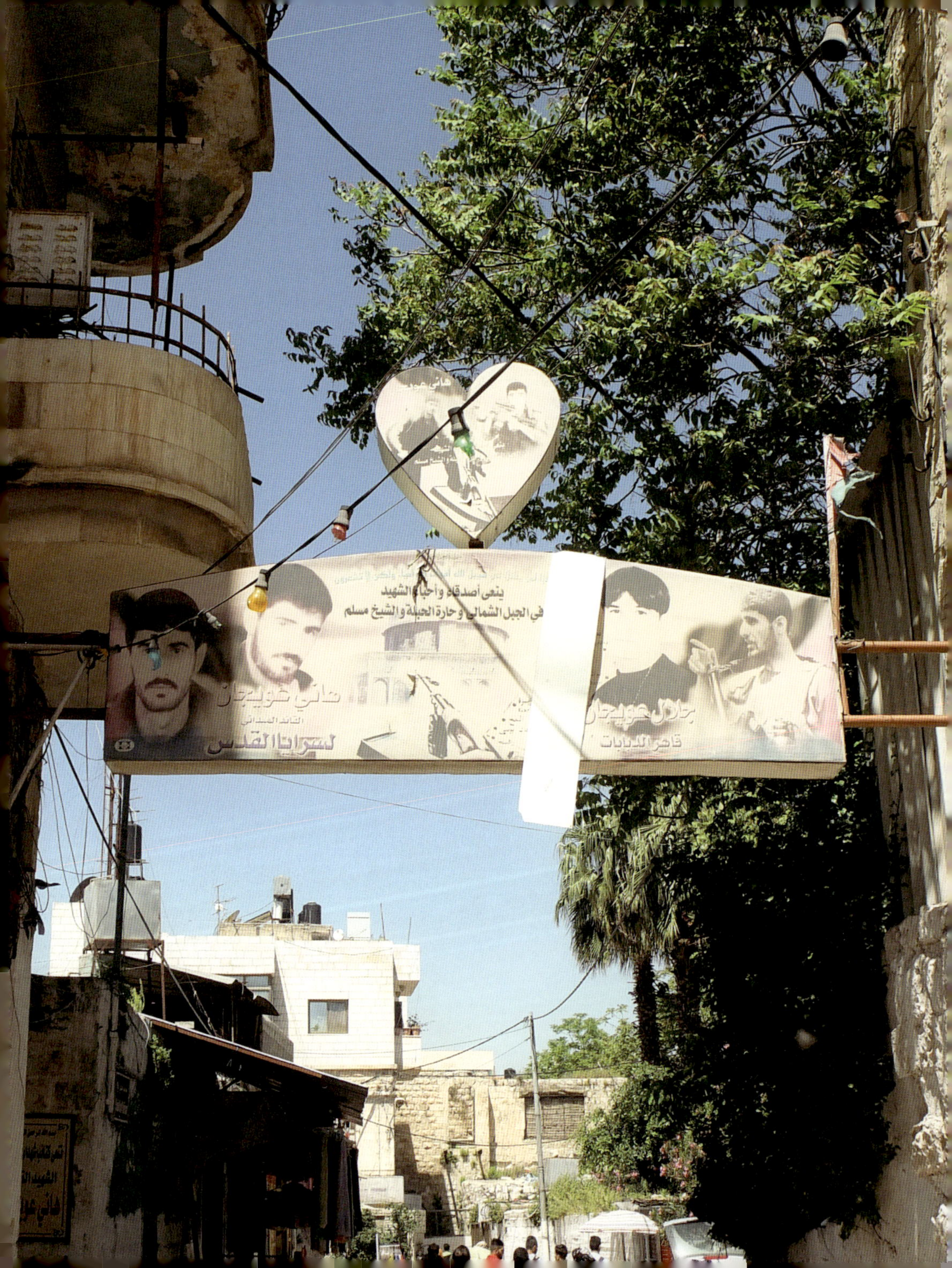

ينعى أصدقاؤه وأحبّاء الشهيد
في الجبل الشمالي و حارة الحبلة والشيخ مسلم
هاني خويلدان
بلال خويلدان
لسرايا القدس

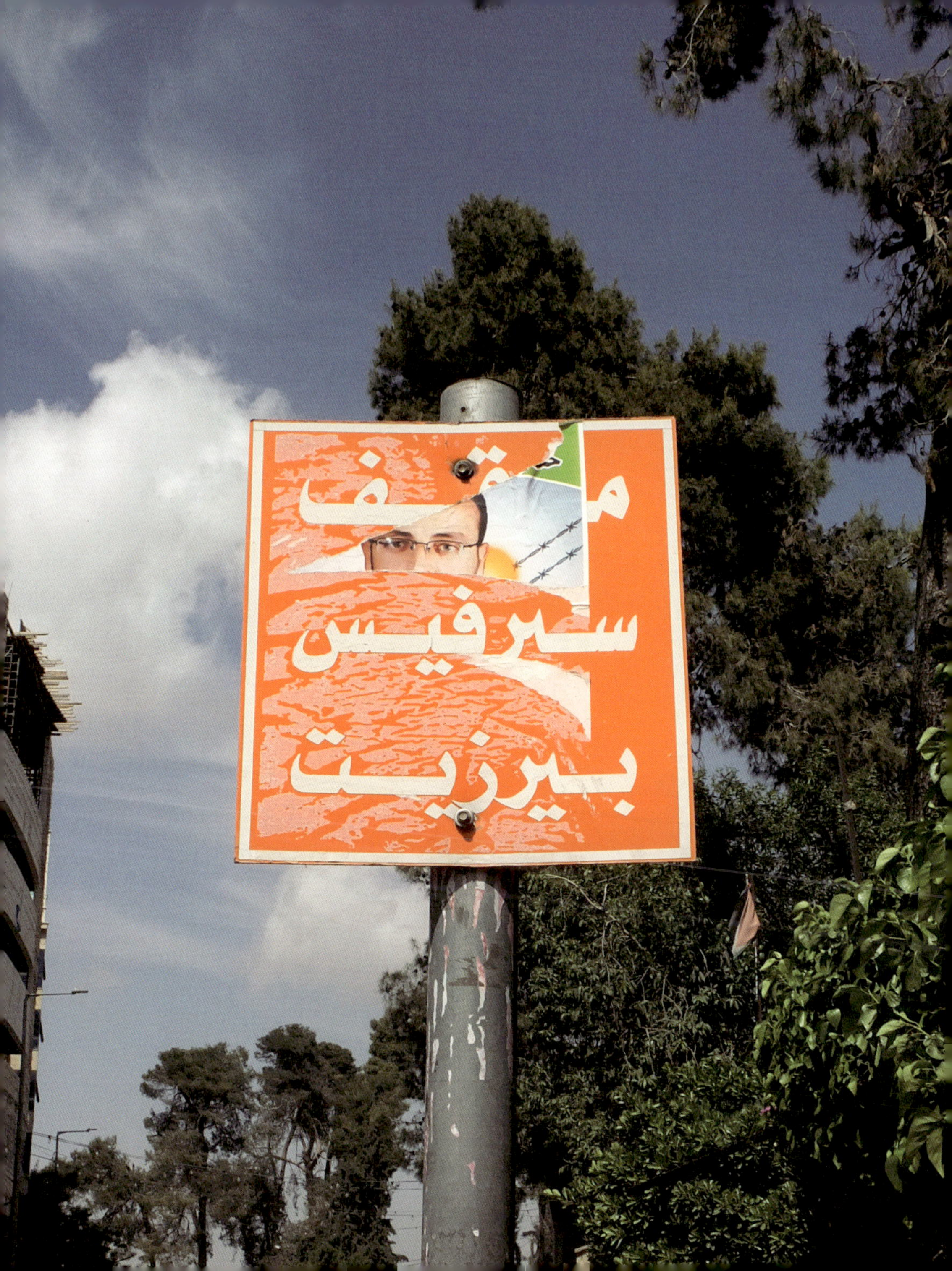
موقف
سرفيس
بيرزيت

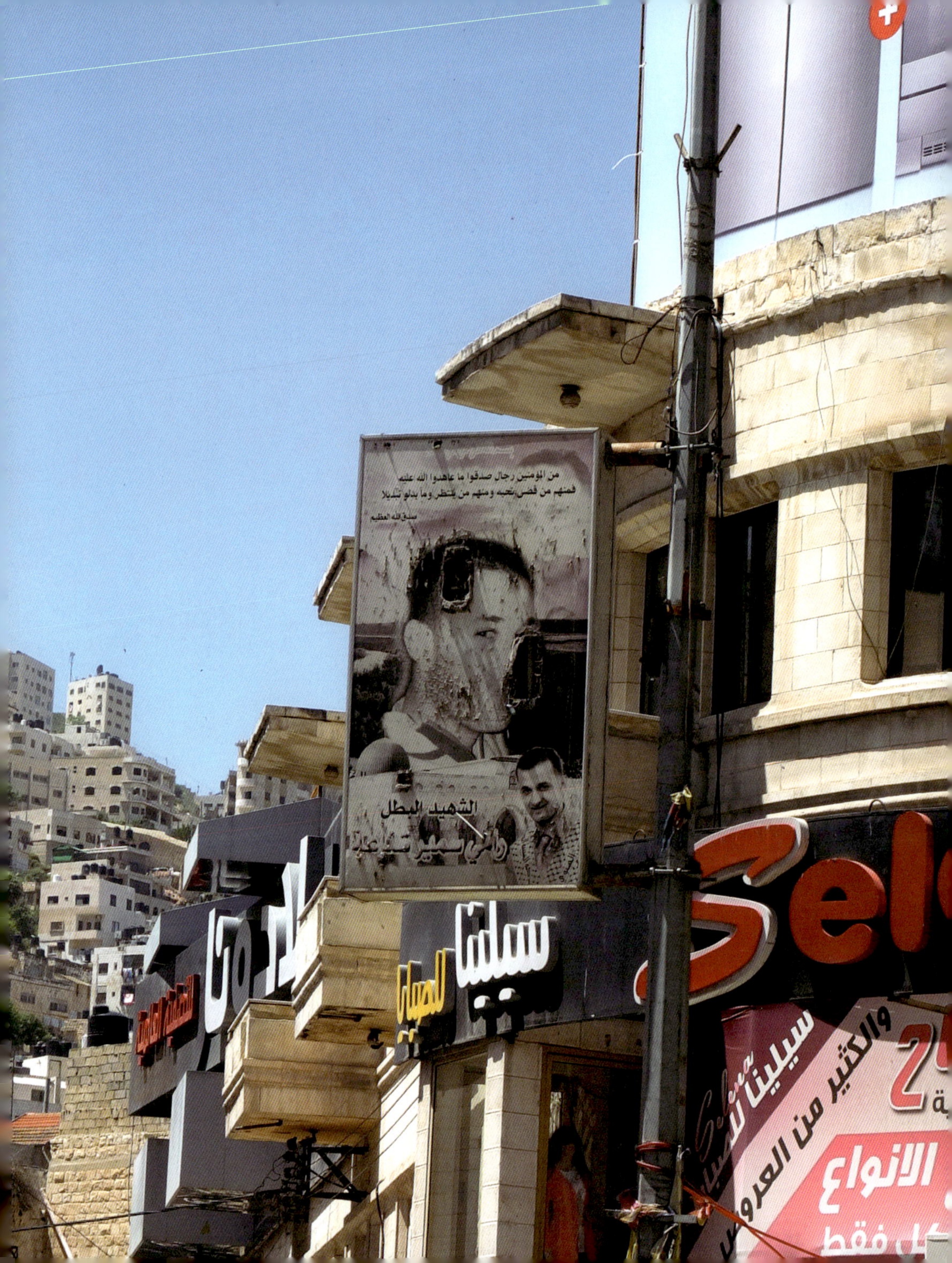

من المؤمنين رجال صدقوا ما عاهدوا الله عليه
فمنهم من قضى نحبه ومنهم من ينتظر وما بدلوا تبديلا
صدق الله العظيم
الشهيد البطل
رامي سمير شاعذا
سليتا للهدايا
Seld
سيليتا للهدايا
والكثير من العروض
2
كل الانواع
فقط

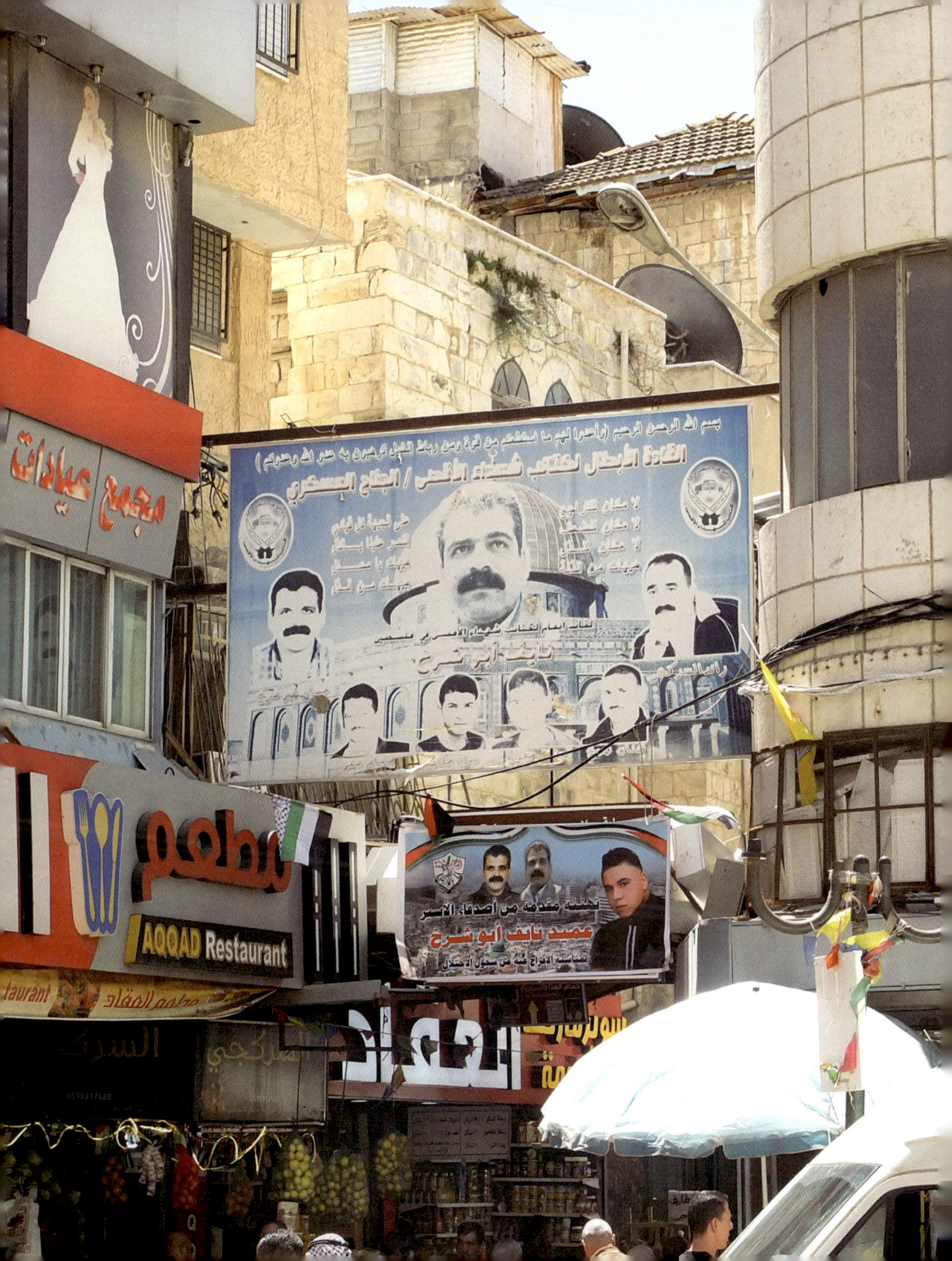
مجمع ميادات
مطاعم
AQQAD Restaurant
taurant المقاد
السد
ماركيتي
العقاد
بسم الله الرحمن الرحيم (واعدوا لهم ما استطعتم من قوة ومن رباط الخيل ترهبون به عدو الله وعدوكم)
القادة الأبطال لكتائب شهداء الأقصى / الجناح العسكري
القائد العام لكتائب شهداء الأسرى في فلسطين
نايف أبو شرح
تهنئة مقدمة من أصدقاء الأسير
عميد نايف أبو شرح
لمناسبة الافراج عنه من سجون الاحتلال

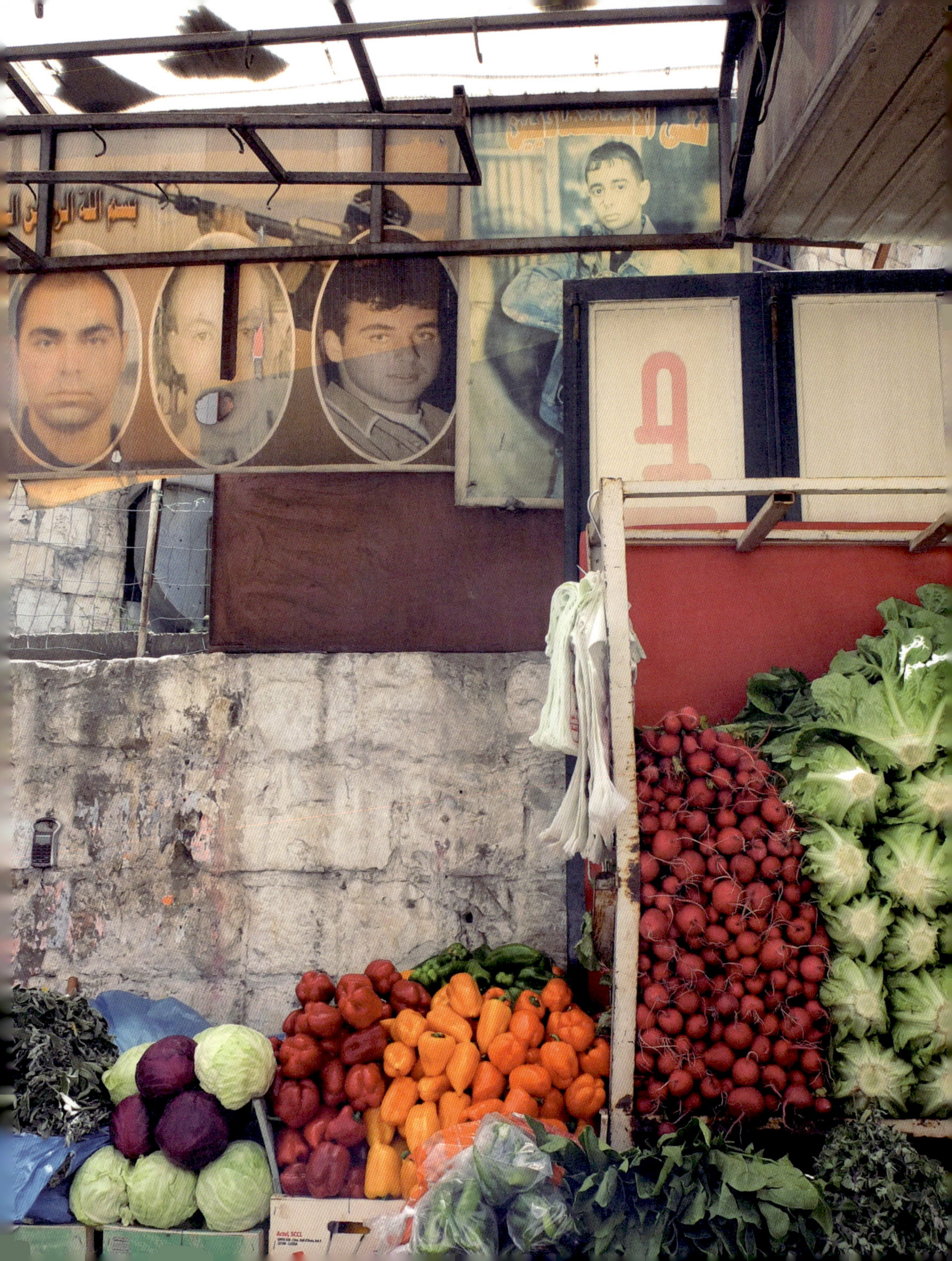

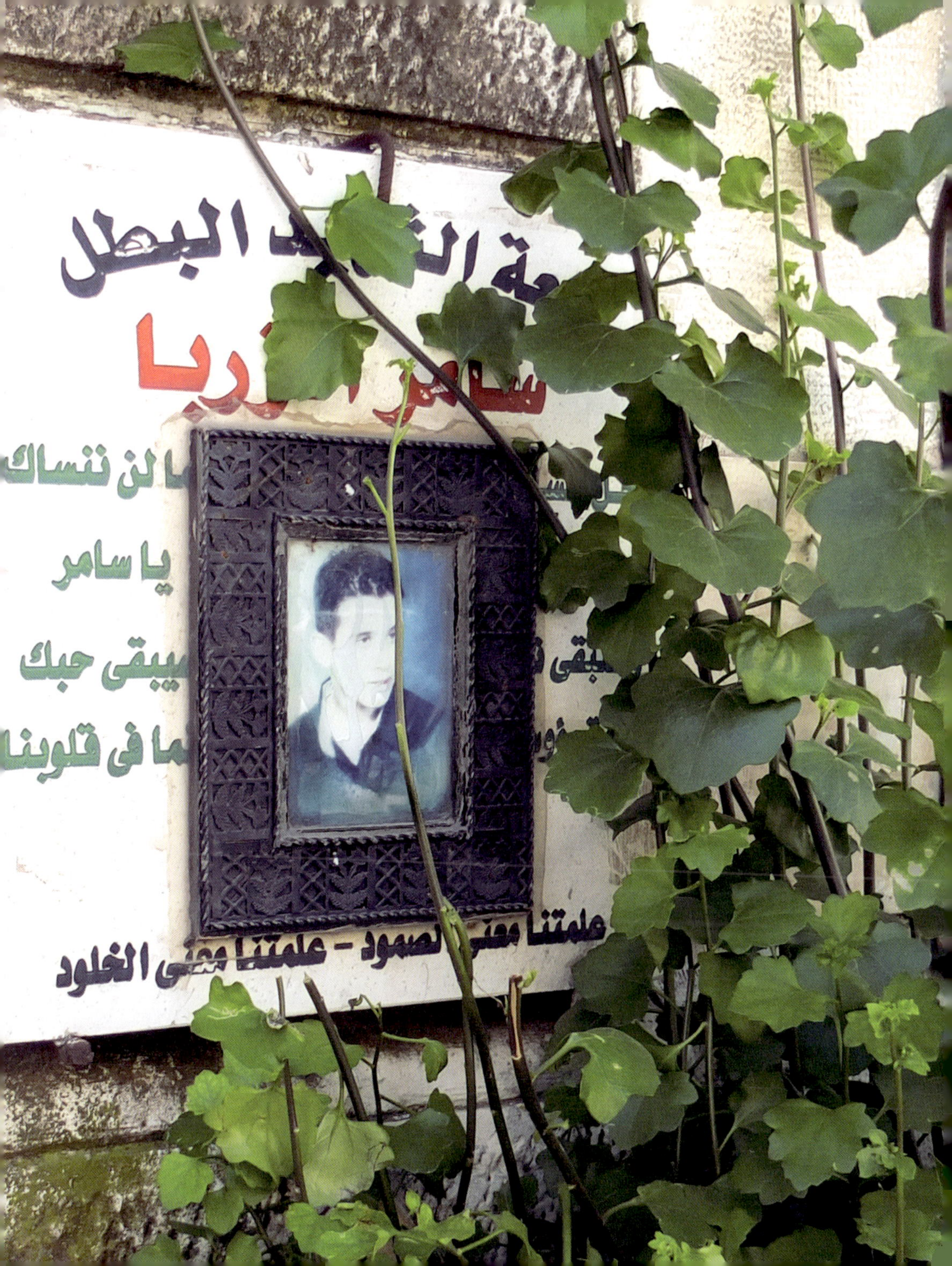
...مة الشهيد البطل
سامر ...
...لن ننساك
يا سامر
يبقى حبك
ما في قلوبنا
علمتنا معنى الصمود - علمتنا معنى الخلود

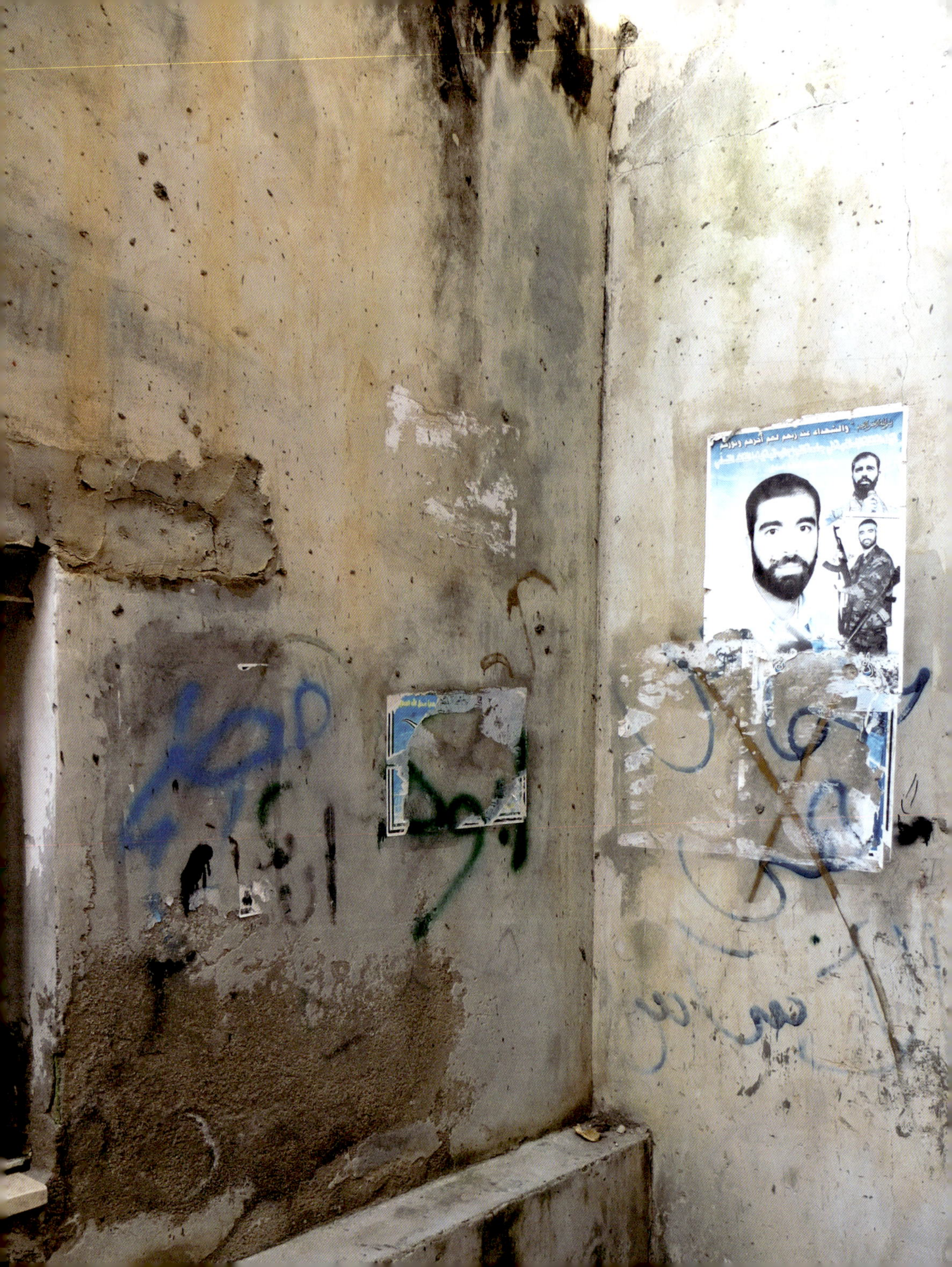
والشهداء عند ربهم لهم أجرهم ونورهم

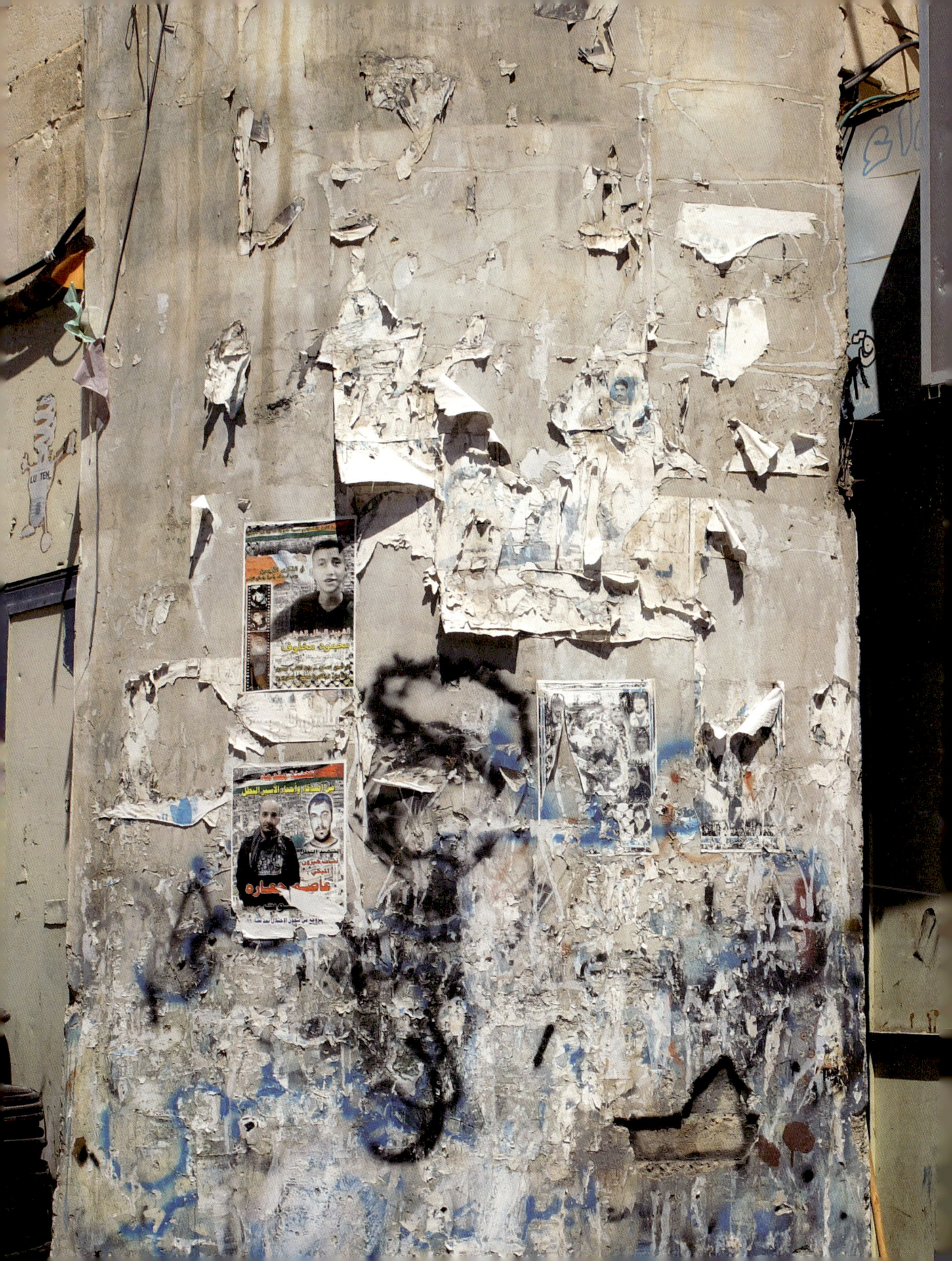

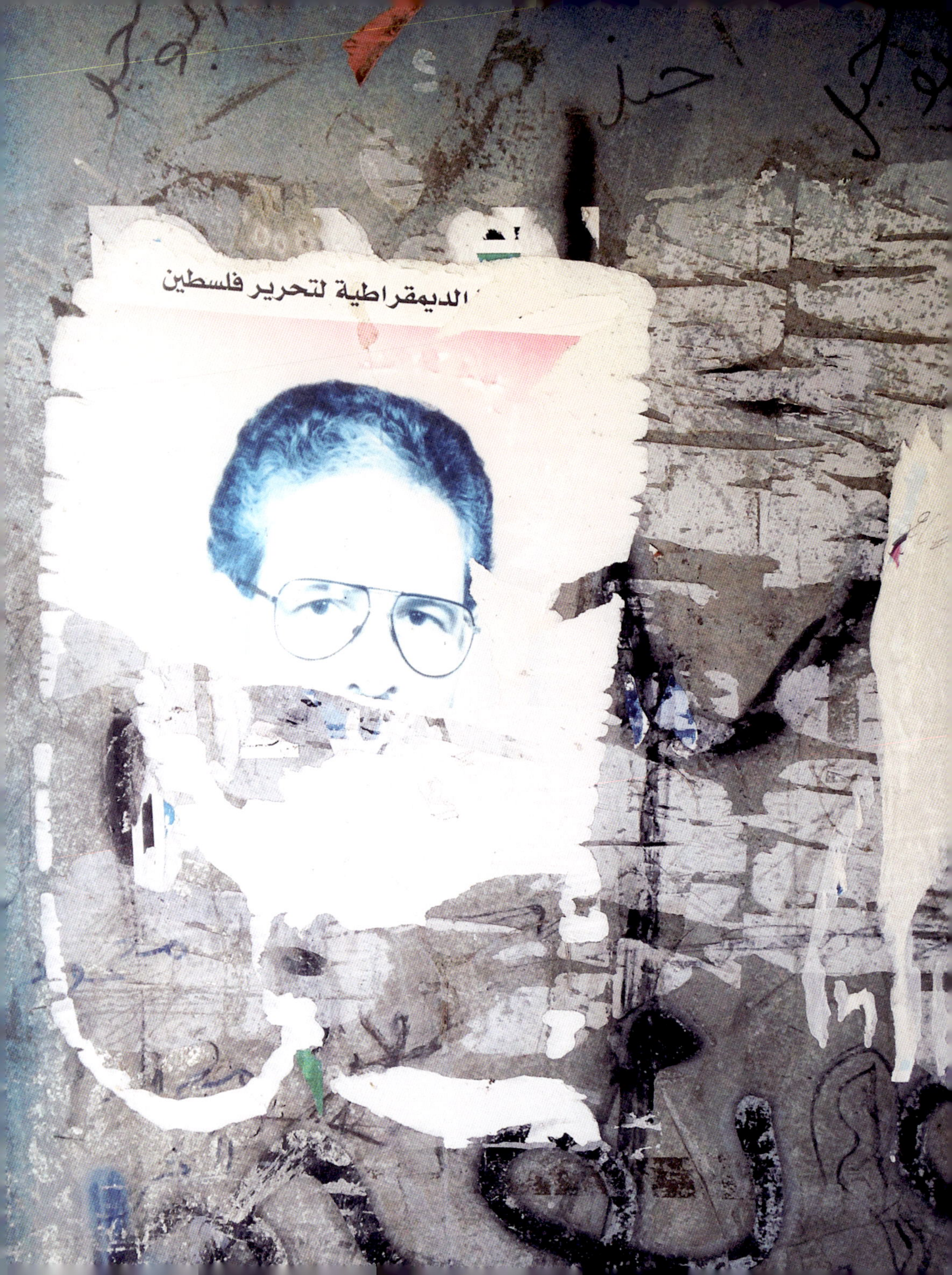
الديمقراطية لتحرير فلسطين

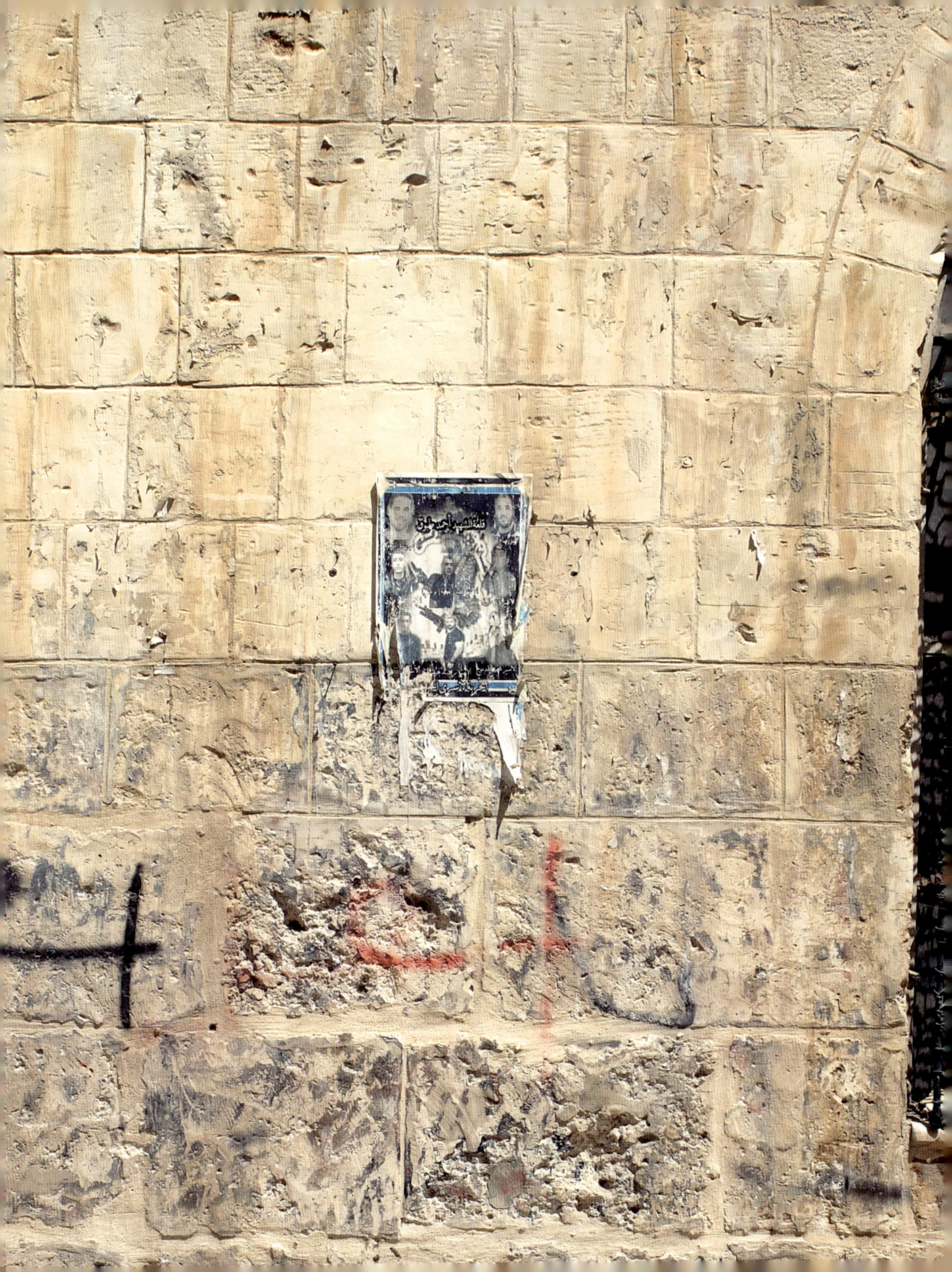

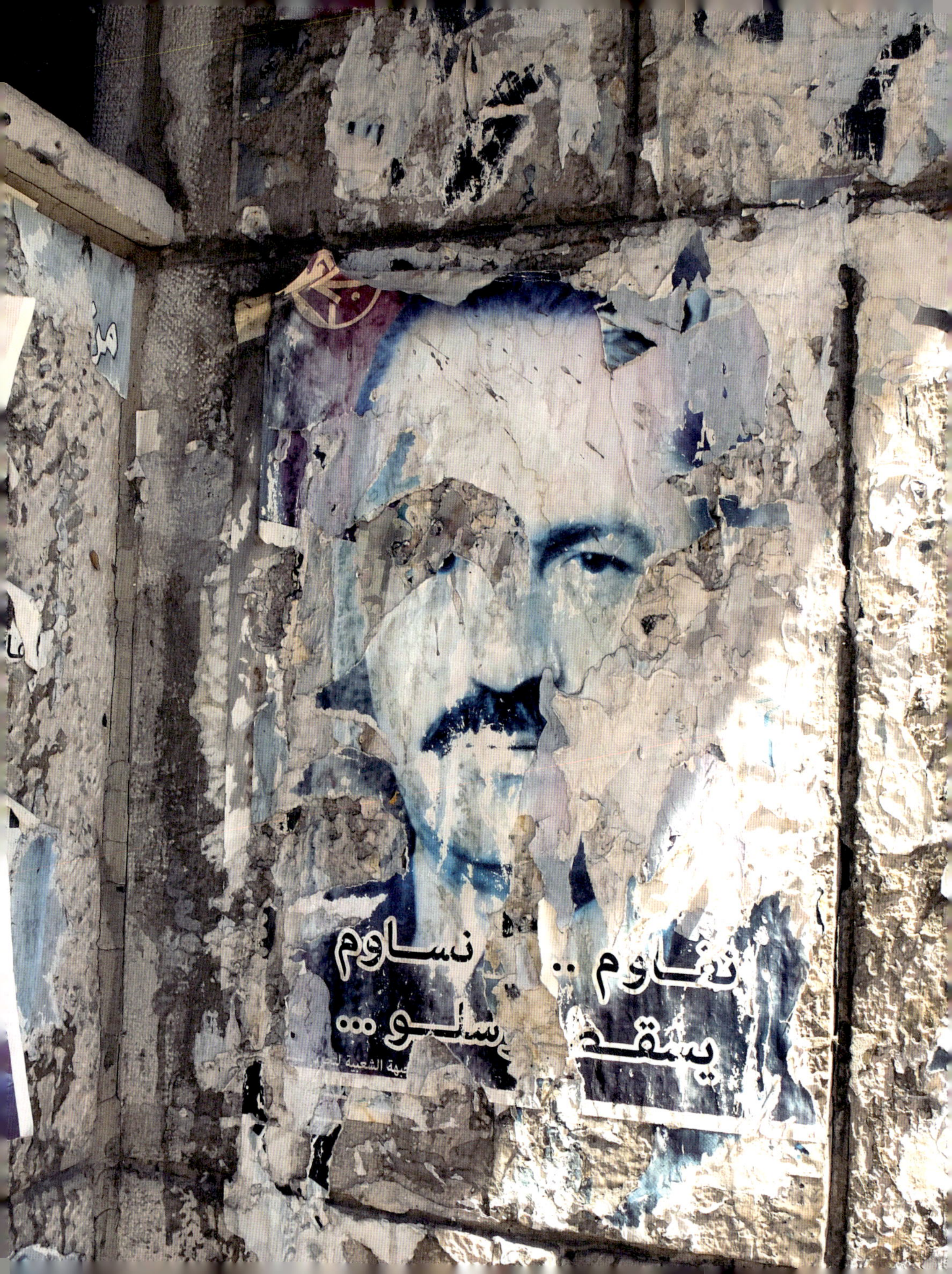
نقاوم .. نساوم
يسقط .. يسلو ...

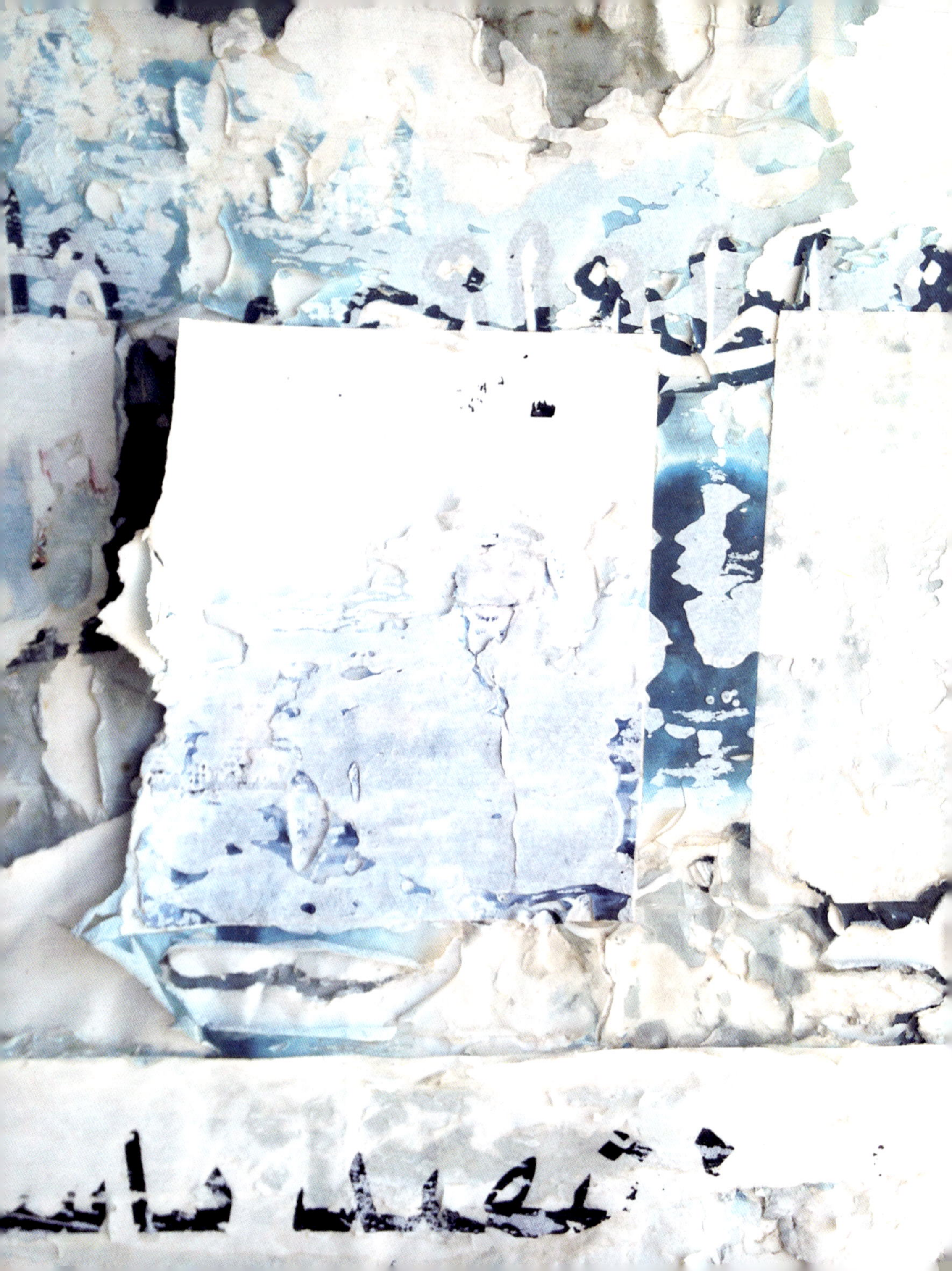

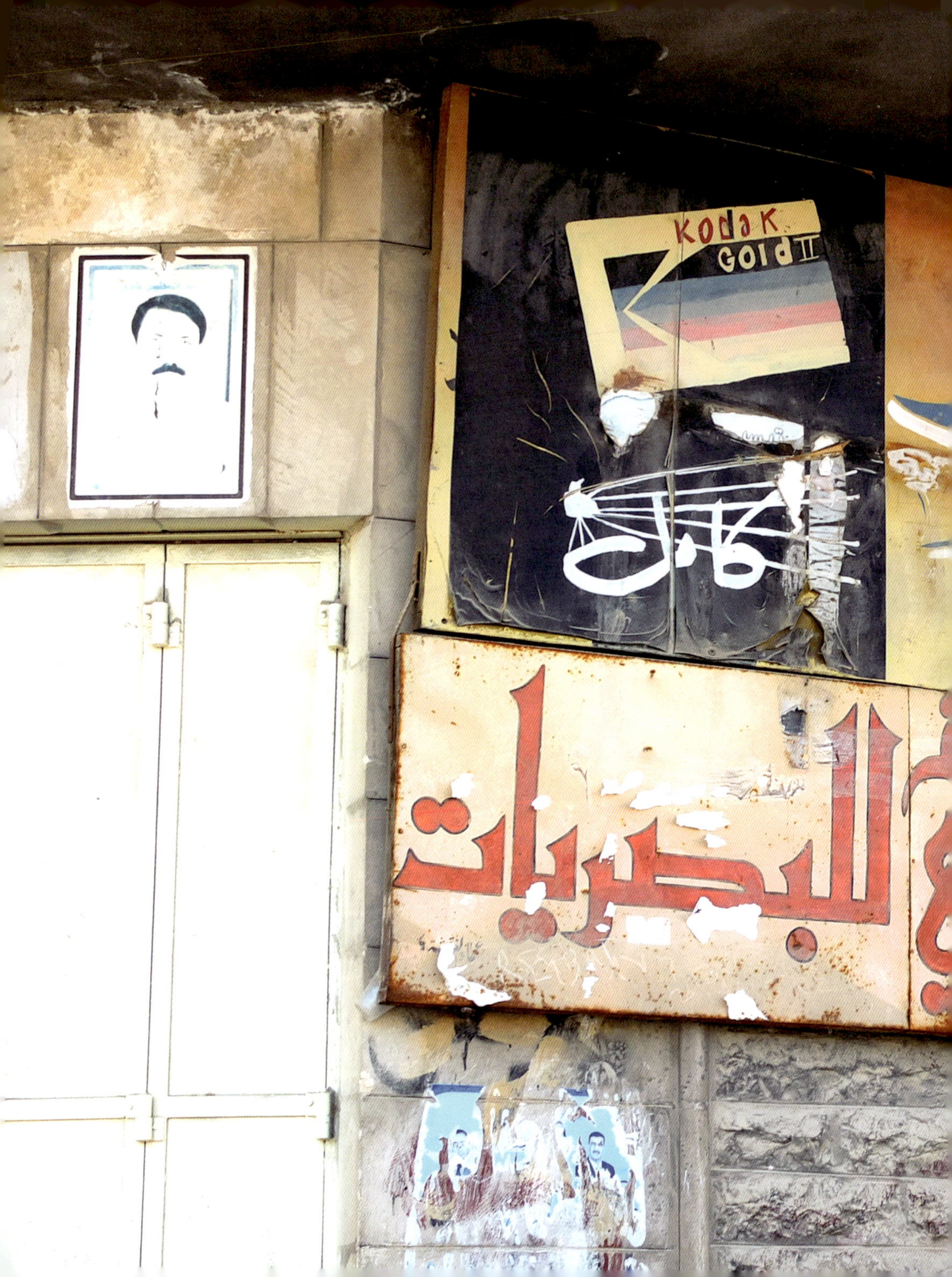
KODAK
GOLD II
كبابجي
الكتريات

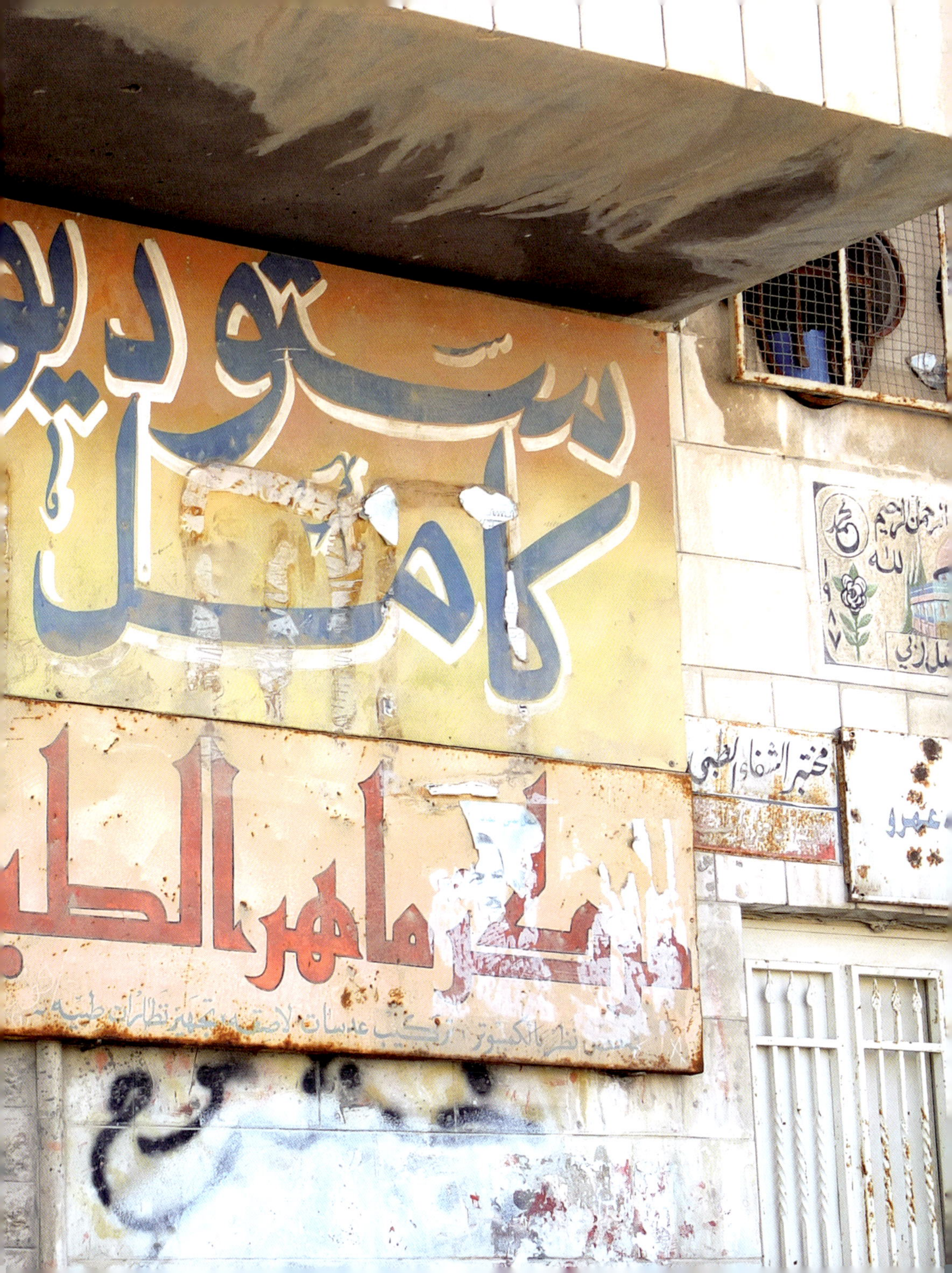

كامل
مختبر الشفاء الطبي
عمرو
نظر بالكمبيوتر تركيب عدسات لاصقة تجهيز نظارات طبية

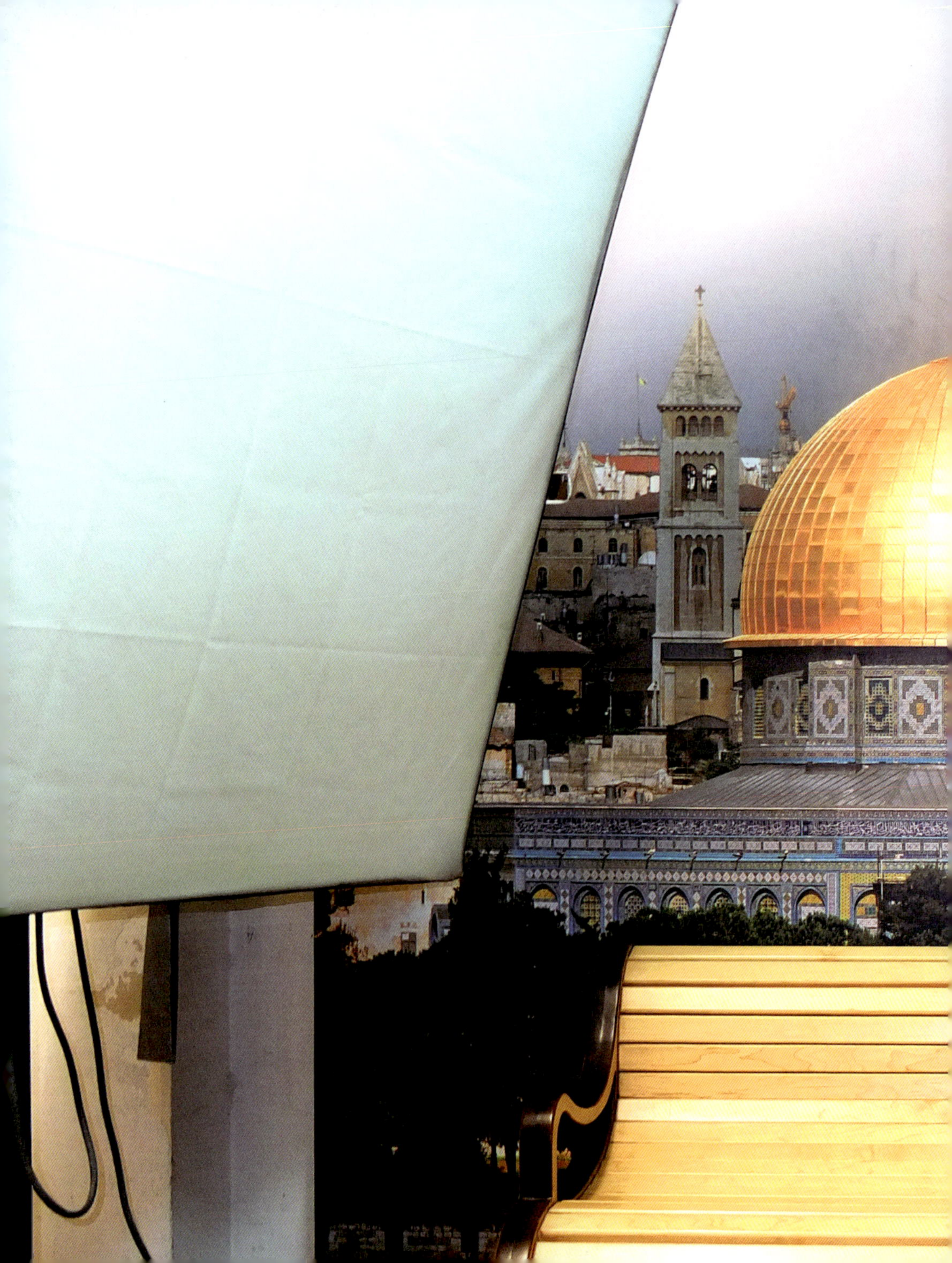

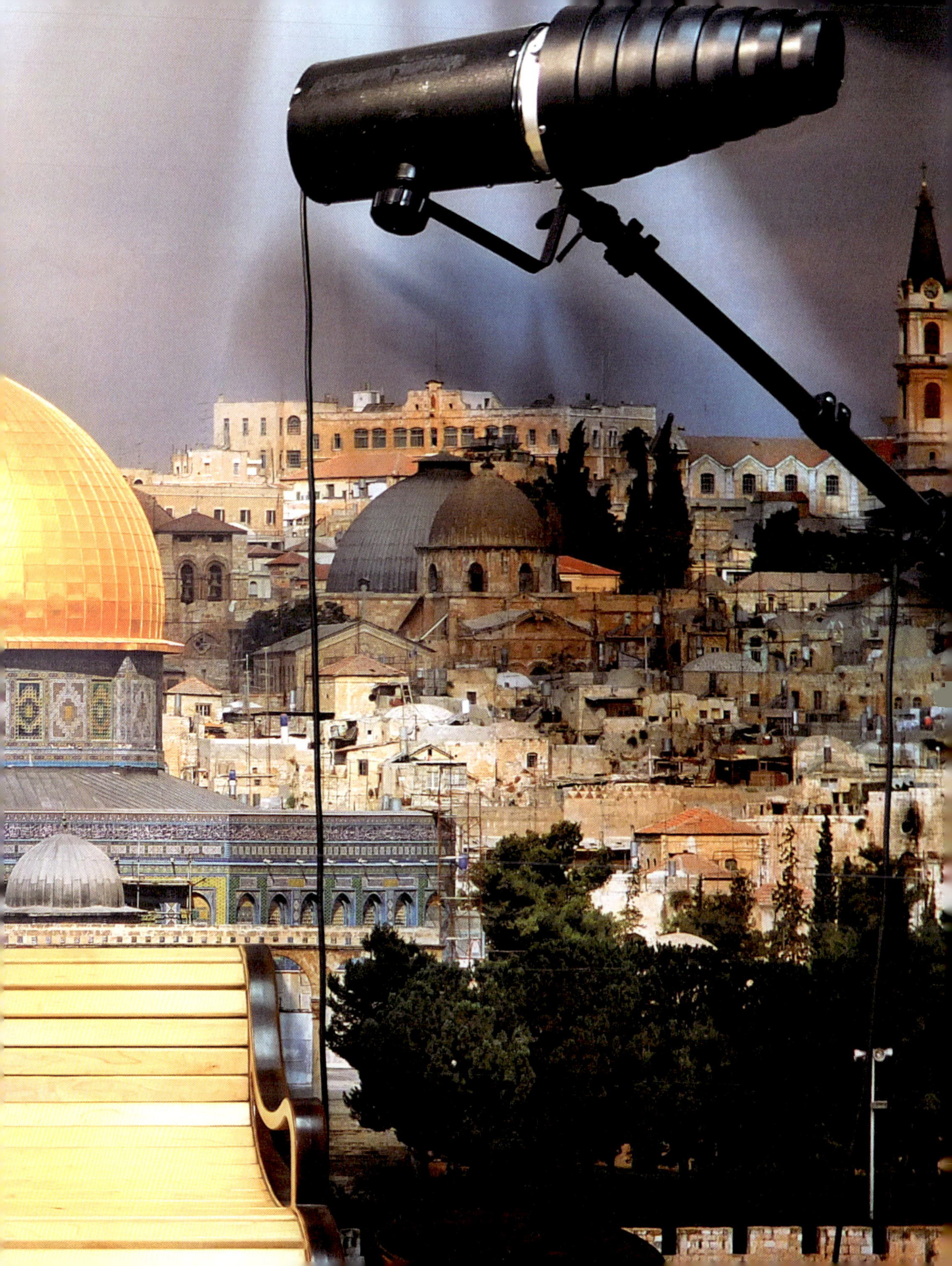

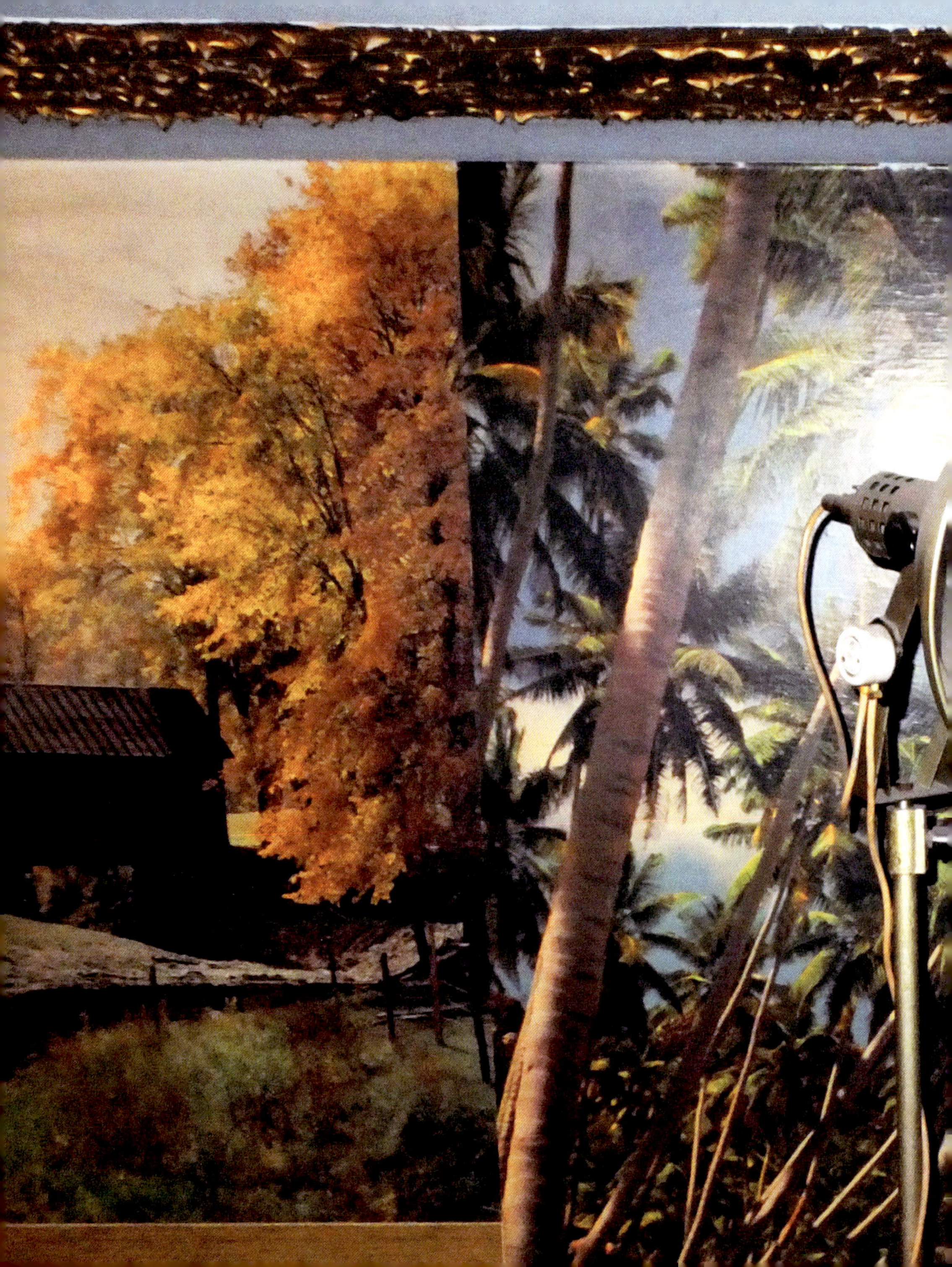

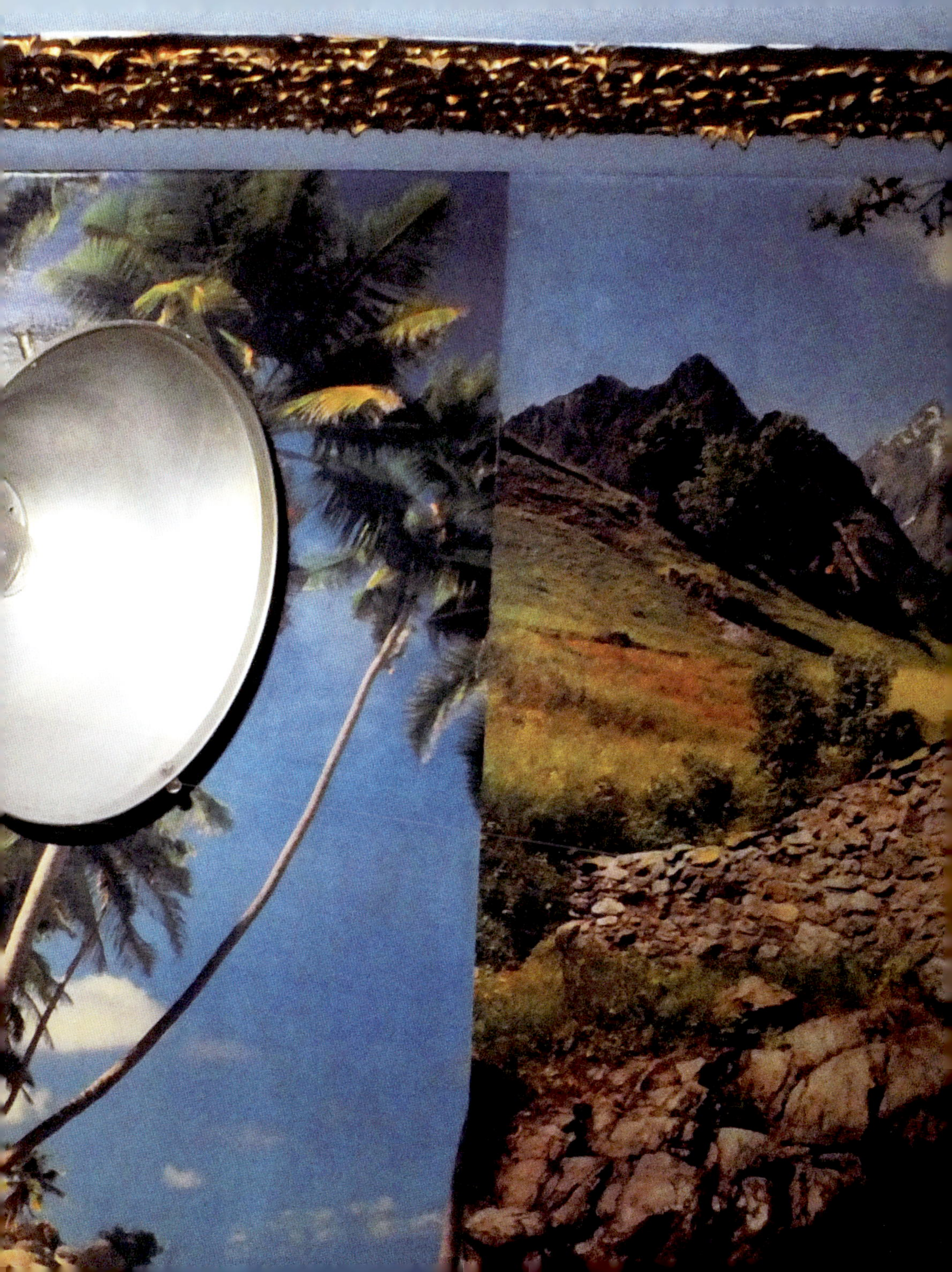

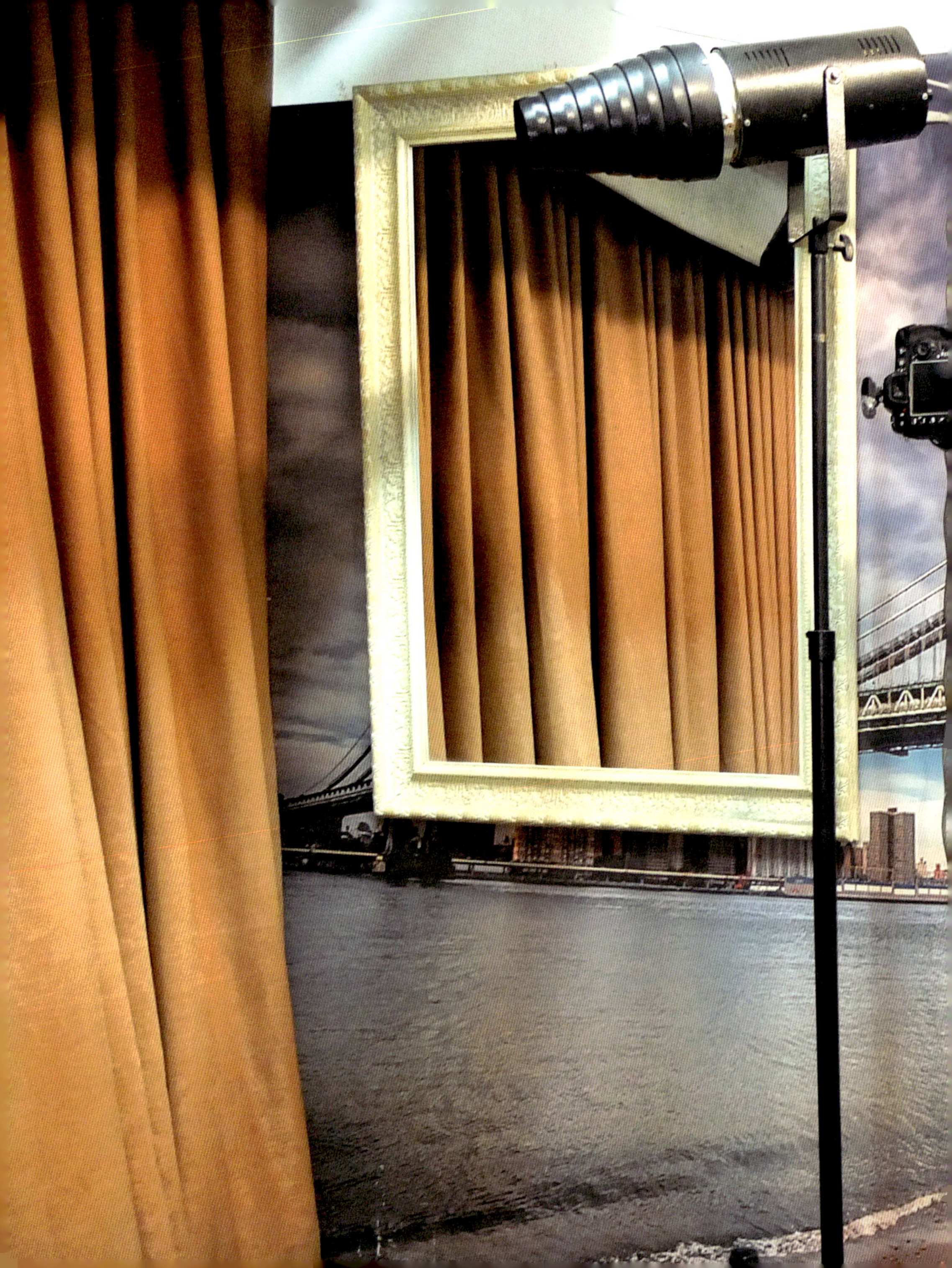

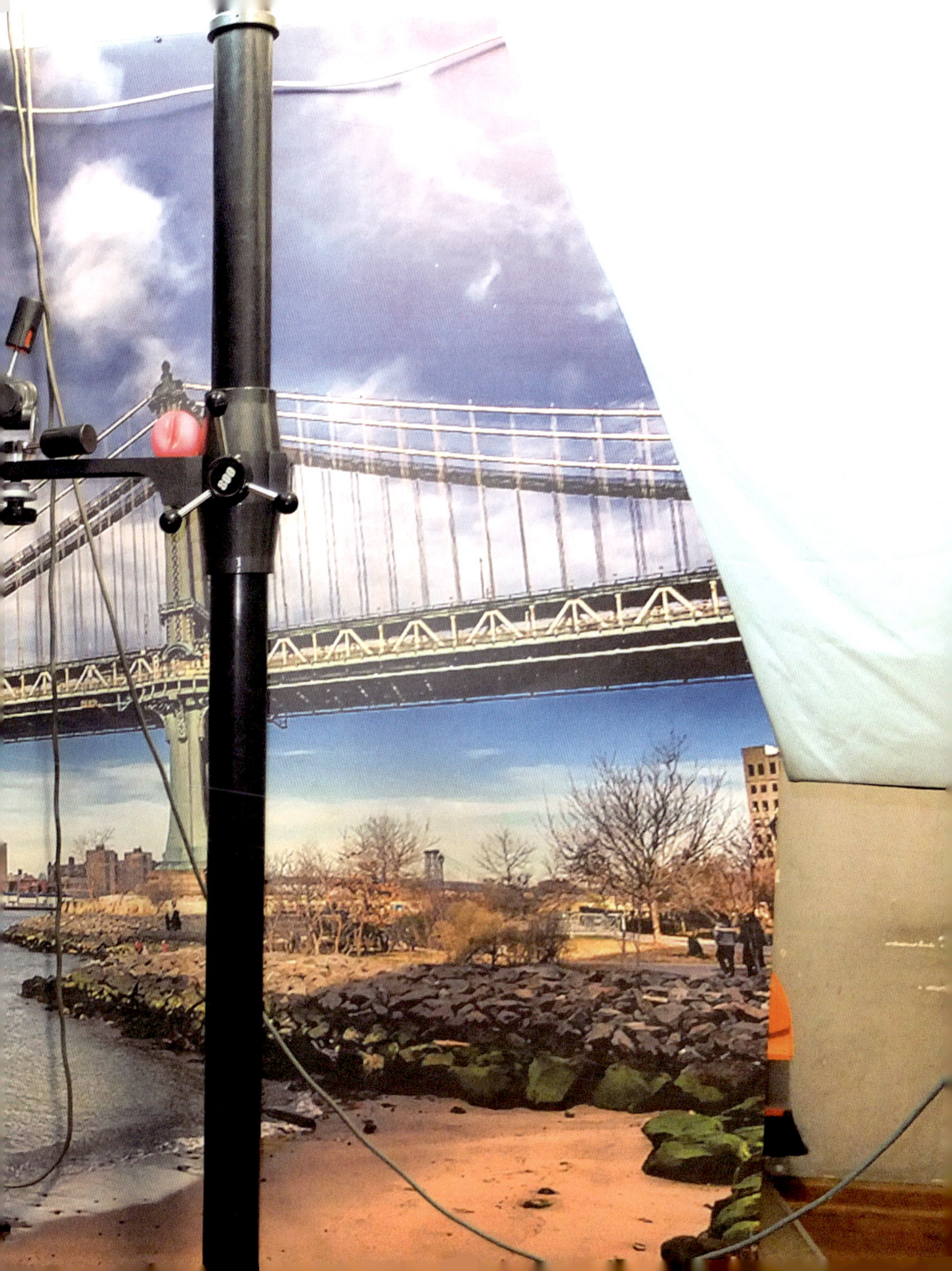

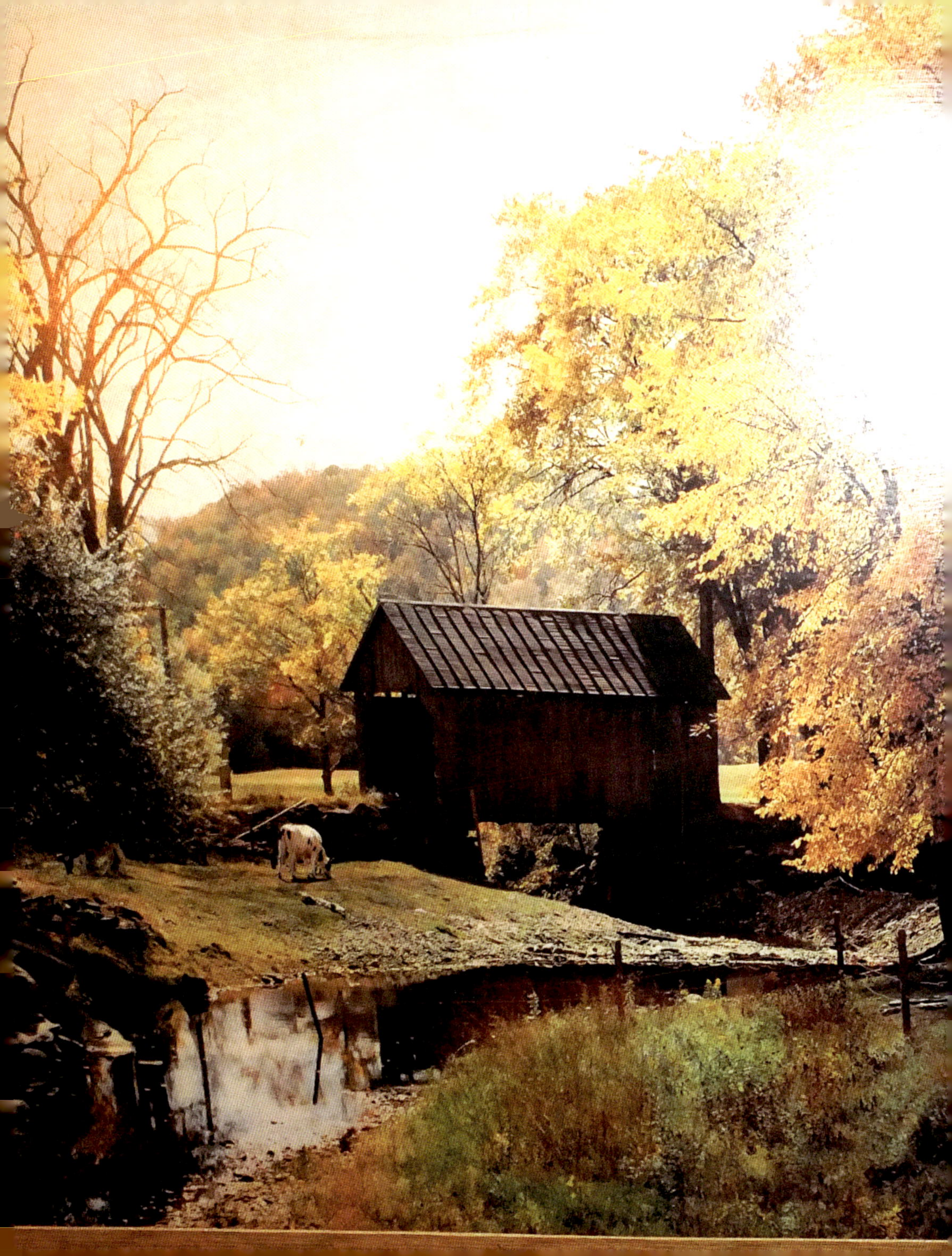

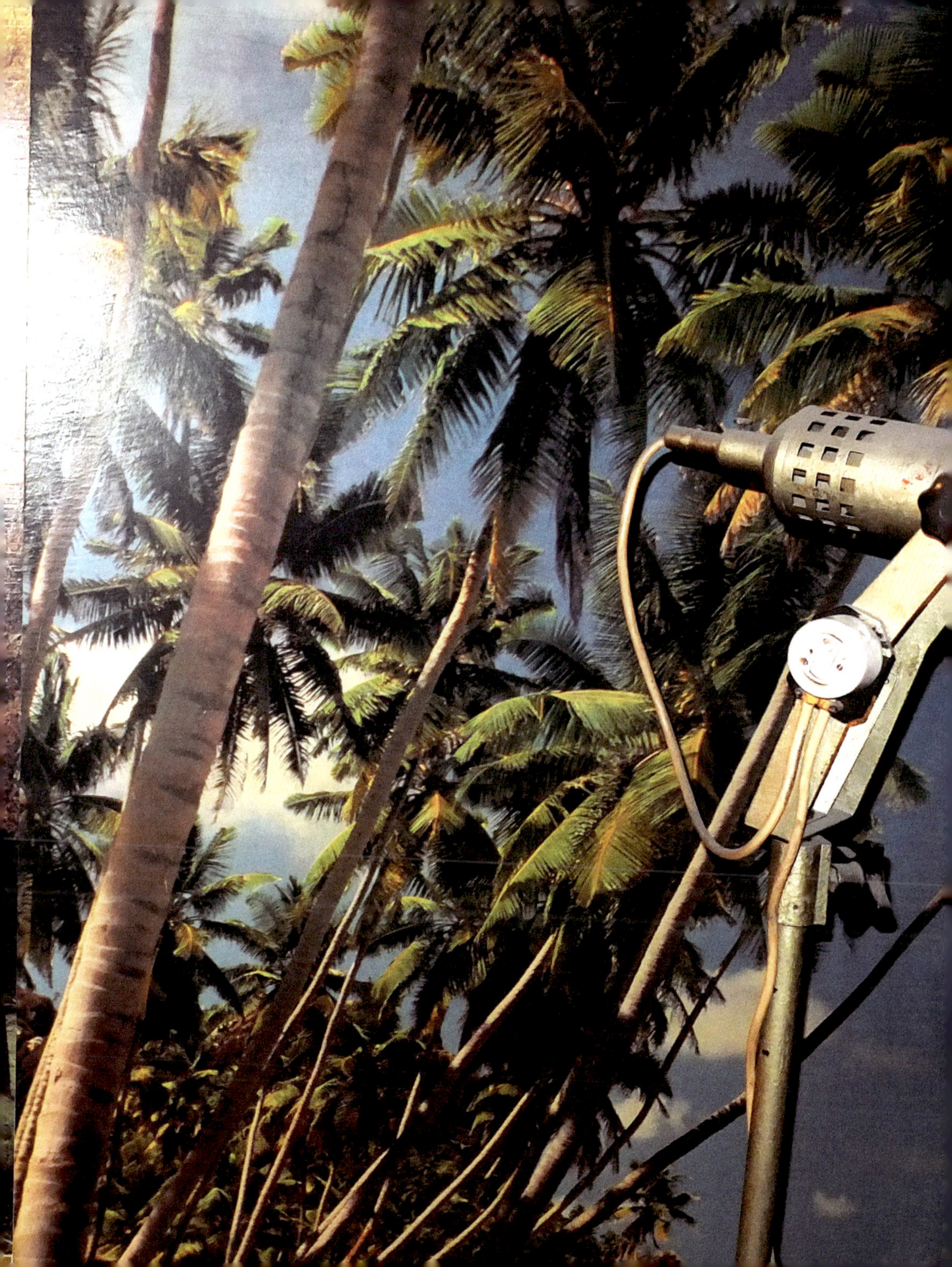

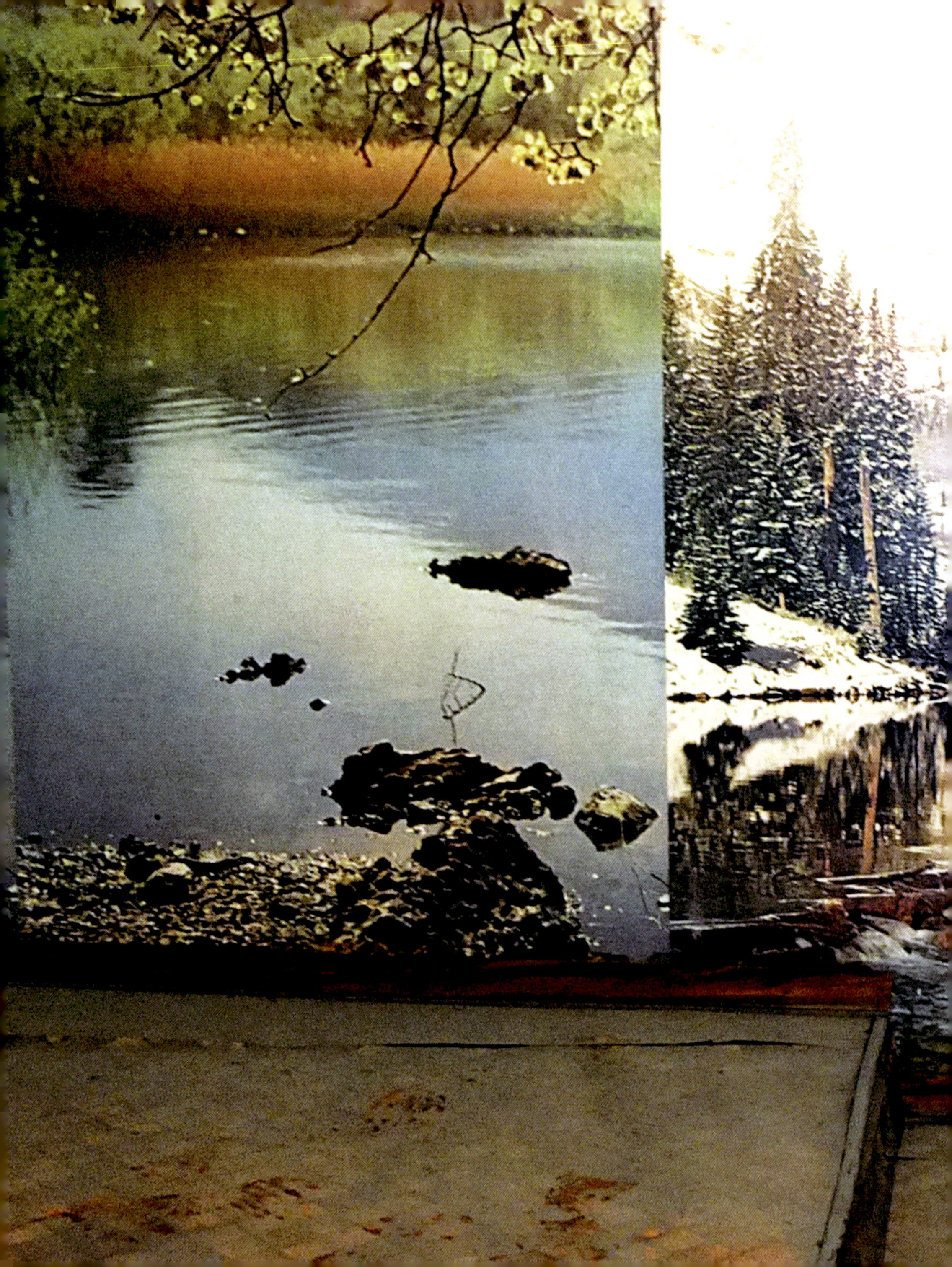

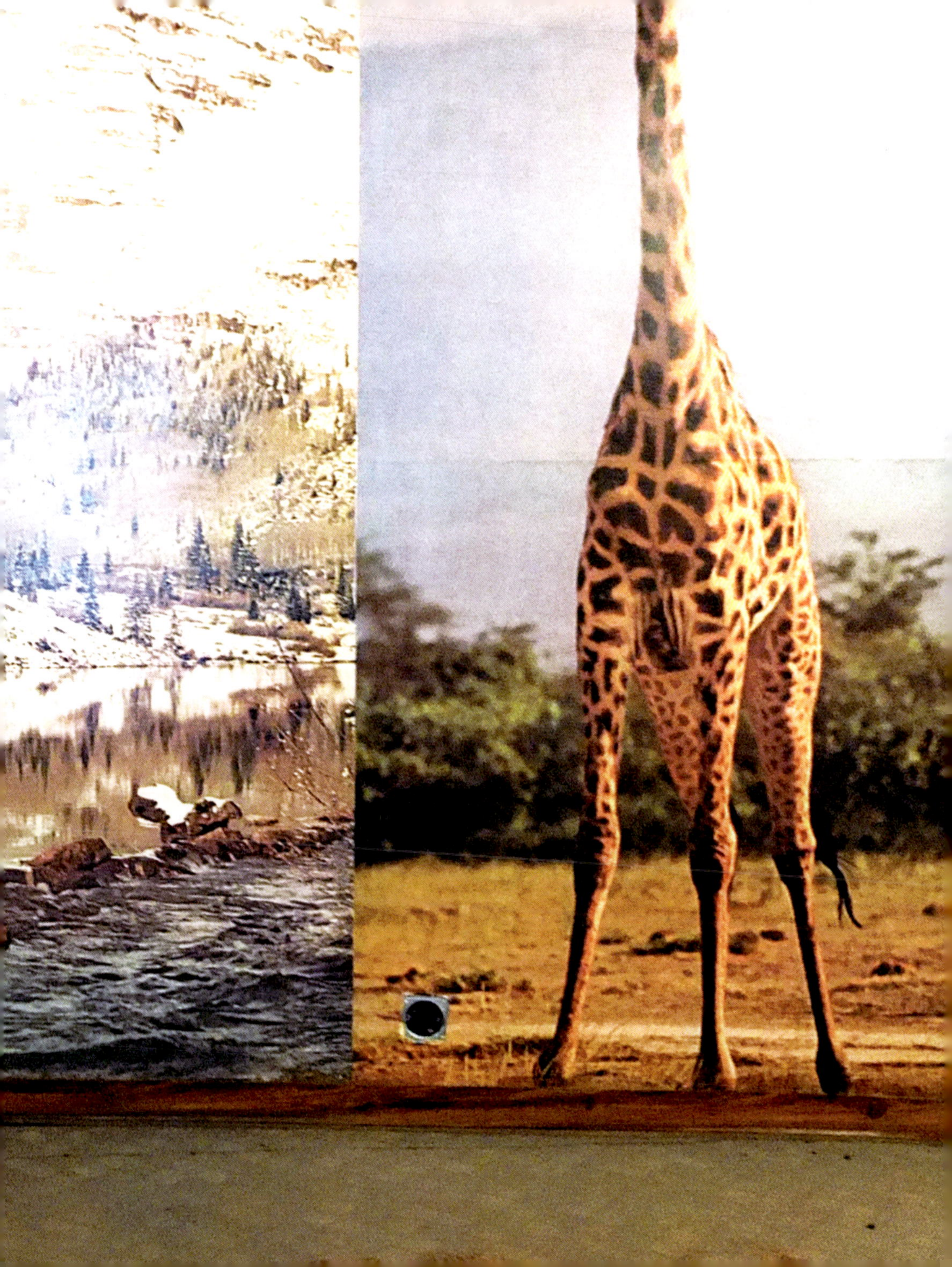

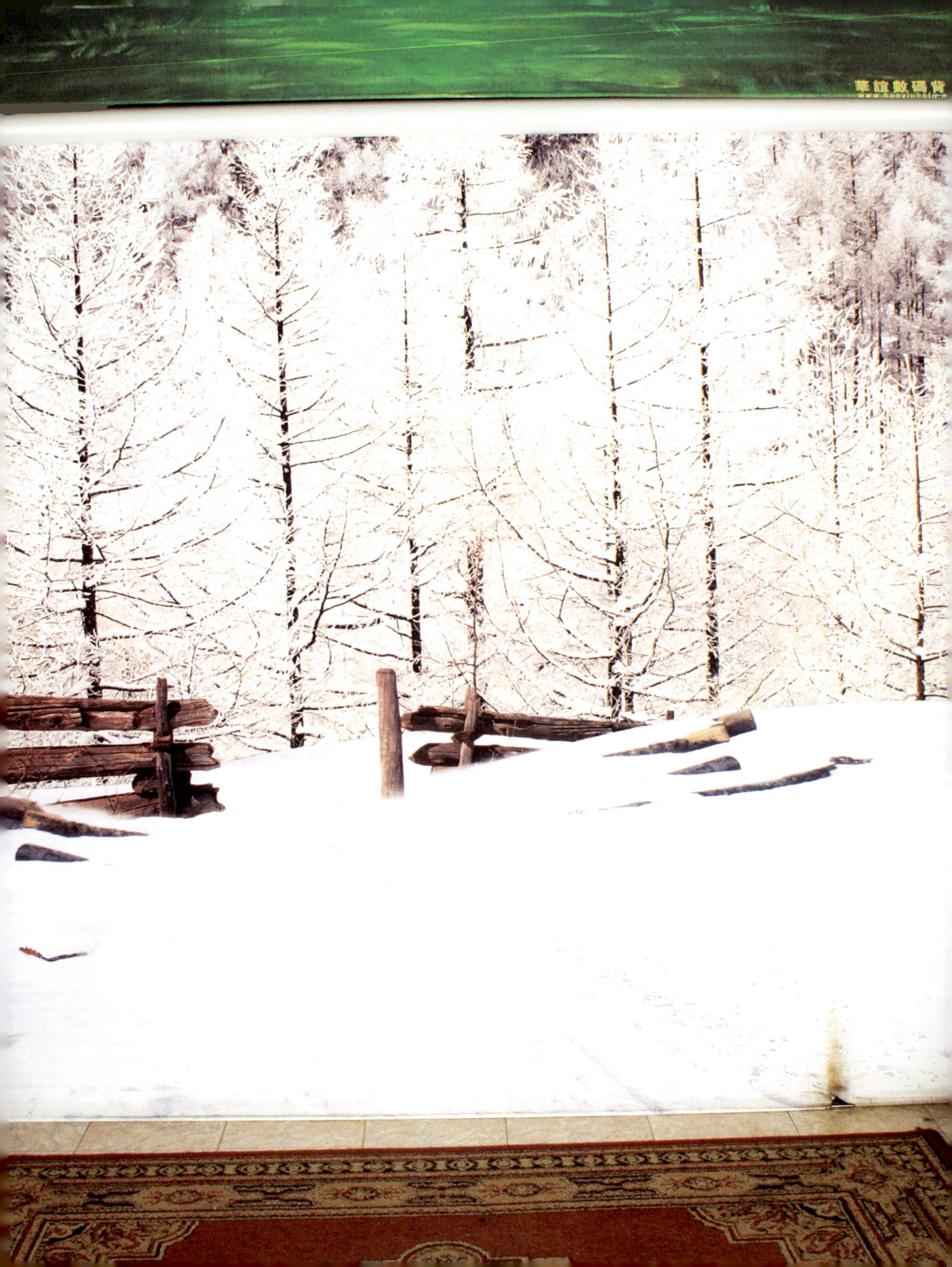

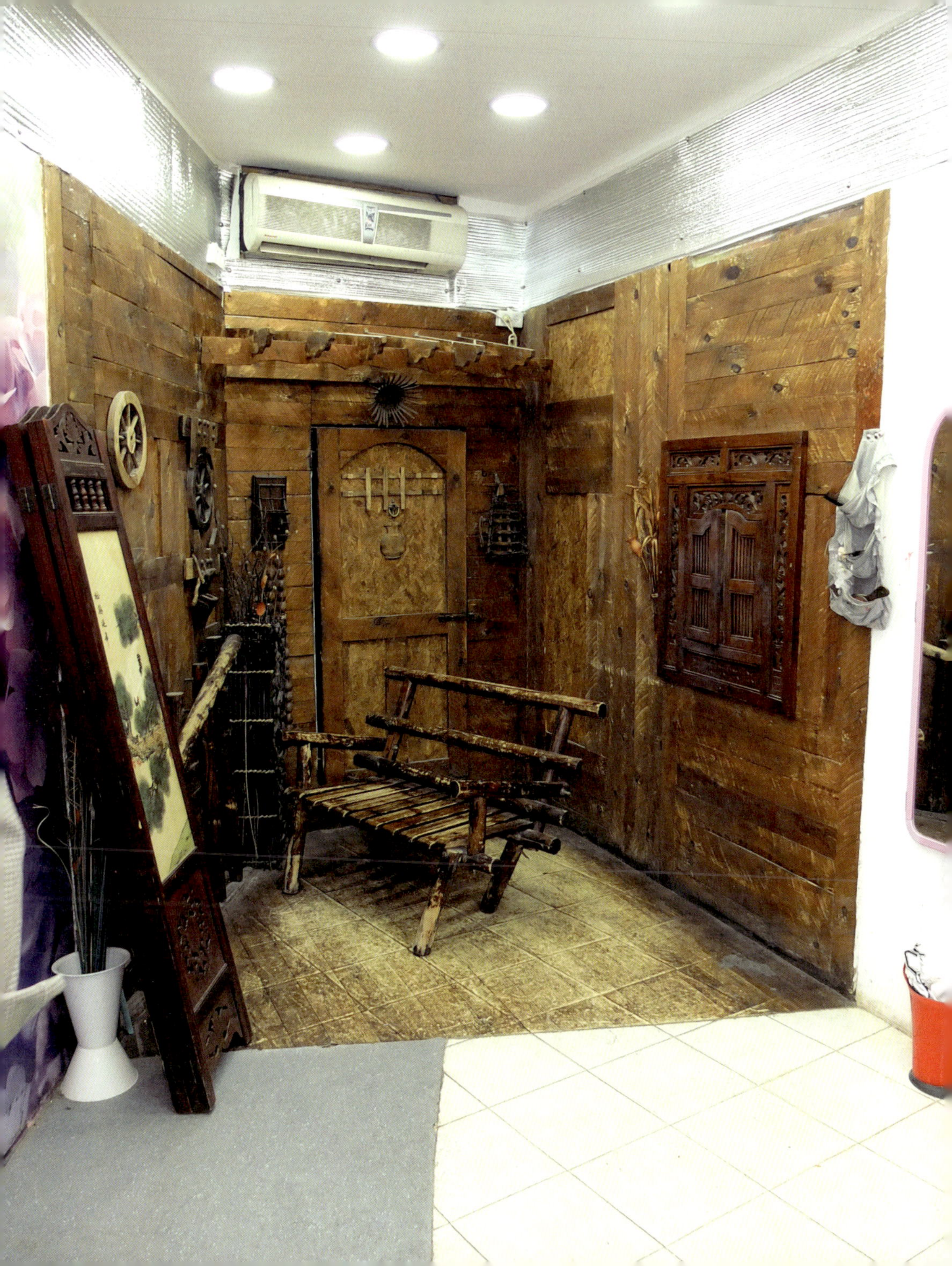

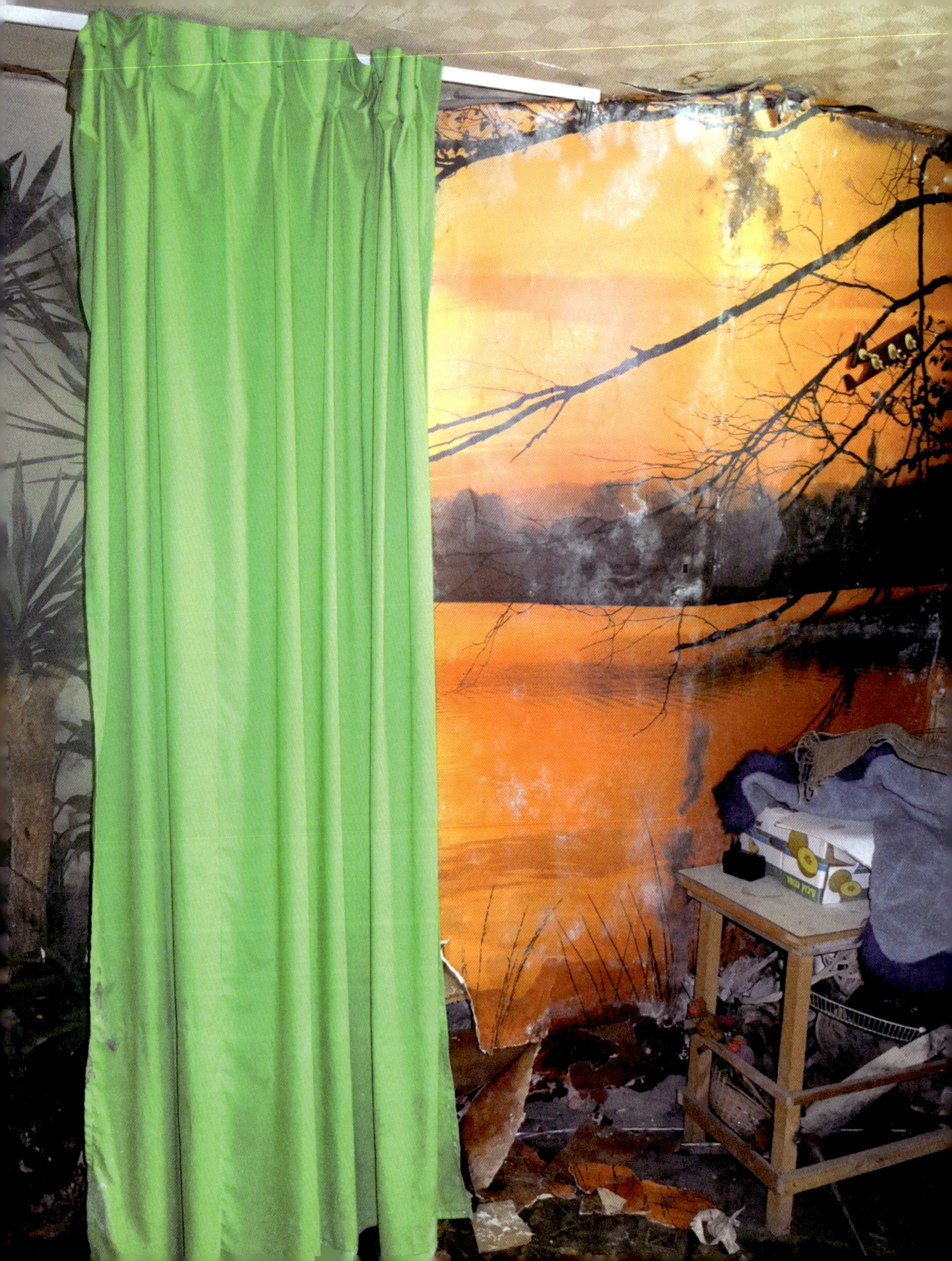

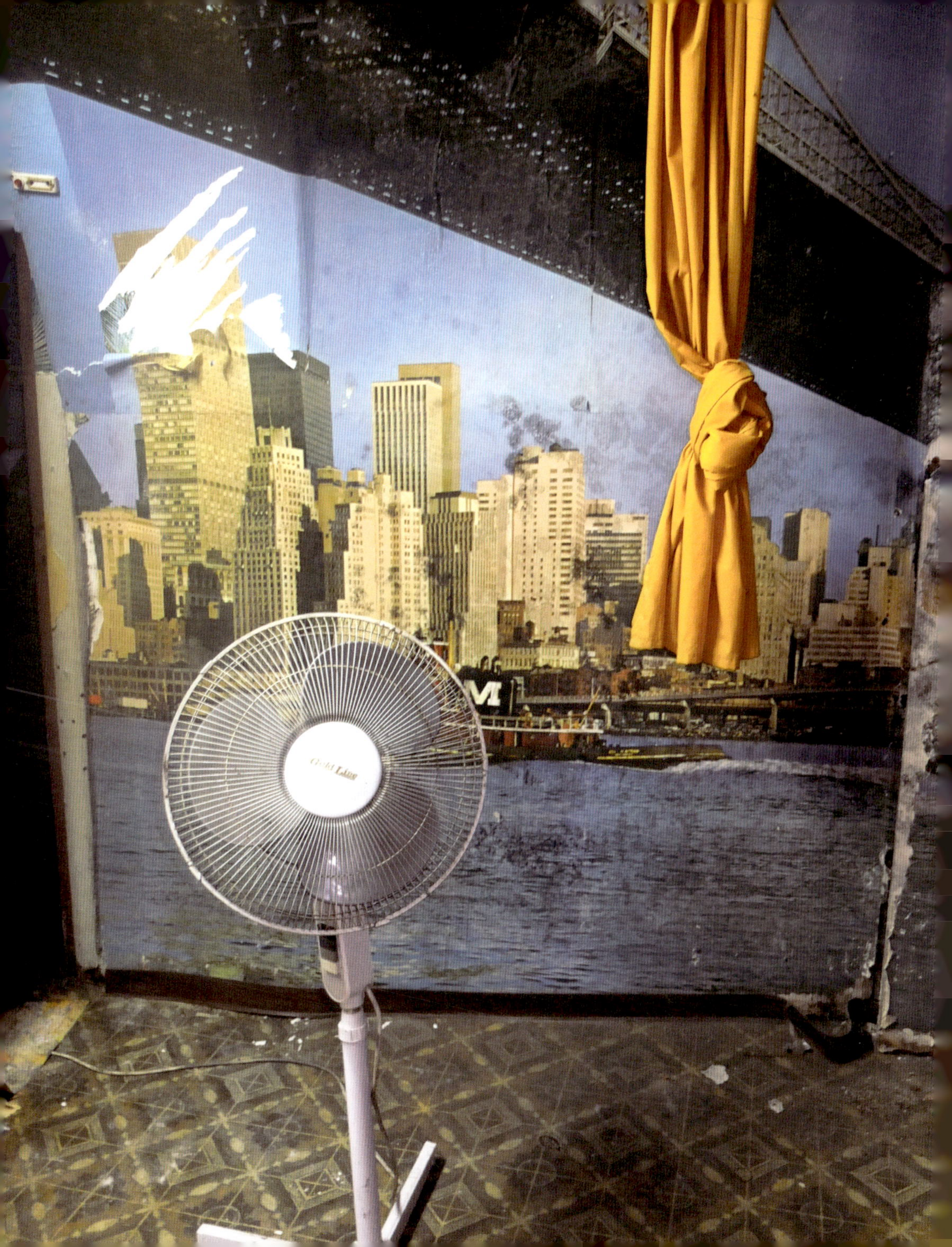

ACKNOWLEDGEMENTS

This book is the culmination of a six year endeavour to document the practice of Studio Portraiture in the West Bank. As an active member of ISM during the prolonged periods of time that I spent there, my priority was always activist work. This project stemmed alongside from seeing the use of Studio Portraiture in the family homes of prisoners and martyrs, who we would visit on a regular basis. Their anonymity must be respected but I would like to extend my gratitude to all of them. Similarly, I worked with a whole range of different activists from around the world whose anonymity must also be respected. I shared some of the most challenging experiences of my life with them, yet in most cases I have never seen them since. I would like to extend my gratitude to all of them, wherever they are.

Azzam Al Shweiki of Studio Chaplin was extremely generous with access to both his archive and life story. His son, Ibrahim, also scanned the negatives from his practice for the purpose of this book. Similarly, the children of Ohannes Shanlikian, who now run Studio Havana in Ramallah, and Garo Nalbandian of Studio Garo in East Jerusalem were central to the development of this book.

Thanks to both Ranin Faidi and Lina Bani Odeh for assisting with and translating many encounters between myself and Palestinian photographers. I would also like to thank two of my heroes, Neta Golan and Abdel K, for everything they have taught me.

With special thanks to Joyce Hardy.

Finally, special thanks must go to both Johnny James Scott and Scott Jackson, for without their charisma, uniqueness, nerve and talent, this project would have been inconceivable.

This project was generously supported by the A M Qattan Foundation, Tawfiq al-Ghussein and Richard Greer.

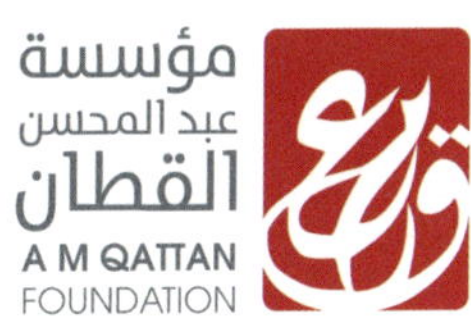

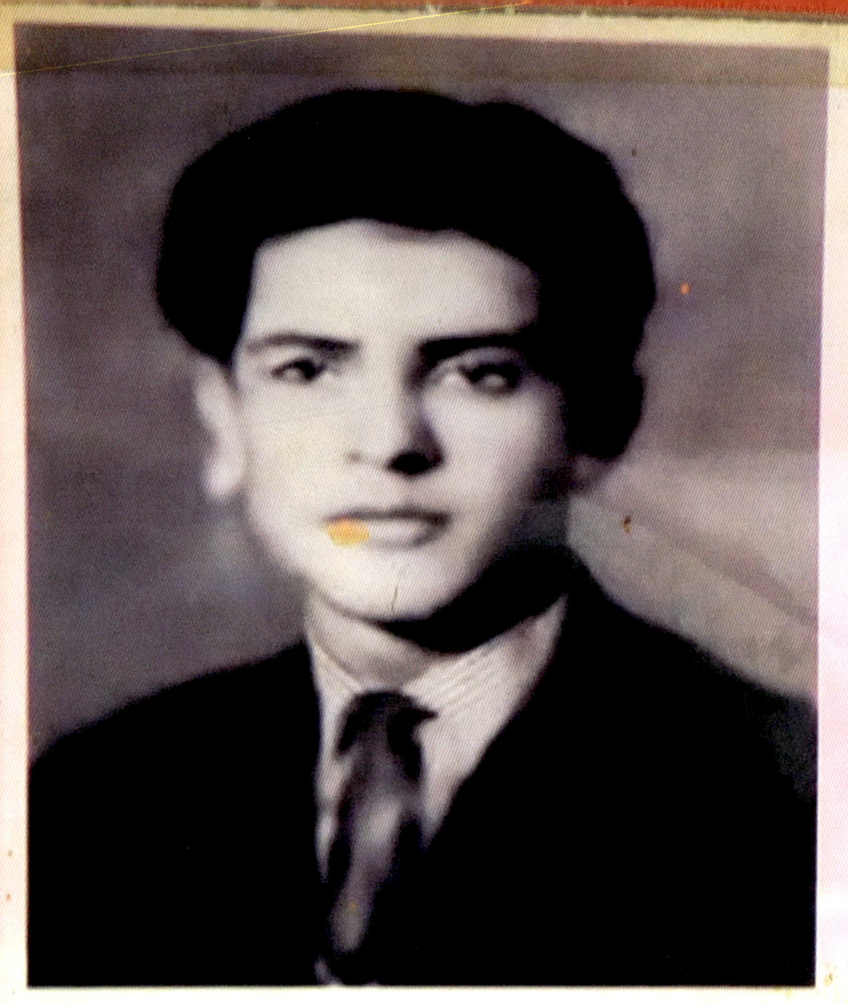

لتالفه) القديمه)

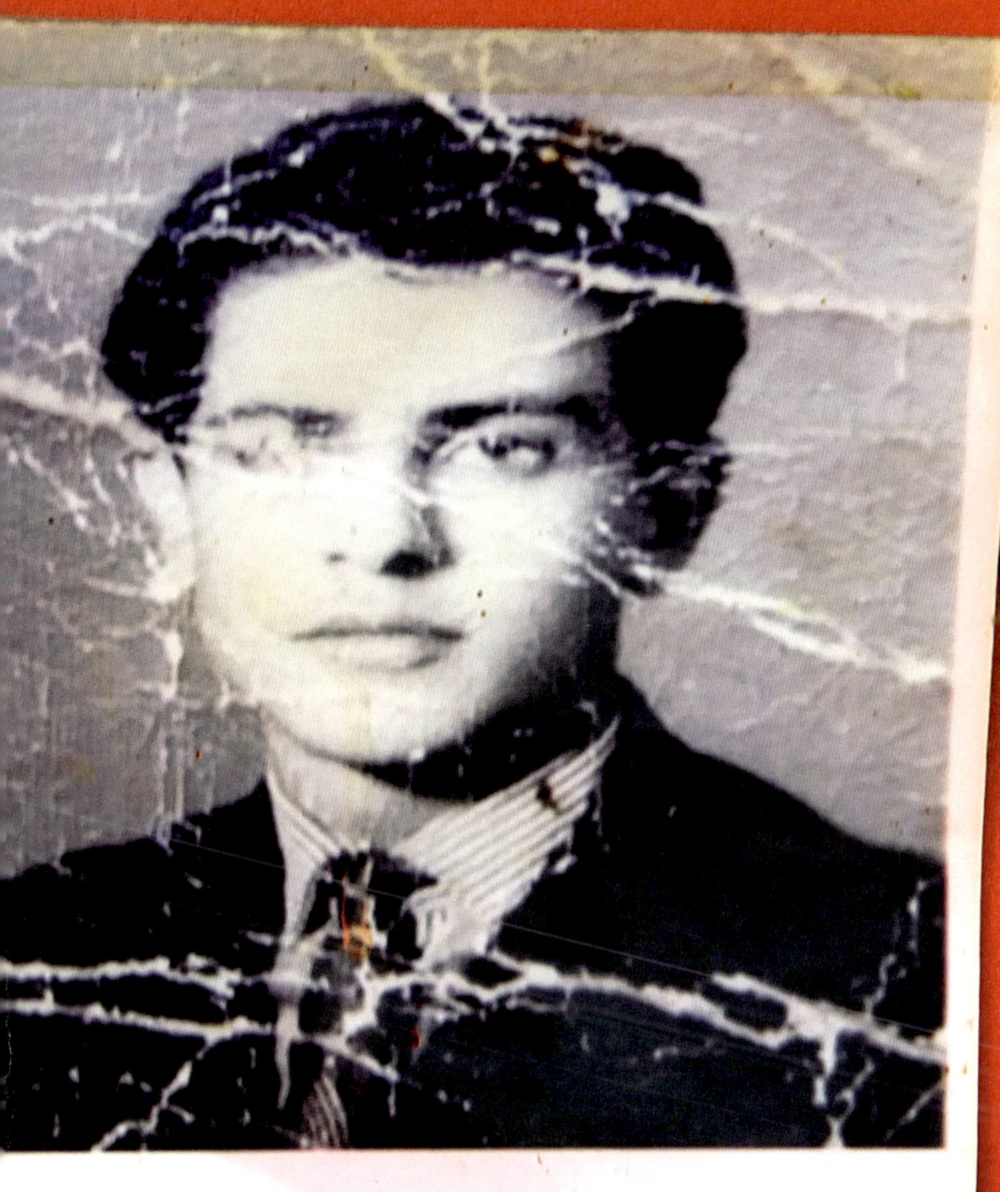
ترميم الصور